INGESTING JESUS

Society of Biblical Literature

Academia Biblica

Saul M. Olyan,
Old Testament Editor

Mark Allan Powell,
New Testament Editor

Number 6

INGESTING JESUS

INGESTING JESUS
Eating and Drinking
in the Gospel of John

Jane S. Webster

Society of Biblical Literature
Atlanta

INGESTING JESUS

Copyright © 2003 by the Society of Biblical Literature

Library of Congress Cataloging-in-Publication Data

Webster, Jane S. (Jane Suzanne), 1953-
    Ingesting Jesus : eating and drinking in the Gospel of John / by Jane S. Webster.
        p. cm. — (Society of Biblical Literature Academia Biblica ; no. 6)
    Includes bibliographical references and indexes.
    ISBN 1-58983-046-6 (alk. paper)
    1. Bible. N.T. John—Criticism, interpretation, etc. 2. Food in the Bible. 3. Drinking in the Bible. I. Title. II. Series: Academia Biblica (Series) ; no. 6.

BS2615.52.W43 2003
226.5'06—dc21

                                    2003005330

07 06 05 04 03 02   5 4 3 2 1

Printed in the United States of America
on acid-free paper

For Tom

Table of Contents

Acknowledgements

There are several people that I would like to thank for their support and encouragement while writing this dissertation. First and foremost, I wish to thank Professor Adele Reinhartz whose important insight and advice at critical moments have enabled this project to take shape. Thanks are also due to Dr. Stephen Westerholm and Dr. Eileen Schuller for their careful reading and helpful suggestions. Megan Webster, Lori Vos, and Michael Fukuchi have offered valuable editorial comments as "interested readers." Thanks also to Katelin Dame and Darla Raper.

This project could not be completed were it not for those who have inspired and encouraged me over the past few years. My husband, Thomas Webster, has been so steadfast in his support and encouragement. He learned to cook so that I could take advantage of my burst of inspiration between 4:00 and 6:30 p.m. (though I suspect that hunger might have something to do with it!). He facilitated a quiet and protected environment, freeing me from the distractions that accompany a busy household. He understood when I opted to work rather than play. He financed my growing library and my trips to conferences. He even agreed to the installation of a hot tub under the stars! Husbands don't get much better than my Tom!

My daughters, Megan and Gillian, have sustained me. Seeing how important this adventure was for me, they respected my need for "thinking time" and my long hours in front of the computer. They adjusted to my random returns to normalcy and my spontaneous need to celebrate esoteric accomplishments. They listened patiently while I tried to make sense of my arguments. They always welcomed snuggles and my questions about their lives. They are the best part of my life.

Finally, the completion of this project would not be possible without the generous funding of the Social Sciences and Humanities Research Council of Canada and the Ontario Graduate Doctoral Fellowships program.

Abbreviations

AB	Anchor Bible
ABD	*Anchor Bible Dictionary*
Bib	*Biblica*
BRev	*Bible Review*
CBQ	*Catholic Biblical Quarterly*
ETL	*Ephemerides theologicae lovanienses*
ET	*Expository Times*
HTR	*Harvard Theological Review*
ICC	International Critical Commentary
JAAR	*Journal of the American Academy of Religion*
JBL	*Journal of Biblical Literature*
JETS	*Journal of the Evangelical Theological Society*
JJS	*Journal of Jewish Studies*
JLT	*Journal of Literature and Theology*
JQR	*Jewish Quarterly Review*
JSNT	*Journal for the Study of the New Testament*
JSNTSup	Journal for the Study of the New Testament: Supplement Series
JSOT	Journal for the Study of the Old Testament
JSOTSup	Journal for the Study of the Old Testament: Supplement Series
JTS	*Journal of Theological Studies*
NICNT	New International Commentary on the New Testament
NT	*Novum Testamentum*
NTD	Das Neue Testament Deutsch
NTS	*New Testament Studies*
RB	*Revue Biblique*
RE	*Revue and Expositor*
RSPT	*Revue des sciences philosophiques et théologiques*
RSR	*Recherches de science religieuse*
SBL	Society of Biblical Literature
SBT	Studies in Biblical Theology
TDNT	*Theological Dictionary of the New Testament*
TS	*Theological Studies*
WBC	Word Biblical Commentary

Introduction

"To eat is human, to digest, divine."
— Charles Townsend Copeland, *Epigram*

In an article titled, "Metaphor and Religion," David Tracy argues that "the study of metaphor may well provide *a* central clue to a better understanding of that elusive and perplexing phenomenon our culture calls religion."[1] All religious traditions are grounded, he observes, on several fundamental root metaphors that define a community's vision of reality. In the Christian tradition, recent interpretations of these root metaphors have undergone methodological revision. First, scholars better appreciate the broad range of modes of being-in-the-world presented in the multitude of New Testament metaphors. Second, they distrust traditional interpretations that merely substitute an "accepted" theological concept, limiting the scope of interpretive possibilities. Third, they are less sure that the historical *Sitz im Leben* of the early Christian community will shed light on the definitive interpretation of metaphors. Fourth, and finally, they have insisted on semiotic, structuralist, semantic and literary critical analyzes to develop a sense of the whole text, and within that text, the sense and meaning of the metaphors. Thus, Tracy argues, religious metaphors should be seen as tensive, dynamic and constructive literary devices that function rhetorically. This challenge is taken up here in a study on the Gospel of John, specifically as it pertains to the cluster of metaphors related to the language of eating and drinking—or what will be called "ingesting language."

Ingesting language is found throughout the Gospel of John and can be divided into two main categories. The first category includes specific references pertaining to food and drink and to the acts of eating, drinking and feeding. It embraces both simple references to food and drink, such as bread, water, fish and wine, as well as metaphorical language drawn from the semantic field of food, drink and ingesting. For example, Jesus refers to himself as the bread of life (6:35, 51) and as the source of living water (4:10–15). The one who believes "drinks" of Jesus and will provide "a river of living water" (7:37–39). Jesus refers to his upcoming death as "drinking the cup that his Father has given him" (18:11). In the last scene in the Gospel, Jesus tells Peter, "Feed my sheep" (21:15–17).

---

[1] *Critical Inquiry* 5, no. 1 (1978): 106, author's italics.

The second category consists of passages describing gatherings in which eating and drinking ostensibly occur, collectively referred to here as "meals." The first meal is a wedding banquet at Cana where, prompted by his mother, Jesus turns six jars of water into fine wine (2:1–11). The second is set in Sychar, where Jesus asks for a drink of water from a Samaritan woman and the disciples bring him food (4:4–42). The third meal takes place on a mountain where Jesus turns five barley loaves and two fish into enough food to satisfy five thousand people (6:1–14). At the fourth meal, Mary, Martha and Lazarus give a supper for Jesus in Bethany. Mary anoints Jesus' feet with ointment and then wipes them with her hair (12:1–8). During the fifth meal, set in Jerusalem the night of his arrest, Jesus washes the disciples' feet and then sends Judas off to betray him (13:1–14:31). The sixth and final meal takes place after Jesus' resurrection, on the shore of the Sea of Galilee. Jesus prepares a breakfast of fish and bread over a charcoal fire and serves it to the disciples (21:1–14). Curiously, not all of these meals feature eating and drinking—some only allude to it—but the repeated use of a meal setting is noteworthy.

The prevalence of eating and drinking language, the references to food and drink, and the narrative context of meals establishes ingestion as a significant literary motif in the Gospel of John. It takes its place among other motifs such as light and dark, above and below, and the good shepherd. While this ingesting language has not gone unnoticed in the history of Johannine scholarship, no study to date has traced the motif through the Gospel, related the various passages to each other, or drawn specific conclusions about the function of the motif in the Gospel as a whole. Without such a study, however, it is impossible to determine how this motif fits into the Gospel's structure and purpose. Limited studies have examined the various metaphors and symbols in isolation or, as Tracy has pointed out, with a theological agenda that restricts the scope of the metaphorical meaning, usually to sacramentalism.[2] In other words, they have not extended the limits of the motif to include the narrative context of meals and language drawn from the semantic domain of ingesting, nor have they attempted to understand the role of the motif in the Gospel narrative. This dissertation is the first attempt to do so.

While not the central focus of this study by any means, any survey of ingesting language in the Gospel of John has implications for the debate about the place of the Eucharist in the Johannine community. Scholars on one side of the debate assume that the fourth evangelist must have known the traditions of the Eucharist; thus, passages that feature bread and wine are thought to be Eucharistic. Scholars on the other side of the debate argue that the evangelist either did not know these traditions or did not approve of them. This question

---

[2] A survey on the state of this question follows on page 12.

will be addressed briefly in the concluding remarks.

The aim of this study is to define the literary motif of ingesting language and its component parts. It will note the use of this language in recurring contexts, demonstrate its role in the Gospel and offer some reflections on its rhetorical function. It will be argued that the ingesting motif is a vehicle for Johannine soteriology. Specifically, ingesting language provides a way to describe both the role of the believer ("to eat and drink Jesus") and the role of Jesus as the one who is incarnate as "flesh" but who must die in order that others might eat and live. In this way, the ingesting motif speaks of soteriology in a microcosmic way, reflecting the Gospel's soteriology as a whole. At the same time, the complex metaphorical language challenges readers to struggle for meaning, to chew it over and, if palatable, to swallow.

It will prove useful at this point to outline the soteriology of the Gospel of John and then to sketch out the way in which ingesting language reflects this larger soteriological construct.

SOTERIOLOGY IN THE GOSPEL OF JOHN

The Gospel of John as a whole describes the way that believers gain eternal life or are "saved." People in the world are understood to be in bondage to their sin, which will lead to their eternal death (8:34–36). Motivated by love, God initiates a rescue plan by sending his son, Jesus, into the world (3:16–17). Jesus dwells among his people (6:50) as the "Word" (1:1–18); he teaches (5:34) and does signs (20:30). Those who believe in Jesus and keep his word (3:15–21, 36; 5:24; 8:51–52) will not die in their sin (1:29; 8:21, 24, 34–36) but will become children of God (1:12) and have eternal life (3:16; 6:47; 11:25–26).

An essential element in this scheme of salvation is the human response: to believe in Jesus. When Jesus is asked by the crowd, "What must we do to perform the works of God?" Jesus responds by saying, "This is the work of God, that you believe in him whom he has sent" (6:28–29). Believing in Jesus is conceived in a variety of ways in the Gospel. For example, believing is "coming into the light" (12:36, 46) or "receiving" Jesus (1:12).

An important metaphor for "believing" is that of "ingesting" Jesus. John 6:40 says that "on the last day" Jesus will raise "all who see the Son and believe in him." John 6:54 says that "on the last day" Jesus will raise all "who eat the flesh (τὴν σάρκα) of the Son of Man and drink his blood." Both those who see and believe and those who eat the flesh of the Son of Man will have eternal life. This phrase "to eat the flesh" recalls the prologue: "In the beginning was the Word, and the Word was with God and the Word was God. . . . And the Word became flesh (σάρξ) and lived among us" (1:1, 14). Though generally thought to mean that Jesus took on human form (became incarnate) and was able to participate in human experience,[3] "the Word became flesh" also hints that Jesus becomes "flesh" or "meat" that is to be eaten.[4] In John 6:53, Jesus emphatically states, "Very truly, I tell you, unless you eat the flesh (τὴν σάρκα) of the Son of Man and drink his blood, you have no life in you." Jesus also claims to be the "bread which has come down from heaven" (6:41, 50–51); again, this bread refers to his flesh (ἡ σάρξ, 6:51). Furthermore, Jesus provides "living water" (4:10, 14; 7:37; 19:34). He says, "Whoever comes to me will never be hungry, whoever believes in me will never thirst" (6:35), and the one who believes will "never taste death" (8:52). Therefore, just as believing in Jesus leads to salvation, so also ingesting Jesus leads to salvation. The Gospel thus uses ingesting language as one way to describe what it means to believe in Jesus.

In order for this "food" to become available for eating, however, Jesus must first die. Again, images of food are used to describe this concept. In referring to his approaching death,[5] Jesus says, "Unless a grain of wheat falls into the earth and dies, it remains just a single grain; but if it dies it bears much fruit" (12:24). This "fruit," or the harvest of grain, is used to make bread, recalling 6:51: "I am the living bread that came down from heaven. Whoever eats of this bread will live forever; and the bread that I give for the life of this world is my flesh." Thus, in order to feed believers the bread of his flesh, Jesus, as a grain of wheat, must first "fall into the earth and die." In addition to this passage, the Gospel presents Jesus as the "Lamb of God" (1:29, 36) who dies at the hour that the lambs are to be sacrificed for Passover (Exod 12:6; John 19:14).[6] The Passover festival, which celebrates a time when the Hebrews are saved from death by smearing lamb's blood on their doorposts and lintels (Exod 12:1–20), includes the slaughter of a lamb and the sharing of its meat. Thus, Jesus is slaughtered and his "flesh" is the substance that is shared with believers; they too are saved from death (6:51–53).[7] Therefore, Jesus' death is necessary for believers to have

---

[3] See, for example, R. Brown, *The Gospel of John (i–ix): Introduction, Translation and Notes* (Anchor Bible 29 and 29a; New York: Doubleday, 1966), 13, 30–32; C. K. Barrett, *The Gospel according to St. John* (2d ed.; Philadelphia: Westminster, 1978), 98; R. Schnackenburg, *The Gospel according to St. John* (3 vols.; trans. K. Smith; New York: Seabury, 1980), 1:265–8.

[4] For the range of meanings for this word, see Walter Bauer, "σάρξ" in *A Greek-English Lexicon of the New Testament* (2d ed.; trans. and adapt. of the 4th ed. by W. Arndt, and F. W. Gingrich; rev. and aug. by F. W. Gingrich, and F. W. Danker from Bauer's 5th ed., 1958; Chicago: University of Chicago Press, 1979), 743.

[5] Brown, *Gospel*, 471–3.

[6] See also 19:29 (cf. Exod 12:22) and 19:36 (cf. Exod 12:46; Num 9:12). For a discussion of the time of Jesus' death as the day and hour of the Passover sacrifice, see Brown, *Gospel*, 882–3, 895–6; W. A. Meeks, *The Prophet-King: Moses Traditions and the Johannine Christology* (Leiden: Brill, 1967), 77; Barrett, *Gospel*, 51.

[7] Note that the "bread of life" discourse is set in the narrative context of Passover (6:4).

eternal life.

Narratives that refer to people gathering to eat and drink emphasize the necessity of Jesus' death. First, meal narratives provide the setting for discussions about the meaning and purpose of Jesus' death. During a meal in Bethany, Mary anoints Jesus' feet with oil bought "for the day of [his] burial" (12:1–8). During another meal on the night before his death, Jesus knows "that his hour had come to depart this world and go to the Father" and he washes the disciples' feet (13:1–11). Second, a number of meal narratives depict Jesus as guest, host and food. At the start of these narratives, Jesus is characterized as a guest, but he quickly becomes a host who offers food and drink. He is the provider of physical food and drink and, as such, one who sustains temporal life. As the narrative proceeds, he is revealed, not just as the *provider* of the food and drink, but as the very *substance* of the food and drink. In other words, it is his flesh, available through death, which gives eternal life. For example, after Jesus miraculously feeds bread and fish to a great multitude, he discusses the need for his death when people come back to him for more "bread from heaven" (6:1–59, especially vv. 30–31, 51). Third, the various meal narratives present the range and the expected response to Jesus' death. Some people are willing to receive what Jesus provides but are unwilling to "eat Jesus' flesh" (6:52–59). Others accept Jesus both as the provider and as the substance of food and drink. To these, Jesus gives the task of feeding others (see, for example, 21:1–19). Thus, in the meal narratives, the Gospel underscores both the importance of Jesus' death and the expected response of believers.

The ingesting motif, therefore, is a vehicle for Johannine soteriology. It provides a way to describe the role of Jesus as the "Word made flesh" who must die in order that others may eat and live. It also provides a way to describe the role of the believer as ingesting Jesus and feeding others.

A NOTE ABOUT METHODOLOGY:
DEFINITIONS

The theoretical approach that is used in this study is situated within the larger framework of literary and, more specifically, narrative criticism. Narrative criticism does not seek to answer questions of history, sociology, form, or sources. It does not seek to define the shape of the community that produced the text, or the historical events that sparked the tradition. Narrative criticism brackets these questions and, instead, focuses on the story that is being communicated and the way in which that story is told.[8]

---

[8] Of course, knowledge of the history and culture of the first century is a crucial aid to understanding John's story-world, but that is a different matter from using elements of the

Within this story, characters act through a plot, respond to and negotiate climax and crisis, develop relationships, and express emotions. They are situated in and proceed through narrative time and space. They speak to each other and interact with each other. On the other hand, the narrator, who ostensibly tells the story, informs the reader—often through direct speech or asides—what the characters think, why they act as they do, and when they misunderstand.[9] They provide explanations and justification; they direct attention. Behind the narrator, however, is the implied author who makes choices such as what to tell, what order to tell it in, what to emphasize, what to ignore, what knowledge to presume, and what proof to use. The narrative elements might thus be divided in two: the "what" of the narrative includes such aspects as characters, plot, and setting; the "how" of the narrative includes such aspects as the point of view, pace, repetition, gaps, parallels, type scenes, focalization, irony, and (of especial interest to this study) figurative language.[10] Figurative language includes metaphors, signs, similes, symbols, and motifs.

Metaphors and similes are means of comparison. A simile compares one thing with another using the word "like" or "as." "Superman is as fast as a speeding locomotive" serves as an example. In a simile, there is no equation of the component parts. Superman is not a locomotive, but he is able to move very fast, so in this way he resembles a locomotive. To say that Superman was as fast as a speeding bullet would not contradict the premise in the first sentence. Superman is as fast as both a bullet and a locomotive.

Metaphors, on the other hand, do imply an equation, for the word "metaphor" literally means "to carry out a change." Unlike similes which use "like" or "as" in a comparison, metaphors use the copula "is" to link a concept or idea with its referent more directly; they speak about one thing or state of affairs in terms that are suggestive of another.[11] We will take as an example the sentence, "The room is an oven." Here, room and oven are equated, or the room

---

text to reconstruct historical events. See D. Rhoads, "Narrative Criticism and the Gospel of Mark," *JAAR* 50 (1982): 413. S. Motyer ("Method in Fourth Gospel Studies: A Way Out of the Impasse?" *JSNT* 66 [1997]: 27–44) argues that narrative criticism must take historical criticism seriously because the narrative presupposes historical reality lying behind the text. See also D. Tovey, *Art and Act in the Fourth Gospel* (JSNTSup 151; Sheffield: Sheffield Academic Press, 1997). The historical basis of the narrative, however important, will not be the main focus of this study.

   [9] R. Alan Culpepper describes the roles of implied author and narrator in *Anatomy of the Fourth Gospel: A Study in Literary Design* (Philadelphia: Fortress, 1983), 1–50.

   [10] "What is communicated is *story*, the formal content element of narrative; and it is communicated by *discourse*, the formal expression element." (S. Chatman, *Story and Discourse: Narrative Structure in Fiction and Film* [Ithaca: Cornell University Press, 1978], 31).

   [11] J. Soskice, *Metaphor and Religious Language* (Oxford: Clarendon, 1985), 53.

"has changed into an oven."[12] But how can that be? If we assume that a room is a place where people can be or live, it is absurd to imagine that someone would be or live in a small compartment used to bake bread. A room and an oven are not the same thing.[13] Yet, if we imagine the characteristics of an oven—say, that it is small, dark, and very hot—we can picture the room as also small, dark and very hot. The characteristics of the oven are applied to the room and we have a clear image not only of the appearance of the room (small and dark), but also of the feel (very hot) and perhaps even the emotional atmosphere of the room (claustrophobic). In this way, the oven serves as a vehicle to carry the meaning of the referent, or what I. A. Richards calls its *tenor* (that is, of the room).[14] The defining characteristics of a metaphor therefore include an equation between one thing and another that "may not normally be expected in a given work, but which may be unusual, unpredictable, and even surprising."[15] To speak metaphorically, then, is to speak of one thing in terms appropriate to another.[16]

The juxtaposition of two disparate images, such as a room and an oven, results in a tension that seeks resolution.[17] Because metaphors are based on likeness in difference and "a system of commonplace associations,"[18] the reader is required to make an educated guess as to which characteristics of the vehicle are to be transferred to the tenor.[19] Because different readers will guess differently, the meaning of the metaphor has infinite possibilities.[20] In our example above, another interpreter might suggest that it is passion that drives

---

[12] E. Roberts, *Writing Themes About Literature* (6th ed., Englewood Cliffs, N.J.: Prentice Hall, 1988), 121–2. J. Culler, "Commentary," *New Literary History* 6 (1974): 219–29, distinguishes two ways of thinking about metaphor. In the philosophical way of thinking, metaphors function, as does all language, to fill the gap between sense and reference. There is usually a one-to-one correspondence between sense and reference. In the rhetorical way of thinking, metaphors are perceived as a problem of incongruity in the text that causes the reader to strive for intelligibility.

[13] Roberts, *Writing*, 121.

[14] *The Philosophy of Rhetoric* (Oxford: Oxford University Press, 1936), 96.

[15] Roberts, *Writing*, 122.

[16] C. Koester, Symbolism in the Fourth Gospel: Meaning, Mystery, Community (Minneapolis: Fortress, 1995), 6.

[17] P. Ricoeur, *Interpretation Theory: Discourse and the Surplus of Meaning* (Fort Worth: Texas Christian University Press, 1976), 50–51. Culler ("Commentary," 229) emphasizes the importance of tension established in metaphors and states that it is the "resistance to replacement operations" that gives literature its power.

[18] P. Ricoeur, "Metaphor and the Main Problem of Hermeneutics," *New Literary History* 6 (1974): 104. Richards (*Philosophy*, 55) argues that the sense of the author's words "are resultants which we arrive at only through the interplay of the interpretive possibilities of the whole utterance," or what he calls the complete "interanimation" of words.

[19] N. Friedman, *Form and Meaning in Fiction* (Athens: University of Georgia Press, 1975), 289–92.

[20] Ricoeur, "Metaphor," 107.

up the emotional temperature in the room. Paul Ricoeur argues that the larger context provides clues to the meaning of a metaphor; a good explanation of the metaphor will then account for all (or most) of the clues.[21] The metaphor will, in turn, contribute to the meaning of the work as a whole, resulting in a hermeneutical circle in which the meaning of both the individual metaphor and the work are enriched.[22] Finally, a metaphor creates new meaning,[23] and tells us something new about reality, especially when it is shocking in its equation of one thing with another.[24] Margaret Atwood's book title *The Edible Woman*,[25] which brings two disparate notions together, provokes such creative re-imagining.[26]

Among the categories of figurative language, signs are distinct from metaphors and similes. As a literary device, a sign signals an event that is about to happen in the narrative.[27] For example, thunder indicates that a storm is approaching, or the presence of the owl anticipates imminent death. The meaning of a sign is determined arbitrarily, sometimes by allusion to the signs of nature, but more often by the text itself.[28] This literary definition is not to be confused with the Johannine use of the term "sign" (σημεῖον), which is a technical term referring to an action of Jesus that points to his identity (20:31). To avoid confusion, the term "sign" will only be used in this study in the Johannine sense.

---

[21] Ibid., 104.

[22] Ibid., 106, 109–10. D. Wead (*Literary Devices in John's Gospel* [Basel: Friedrich Reinhart Kommissionsverlag, 1970], 73) notes that metaphors and double meanings are distinct. In metaphors, the various aspects of meanings merge to create something new. In double meanings, two aspects of meaning are held separately and do not create something new.

[23] Ricoeur, *Interpretation*, 52–53; Roberts, *Writing*, 122.

[24] R. Kysar ("Johannine Metaphor—Meaning and Function: A Literary Case Study of John 10:1–8," *Semeia* 53 [1991]: 98–99) says that the resulting "irresolvable paradox" shocks the reader into a new kind of experience.

[25] Toronto: McClelland & Stewart, 1969.

[26] D. Davidson ("What Metaphors Mean," *Critical Inquiry* 5, no. 1 [1978]: 31–47) argues that metaphors evoke associations that are limitless; that is what keeps them alive. Thus, metaphors cannot be dependent on their historical context or they would not be metaphors. See J. Derrida, "White Mythology: Metaphor in the Text of Philosophy," *New Literary History* 6 (1974): 12; Ricoeur, "Metaphor," 100. On the other hand, if a metaphor is over-used or has a one-to-one correspondence, it is a dead metaphor, because it no longer has the power to evoke new meanings. For example, the "leg of a table" is a dead metaphor. See R. Wellek and A. Warren, *Theory of Literature* (3d ed., New York: Harcourt Brace & World, 1956), 196.

[27] P. Wheelwright, *The Burning Fountain: A Study in the Language of Symbolism* (Bloomington: Indiana University Press, 1954), 20.

[28] J. Painter, "Johannine Symbols: A Case Study in Epistemology," *Journal of Theology of South Africa* 27 (1979): 33.

The distinction between metaphor and symbol is more difficult.[29] René Wellek and Austin Warren argue that if an image appears once, it is a metaphor. If it recurs persistently, both as presentation and representation, it becomes a symbol or a part of a symbolic (or mythic) system.[30] However, metaphors and symbols are distinct because of the nature of their tenor. A metaphor has both a vehicle and a tenor or referent; it is the role of the reader to understand the relationship between the two. With symbols, however, the tenor is implied; only the vehicle is supplied in the form of an object, an action, a pattern or a person, each of which stands for something in its own right. It is the task of the reader to discover which tenor is meant. This tenor may be identified by either external or internal relationships. External relationships are established through other works by the same author, universal experience, historical, literary and textual conventions and archetypal patterns.[31] Internal relationships are established within the text by other similes, metaphors, structural emphasis, arrangement, position, development, selection, inclusion, and recurrence.[32] Once a relationship is established which locates the symbol (vehicle) in its appropriate tenor, then mere mention of the vehicle will call forth the whole complex of contexts and metaphors that establish the relationship in the first place.[33] Thus, as the reader proceeds through the text and sees the symbol in a variety of contexts, the meaning of the symbol develops and expands, evoking new meanings and ideas.[34] These new meanings and ideas do not always confirm the perceived meaning of the symbol. Often, they challenge the previous conceptual idea of the symbol and force readers to reassess and adjust their thinking in order to bring some measure of coherence to the meaning of the

---

[29] On the difference between metaphor and symbol, see Ricoeur, *Interpretation*, 45–69, especially 63–69.

[30] Wellek, *Theory*, 189.

[31] Although this study will note literary traditions that shape the symbolic language where they apply, no account will be given of universal experience or archetypal patterns. For a full discussion of these external relationships, see C. Jung, *Psychology and Religion* (New Haven: Yale University Press, 1938); E. Goodenough, *Jewish Symbols in the Greco-Roman Period* (Princeton: Princeton University Press, 1988); P. Diel and J. Solotareff, *Symbolism in the Gospel of John* (San Francisco: Harper & Row, 1988); P. Diel, *Symbolism in the Bible: The Universality of Symbolic Language and Its Psychological Significance* (translated by N. Marans; San Francisco: Harper & Row, 1986). As the author of the Gospel of John cannot be determined with certainty, no comparison will be made with either the Johannine Epistles or the Book of Revelation.

[32] Friedman (*Form*, 291–4) discusses these relationships in detail. He identifies archetypal patterns and other works of the author as the only two external relationships and inexplicably includes the others in the list of internal relationships.

[33] Friedman, *Form*, 293.

[34] R. Wade Paschal, Jr., "Sacramental Symbolism and Physical Imagery in the Gospel of John," *Tyndale Bulletin* 32 (1981): 153.

symbol. Sometimes coherence is impossible and the reader must be satisfied with ambivalence, which, in itself, can be both positive and productive.[35] Figurative or symbolic language can, therefore, do more than explain; it can challenge the reader to think, to probe and to interpret.[36] In short, a symbol is defined as a literary device that both stands for something in its own right (presentation) but also points beyond itself to something that defies clear and definitive perceptual expression (representation).[37]

William Freedman distinguishes literary motifs from literary symbols. He argues that literary symbols are single, unchanging elements, such as the turtle in the opening pages of John Steinbeck's novel *Grapes of Wrath* which foreshadows the slow movement of the Okies across the country.[38] In contrast, a motif, while it may appear as something described, more often forms part of the description, even when the symbolized referent is not immediately involved. For example, if there were frequent references to Tom Joad's turtle-neck sweater, or to the hard shell of Ma Joad, or to things tortoise-like or turtle-like, and if these references were found outside of the narrative context of the family's slow movement westward, this cluster of references, which Freedman calls an "associational cluster," would form a motif.

> A motif, then, is a recurrent theme, character, or verbal pattern, but it may also be a family or associational cluster of literal or figurative references to a given class of concepts or objects, whether it be animals, machines, circles, music, or whatever.[39]

Like individual symbols, motifs accumulate meaning throughout the text and seem to represent more than their mere literal referent.

According to Freedman, a motif is identified by a number of factors. First and most importantly, a motif is identified by the frequency with which it occurs in the work beyond sheer necessity and coincidence. It must recur often enough to leave a lasting impression on the reader, at least subliminally. Second, equally important, it must also appear in contexts where it is not demanded, where another expression or phrase might easily replace it.

---

[35] Ricoeur, *Interpretation*, 47; see the discussion in F. Dillistone, *The Power of Symbols in Religion and Culture* (New York: Crossroad, 1986), 165–6.

[36] Paschal, "Sacramental," 153.

[37] L. Jones, *The Symbol of Water in the Gospel of John* (Sheffield: Sheffield Academic Press, 1997), 19; Wellek, *Theory*, 189; Dillistone, *Power*, 33. Cf. Wheelwright, *Fountain*, 24. "The paradox of symbols is that they represent something else while they continue to remain themselves" (M. Eliade, *The Sacred and the Profane: The Nature of Religion* [trans. W. Trask; New York: Harper & Row, 1961], 12).

[38] New York: Penguin, 1992. Other examples include Melville's white whale, the New Testament's cross, or Hawthorne's scarlet letter.

[39] W. Freedman, "Literary Motif: A Definition and Evaluation," *Novel* 4 (1971): 127. E. K. Brown (*The Rhythm of the Novel* [Toronto: University of Toronto Press, 1950], 85) suggests that the physical setting of a narrative might also be included in this collection.

The effectiveness of a motif is determined by five factors. The first is the rate of recurrence; the more often the motif recurs, the deeper impression it is likely to make on the reader. The second factor determining effectiveness is avoidability and unlikelihood. If a reference is uncommon in a given context, it is more likely to strike the reader, either consciously or unconsciously. The third factor is the significance of the context in which the motif occurs. A motif that prominently appears at most of the climactic points in the narrative makes a greater impact than a motif that appears only in less central passages. The fourth factor that increases the impact of the motif is the degree to which all occurrences of it cohere into a recognizable unit. The fifth factor, which concerns only those motifs that function symbolically, is "the appropriateness of the motif to what it symbolizes."[40]

A literary motif draws attention to itself through repetition and evokes lively interest and engagement from readers. Its primary function, however, is to act symbolically.[41] Indeed, Freedman claims that motifs "perform a synecdochic function." That is, the literary motif represents in microcosm that which the literary work accomplishes on a larger scale, and that which human experience accomplishes in general.[42] In this way, motifs reflect the (often unconscious) preoccupation of a society or its particular members.[43] At the same time, symbolic language participates in the creation of new self-understanding.[44]

It is this last dimension that makes symbolic language so important in religious texts. Symbols that arise in religious contexts are often understood to connect the everyday with the primordial world. Ricoeur says that symbols "hesitate on the dividing line between *bios* and *logos*" and are thus "bound to the cosmos."[45] Paul Tillich argues that symbolic language must be used to refer to transcendence, for transcendence is essentially unknowable.[46] Craig Koester believes that symbolic language "provides a way to span the distance without collapsing the distance."[47] Thus, when readers who accept the authority of the text interpret its symbolic language, they also reassess and reconstruct their authoritative transcendent worldview, often in opposition to their present "earthly" worldview. While this study will explore the rhetorical potential of the

---

[40] Freedman, "Motif," 126–7.

[41] Ibid., 124.

[42] Ibid., 129; see also Friedman, *Form*, 293.

[43] Freedman, "Motif," 124; cf. Friedman, *Form*, 290.

[44] D. Rasmussen, *Symbol and Interpretation* (The Hague: Martinus Hijhoff, 1974), 88.

[45] Ricoeur, *Interpretation*, 59, 61; Dillistone, *Power*, 13–14.

[46] P. Tillich, *Dynamics of Faith* (New York: Harper & Row, 1957), 41–47. In this sense, A. J. Heschel (*Who Is Man?* [Stanford: Stanford University Press, 1965], 1–2) agrees with Tillich but warns that symbols should be chosen very carefully, knowing always that symbols of the transcendent are always partial and imperfect.

[47] Koester, *Symbolism*, 28.

literary motif in general terms, it will mainly focus on the literary construction and coherence of the ingesting motif as a vehicle for soteriology.[48]

Figurative language in general and symbolic language specifically are used to expand the meaning and interest of the simple narrative. Similes instruct through comparison. Metaphors create new concepts by referring to one thing in language appropriate to another. Symbols refer both to themselves and to something else more abstract. Motifs remind the reader repeatedly of the central preoccupation of the text. In all this, the responsive reader endeavors to construct some degree of coherence between the narrative and its discursive elements.[49] These definitions will give shape to the following study.

A NOTE ABOUT METHODOLOGY:
PARAMETERS FOR THIS STUDY

This dissertation takes as its starting point the well-established premises that the Gospel of John is a clearly defined literary document[50] and that it uses figurative language with the intent to convey meaning. In order to explore the range of this meaning, this study will take into consideration both external and internal referents for the metaphorical language. The social environment in which the Gospel was produced[51] provides the context for external referents and may include literature produced and/or used by first-century Jews and Christians. Biblical material is particularly important in this respect because the Gospel is demonstrably dependent on it.[52] That is, the author of the Gospel assumes that the reader has some previous knowledge of Jewish scripture and

---

[48] Compare other studies that focus on the expected response of the reader, such as J. Staley, *The Print's First Kiss: A Rhetorical Investigation of the Implied Reader in the Fourth Gospel* (Atlanta: Scholars Press, 1988) and Kysar, "Metaphor," 81–111.

[49] The literary theory of symbolic language as it is presented here is drawn from the analysis of modern literature, especially the modern novel. These theories will, in turn, be used in an analysis of an ancient text. While this may seem to be anachronistic because of the span of literary history, modern literary criticism does supply working definitions, categories and tools that will help to shape an analysis of ancient literature. See R. Morgan, *Biblical Interpretation* (Oxford: Oxford University Press, 1988), 227–9.

[50] The Greek New Testament UBS 4th edition serves as the basis for this study. English citations are either my own translation or the NRSV.

[51] Most likely originating in Ephesus, this Gospel is addressed to those who are familiar with both Palestinian Jewish and Greco-Roman culture. See R. Brown, *An Introduction to the New Testament* (New York: Doubleday, 1997), 371–3. The text was probably written over time and was completed near the end of the first century. See Brown, *Introduction*, 375; Schnackenburg, *Gospel*, 1:59–74; and P. Perkins, "The Gospel according to John," in *The New Jerome Biblical Commentary* (ed. R. Brown, J. Fitzmyer, R. Murphy; London: Geoffrey Chapman, 1989), 942–7.

[52] Brown, *Gospel*, lix–lxi.

its religious themes. Therefore, this study will consider the use of words and ideas in texts that were known to have influenced the Gospel of John because they are either directly or indirectly cited, such as Second Isaiah, Psalms 22 and 69, or Zechariah.[53] To a much lesser extent, this study will consider the Apocrypha, Pseudepigrapha, the writings of Josephus and Philo of Alexandria, and the Qumran material as other possible windows into the religious thought-world of the author and reader of the Gospel of John.[54] Greco-Roman literature which pre-dates 100 C. E. and concerns eating practice will also be considered when appropriate. However, while this study recognizes the importance of the historical location in the generation of the Gospel of John, it also appreciates the fact that texts often do more than *reflect* their generative historical context. They *create* imagined, ideal social contexts that are quite different from their generative locations.[55] Therefore, this study will use these texts to assist in the interpretation of the Johannine ingesting motif with both discretion and humility.

The dependence of John on other New Testament texts continues to be highly debated, and rather than assume dependence, this study will confine itself to the known "literary world" of the Johannine narrative. This means, for example, that because there is no explicit reference to the Eucharist in the Gospel of John, this study will not assume that the thanksgiving for the bread and fish in John 6 relates to Eucharist traditions known to the Synoptic Gospels and Paul.[56] But because these traditions *may* stand behind John 6, this question of the Eucharist will be treated separately in the conclusion.

This study will therefore focus on the Gospel of John itself and on the biblical allusions it uses. It appreciates the static, synchronic role of structure,

---

[53] See J. Beutler, "The Use of Scripture in the Gospel of John," in *Exploring the Gospel of John: In Honor of D. Moody Smith* (ed. A. Culpepper and C. Black; Louisville, Ky.: Westminster John Knox, 1996), 147–62; A. T. Hanson, "John's Use of Scripture," in *The Gospels and the Scriptures of Israel* (ed. C. Evans and W. Stegner; JSNTSup 104; Sheffield: Sheffield Academic Press, 1994), 358–79; M. Hengel, "The Old Testament in the Fourth Gospel," in *The Gospels and the Scriptures of Israel* (ed. C. Evans and W. Stegner; JSNTSup 104; Sheffield: Sheffield Academic Press, 1994), 380–395; D. Clark, "Signs in Wisdom and John," *CBQ* 45 (1983): 201–9; M. Daly-Denton, *David in the Fourth Gospel: Johannine Reception of the Psalms* (Leiden: Brill, 2000).

[54] See Brown (*Gospel*, lii–lxiv) for a summary of the influences on the religious thought in the Gospel of John.

[55] F. Jameson, The Political Unconscious: Narrative as a Socially Symbolic Act (Ithaca: Cornell University Press, 1981).

[56] Schnackenburg (*Gospel*, 3:6), for example, assumes that the Gospel of John must know the Synoptic tradition because it leaves out details that are necessary to understand the story. With a note of caution, Painter ("Symbols," 26) says that unproven dependence is not the same as independence. See U. Wilckens, *Das Evangelium nach Johannes* (NTD 4; Göttingen: Vandenhoeck & Ruprecht, 1998).

metaphors, symbols and literary motifs that shape the presentation of the content. At the same time, it acknowledges the narrative elements of the Gospel that present the content in diachronic fashion, demonstrating development of themes over narrative time and space. Moreover, this study recognizes the role of the reader in the interpretation process, noting that, while the text in its final form has remained more or less fixed, the thought-world of its readers has not remained static. Conceding that each reader's subjectivity influences an interpretation and that diverse and varied interpretations may be equally valid, all observations and conclusions in this study are made with humility.

A SURVEY OF PREVIOUS STUDIES
ON JOHANNINE SYMBOLISM

Most modern discussions of Johannine symbolism start with the work of C. H. Dodd who states that the Gospel of John is meaningless unless it is understood to function symbolically. Indeed, the language is so symbolic that the symbol is absorbed by the thing signified.[57] Thus, the meaning of the symbol cannot be derived from its place in ordinary experience; it must be derived from the worldview of the evangelist. This worldview, according to Dodd, is influenced by Pauline thought, Rabbinic Judaism in part, Hellenistic Judaism and, less directly perhaps, Paganism, Gnosticism, and Platonism. Thus, John's references to water stand simultaneously for the water of Christian baptism, the Jewish notions of Torah, Wisdom, and the Holy Spirit, and the Gnostic concept of lower creation. The narratives of the first twelve chapters of John also require symbolic interpretation, for the "signs" are partly explained by the discourses that accompany them.[58] The narratives are thus both factual and symbolic of a higher truth.[59] Binding the whole work together, Johannine symbols disclose a worldview that sees the events and things of the world as living and moving images of the Eternal, revealed most succinctly in the person of Jesus. Dodd thus underlines the importance of reading the Gospel of John as a symbolic text.

Building on these foundations, Wayne Meeks argues that even geographical place names, such as Galilee and Judea, are symbolic. He concludes that the Gospel of John emphasizes the conflict between Jesus' origins in Galilee and eschatological expectations in Judea, thus reflecting traditions arising in the

---

[57] C. H. Dodd, *The Interpretation of the Fourth Gospel* (Cambridge: University Press, 1953), 133–43, especially 137. A similar argument is expressed by J. Leal, "El simbolismo histórico del IV Evangelio," *Estudios Bíblicos* 19 (1960): 329–48.

[58] Ibid., 141–2.

[59] Ibid., 142–3.

early Johannine community.[60] In a later study, Meeks uses the ascent-descent motif to demonstrate the way in which motifs reconstruct a new worldview by establishing oppositions. "The book defines and vindicates the existence of the community that evidently sees itself as unique, alien from this world, under attack, misunderstood, but living in unity with Christ and through him with God."[61] Meeks thus demonstrates the social function of symbolic language in the Gospel of John.

David Wead's dissertation, titled *The Literary Devices in John's Gospel*,[62] examines metaphors and symbolic language and pays particular attention to the "I am" sayings that "cover the majority of the important concepts and the essential proclamations of the messianic role of the Christ found in the Gospel." Against Rudolf Bultmann's and Eduard Schweizer's claims that the "I am" sayings are fixed symbolic titles, Wead argues that these sayings are metaphors that conjoin known elements (gate, good shepherd, vine, bread, etc.) with an unknown element (the Christ). These metaphors are explained in the context of the larger discourse. For instance, Jesus uses a biblical reference, such as the manna, and reinterprets it by describing himself as "the bread of life." Whereas symbols and titles are fixed entities, statements such as "I am the bread of life" are more fluid; on this basis, Wead identifies them as metaphors.[63] "The metaphors are then developed to emphasize to the hearer or reader the characteristics or qualities of each element which become important for the union."[64] This union of terminology, Wead stresses, is a rich source for Johannine Christology.[65]

Wead also addresses the importance of the Johannine signs, events that illuminate messianic salvation but require explanation. They serve to authenticate the person and mission of Jesus, and as such, push witnesses to choose either for or against him. "Jesus gives and is the sign."[66] Wead cautions against always reading signs as symbols, however, for the author of John frequently points out symbolic elements by explaining them. If an object or

---

[60] "Galilee and Judea in the Fourth Gospel," *JBL* 85 (1966): 159–69. For another study focusing on the symbolic use of geographical and chronological information, see Wilckens, *Evangelium*.

[61] W. Meeks, "The Man from Heaven in Johannine Sectarianism," *JBL* 91 (1971): 70.

[62] Basel: Friedrich Reinhart Kommissionsverlag, 1968.

[63] Here, Wead (Literary, 83–6) agrees with P. Borgen, Bread from Heaven: An Exegetical Study of the Concept of Manna in the Gospel of John and the Writings of Philo (Leiden: Brill, 1965), 59–98.

[64] Wead, *Literary*, 94.

[65] G. Stemberger, *La symbolique du bien et du mal selon Saint Jean* (Paris: Seuil, 1970), also argues that Johannine symbols are Christological in nature and that they convey the same ethical imperative calling the reader to believe in Jesus.

[66] Wead, *Literary*, 29.

event is not explained, it is not a symbol, according to Wead. Since some signs are explained (the Feeding of the Multitude, for example) and others are not (the Wedding at Cana), it is not clear that signs should be interpreted as symbols beyond the parameters that the author has set.[67] Wead emphasizes the importance of clear definitions for symbols as literary devices, but his limits rule out multiple meanings, an imposition that does not do justice to the profundity of the Gospel.

Observing that studies of Johannine symbolism are often avoided because they might challenge historicity, Sandra Schneiders argues that it is "only in terms of symbol, correctly understood, that we can understand John's presentation of the incarnation as salvation."[68] She distinguishes the literary use of "sign" and "symbol" in the Gospel of John. A symbol, she says, is "1) a sensible reality 2) which renders present to and 3) involves a person subjectively in 4) a transforming experience 5) of the mystery of the Transcendent."[69] In contrast, a sign (as a literary definition, not as the Johannine σημεῖον) is a sensible reality which merely points to an absent reality totally other than itself. Whereas a symbol is multi-faceted, a sign designates the known by means of an unambiguous one-to-one correspondence. Unlike a symbol, a sign does not require the commitment necessary for a transforming experience. Finally, a sign cannot mediate the personal or some aspect of the personal existence of life such as love, life or truth; only a symbol can do that. As a symbol, therefore, Jesus is the "sensible locus of relationship with God" and his σημεῖα ("signs") and ῥήματα ("words") are the symbolic expressions of his identity as the Son of God (5:1–18; 7:21; 14:10).[70] After Jesus is no longer historically present, the believing community becomes the "sensible locus of relationship with God" for they are "children of God" (1:12; 11:52); by their words and deeds (14:12), they become the continuing present reality of a transcendent mystery.[71] Thus, according to Schneiders, salvation is presented as a symbolic revelation that does not change. Only its expression changes: first it is through Jesus; then it is through the church. In this way, Schneiders values the literary and historical function of symbolic language.

In a significant study of John 9, John Painter argues that the Gospel of John draws its symbols from the human experience of the world, a world that

---

[67] Ibid., 27–29.

[68] S. Schneiders, "Symbolism and the Sacramental Principle in the Fourth Gospel," in *Segni e sacramenti nel Vangelio di Giovanni* (Rome: Editrice Anselmiana, 1977), 226. See also "History and Symbolism in the Fourth Gospel," in *L'Evangile de Jean* (ed. M. de Jonge; Gembloux, Leuven University Press, 1977), 371–6.

[69] Schneiders, "Symbolism," 223.

[70] Ibid., 228–9.

[71] Ibid., 229–35.

manifests its creator through the λόγος.[72] Those things that give life, such as
bread, water and light, symbolically point to Jesus who also sustains life. "The
world is a storehouse of symbols which can become bearers of the revelation if
they are *seen* to point beyond themselves to the revealer and through him to
God."[73] The function of the symbols thus depends on their perception by the
reader. Painter argues that these symbols are regularly drawn from Judaism and
reapplied to a Christological context. For example, "John contends that Jesus,
not the Law, gives man sight, perception, light, understanding and life."[74] In
this way, John's "use of symbols is intended to attack the root of unbelief and to
make a new and growing knowledge of God possible."[75] The Gospel establishes
a dualistic structure that forces the reader to choose for or against the revealer,
and consequently, for or against Judaism.[76] Moreover, according to Painter, the
symbolic use of bread, wine and water is not necessarily symbolic in a
sacramental sense, if by "sacramental" we mean to refer only to the Eucharist
and baptism. Indeed, the Gospel's use of these symbols might suggest an
attempt to correct or to reinterpret various symbols as they relate to sacramental
understanding.[77] Painter's study is thus important for two reasons: first, he
emphasizes the rhetorical function of symbols; second, he challenges the view
that all references to water, bread and wine relate to the sacraments.

Calling renewed attention to the symbols in John, Xavier Léon-Dufour
argues that a symbolic reading *must* serve as a complement to other approaches
to the study of the Gospel; to read the text only historically, or only
symbolically, limits our ability to appreciate its significance.[78] According to
Léon-Dufour, symbols do not have a fixed inherent meaning, for their meaning
is determined by their cultural and literary context. For this reason, he calls
them "symbolic operations." Symbolic operations are required on more than
one level. For example, bread may be understood both on an earthly or spiritual
level (physical or spiritual nourishment) and on a Jewish or Christian level
(manna or Eucharistic bread). "The authentic reading of the Gospel supposes
that the two levels of symbolism be maintained in a dialectical relationship, that
is, neither one nor the other should drive its opposite number from the field."[79]
By giving one level primacy, we lose the full meaning of the text. This is most

---

[72] "Symbols," 26–41.
[73] Ibid., 40 (Painter's italics).
[74] Ibid., 41.
[75] Ibid., 40.
[76] Ibid., 36.
[77] Ibid., 31.
[78] X. Léon-Dufour, "Towards a Symbolic Reading of the Fourth Gospel," *NTS* 27
(1981): 439–56 (Léon-Dufour's emphasis).
[79] Ibid., 441.

evident with reference to Jesus: he is both human and divine, both historical and transcendent, and both physical and spiritual. Denying one aspect in the pair negates the basic theological premise of the Gospel that the Messiah is both Jesus and the Son of God (cf. John 20:31). Léon-Dufour's most significant contribution to the study of Johannine symbolism is his stress on reading symbols on several levels at the same time, without negating one in favor of the other. In this way, the full significance of symbols in both their Jewish and their Christian contexts is appreciated.

In an important and influential study, *Anatomy of the Fourth Gospel: A Study in Literary Design*, R. Alan Culpepper discusses the role of symbols in the "implicit commentary," or the "sub-surface signals," of the Gospel of John. "Traffic on the Gospel's subterranean frequencies," he says, "is so heavy that even the perceptive reader is never sure he or she has received all the signals the text is sending."[80] By closely defining metaphors, symbols, and motifs, and by being sensitive to the interplay of their movement and development in the narrative as well as in their relationship to each other, Culpepper analyzes the function of symbolic language in the Gospel as a literary whole.[81] Three core symbols which represent both Jesus and all that sustains life—namely light, water and bread—are discussed in detail; these symbols are progressively disclosed throughout the narrative by repetition and variation, providing only flashes of meaning here and there.

> John's development of the symbolism of water, like that of light, moves from earlier contexts in which its meaning and associations are more clearly defined, even if they change from one passage to another, to the point where the author assumes that mere references to the symbol, or words or images connected with it, will evoke the same rich constellation of earlier references and associations. The impact is profound and moving, for the symbols increasingly elude efforts to interpret them and thereby invite further contemplation.[82]

Therefore, the author of the Gospel uses symbolism to tell the reader that things are more than they seem, that abstract realities lie behind concrete objects.[83] Citing Edward K. Brown, Culpepper claims that words and scenes have a "surplus of meaning" that is never fully exhausted.[84] It is up to the reader to make some sense of the symbolic language. In addition, symbolic language, which is often dualistic, points to the central conflict between Jesus who is "from above" and those "from below" who cannot or will not recognize his identity. As readers begin to understand and accept the symbols of the world

---

[80] Culpepper, *Anatomy*, 151.
[81] Ibid., 188–9.
[82] Ibid., 195.
[83] Ibid., 199.
[84] Brown, *Rhythm*, 45–46.

above, they distance themselves from the world below. That is not to say, warns Culpepper, that the world is inherently evil or opposed to the world above; the Gospel represents the world below as a creation of Jesus the λόγος and thus as a reflection of the higher mysteries. In this way, all of concrete reality is essentially sacramental; the ecclesial sacraments have no exclusive claim to this function.[85] As a result, the Gospel invites constant re-reading and struggling with the text to the end that readers begin to share the perception of meaning with the author,[86] a perception that is but a glimpse of a different reality. In this way, symbols are "often the ladder on which readers, like the angels of Jacob's dream, may ascend and descend while moving to and from the heaven opened by the story" (cf. 1:51).[87] Culpepper thus identifies patterns of symbolic language in the Gospel of John and reflects on their larger rhetorical potential.

Dorothy Lee focuses on the complex interplay of symbol and narrative in her examination of six "symbolic narratives" in the Gospel of John.[88] Each narrative develops a different symbol; the symbol in turn draws out the narrative. The narrative proceeds through five stages. First, the narrative begins by presenting a miracle or a sign, such as bread or healing, or by establishing an image such as water. Second, a character responds in such a way as to express misunderstanding: by understanding the symbol literally, they misunderstand both the symbolic meaning of the sign and Jesus as the one who provides the sign. Third, the character struggles to understand, and Jesus explains with a series of clarifying statements. Fourth, the character either accepts or rejects the symbolic understanding of the sign, choosing either belief or unbelief. Fifth, the narrative concludes with a confession of faith and/or an explicit statement of rejection by Jesus.[89] In theological terms, these narratives reveal the manner in which material realities become understood as divine, reflecting the larger narrative pattern of the divine made flesh in Jesus. Lee thus focuses on the symbol's articulation within the discourse (semantic) and the symbol's relationship to life (non-semantic); both have their parallels in the basic theological outlook of the Gospel. Accordingly, she can say that σάρξ ("flesh") and δόξα/πνεῦμα ("glory"/"spirit") are not in opposition to each other, but relate to each other as symbol relates to reality. "What is intended by the narrative is the re-appropriation of σάρξ to become symbolic of the divine." This re-appropriation occurs only through the narrative form.[90] Lee concludes

---

[85] Culpepper, *Anatomy*, 199–201.

[86] Ibid., 202.

[87] Ibid., 181.

[88] D. A. Lee, *The Symbolic Narratives of the Fourth Gospel: The Interplay of Form and Meaning* (Sheffield: Sheffield Academic Press, 1994).

[89] Ibid., 12–13.

[90] Ibid., 230–231.

that when readers accept Jesus as the symbol of God, they embrace not only God but also their "own identity as belonging to God and made in God's image, finding there a new self-understanding."[91] In this way, Lee appreciates both the interplay between symbols and their narrative context and the role of symbolic language in constructing identity.

Craig Koester has conducted the most recent comprehensive study of Johannine symbolism by drawing out the literary, sociohistorical and theological aspects of the text. Building on the work of literary theorists, he defines a symbol as (1) an image that can be perceived by the senses, such as bread, wine or water, (2) an action, like the foot-washing, that contradicts regular patterns of behavior, or (3) a person who is understood to have transcendent significance, especially when an individual is addressed in the plural, like Nicodemus.[92] Koester further distinguishes between core symbols, which convey transcendent realities most clearly, and supporting symbols, which contribute to the development of these core symbols. Light is a core symbol; daytime and the ability to see are supporting symbols. Core symbols "occur most often, in the most significant contexts in the narrative, and contribute most to the Gospel's message."[93] Koester also points out that many symbols are identified by their incongruity or contradiction; for instance, the Gospel cannot possibly mean that Jesus is baked flour and water when it refers to him as "the bread of life." Other symbols become evident in the context of a misunderstanding among characters in the narrative. The Samaritan woman looks for the water that Jesus offers without realizing that he is referring to a transcendent reality—that is, himself. Some terms acquire symbolic overtones when they become a part of recurring motifs; for example, darkness and night take on new meaning after Jesus says, "I am the light of the world" (8:12).[94] According to Koester, the underlying structure of these Johannine symbols is twofold: first, they say something about Christ, and second, they say something about the disciples. For example, Jesus is the light of the world and the disciples are called to walk in the light (8:12). As the seed that falls to the ground, Jesus must die to give life (12:24); similarly, the disciples must die to the self through service to Christ, resulting in everlasting life (12:25–26).[95] The interpretation of Johannine symbols must consider its literary context (within both the Gospel and the literature of antiquity) and its social and cultural setting. Based on the interpretation of symbols in their sociohistorical context, Koester challenges "the idea that Johannine Christianity was an introverted sect

---

[91] Ibid., 231.
[92] Koester, *Symbolism*, 4.
[93] Ibid., 5.
[94] Ibid., 9.
[95] Ibid., 13–15.

whose symbolic language would have been opaque to the uninitiated."[96] Rather, Johannine symbolism would have been accessible to a wide range of people and functioned both to develop a sense of group identity and to motivate the community to engage in missionary activity. In all this, Koester emphasizes the centrality of the death of Jesus for understanding Johannine symbolic language, for Jesus is "at the heart" of every symbol.[97] Koester concludes that Johannine symbols, which are drawn from this world, transcend their earthly meaning to provide a glimpse of higher reality.

Building on the work of Culpepper and Koester, Larry Paul Jones considers the symbol of water in the Gospel of John as an expanding symbol, that is, one whose meaning is disclosed bit by bit over the course of the narrative.[98] Two aspects of water are developed. First, water is used to demonstrate Jesus' mastery (he walks on it and turns it into wine). Second, water represents purification and the invitation to a new beginning (seen in the offer of baptism in water and spirit, of living water, of healing through washing, and of foot-washing).[99] In sum, water symbolizes primarily the Spirit, and so also Jesus; to accept the washing or the drink of living water thus means to accept Jesus.[100] "The symbol of water gently but persistently encourages every reader to take (or to reaffirm) that step of faith."[101] This does not necessarily require the sacrament of baptism, Jones concludes, for the Gospel's "interest in the sacraments, like interest in everything else, [is] secondary to faith."[102] This study of the use of water is the first to trace systematically the development of a single symbol throughout the Gospel.

Bruce Malina and Richard Rohrbaugh interpret Johannine symbols from a social-scientific approach by focusing on the social context in which language, especially symbolic language, is constructed. They argue that the Gospel of John likely arose in the context of an "antisociety," a community that saw itself in opposition to their surrounding environment. This community used new words ("relexicalization") to refer to some reality that is not ordinarily described with those terms—such as "abiding in" and "believing into" Jesus—in order to provoke a response of faith and thus membership in the community. It built contrasts between such things as spirit and flesh, above and below, life and death, light and darkness, this-world and not-of-this-world, freedom and slavery, truth and lie, love and hate, in order to create and sustain opposing

---

[96] Ibid., xi.
[97] Ibid., xi, 1–5.
[98] Jones, *Water*, 13.
[99] Ibid., 229.
[100] Ibid., 230.
[101] Ibid., 231.
[102] Ibid., 237.

modes of living and being. It emphasizes interpersonal and textual modes (who speaks to whom, and how they speak) instead of ideational modes (what is being said). In this way, social values are placed in the foreground of the text.[103] According to Malina and Rohrbaugh, then, John uses complex metaphorical language ("anti-language") to separate members of the Johannine community from the society around them on the basis of highly distinctive social values. Unfortunately, both the society that produced this text and the society against which it defines itself are far distant from the modern reader, so Malina and Rohrbaugh set out to provide some insight into the social system in which John's language is embedded.[104] What is particularly significant about Malina and Rohrbaugh's study is its focus on the social influence of metaphorical language both in the formation of the anti-language and, through it, the formation of a community's self-identity. The study highlights the rhetorical value of language in both reflecting and creating community solidarity.

To summarize, Dodd emphasizes the multi-leveled potential of symbols, the various levels of which Léon-Dufour attempts to hold concurrently. Meeks, and Malina and Rohrbaugh point to the social location and function of symbolic language. Wead, Schneiders, Painter, Culpepper, Koester, and Jones address more directly the rhetorical function of symbolic language, and Lee introduces the interplay of symbol and narrative. These studies have made important contributions to the study of figurative language in the Gospel of John but only Jones' study of water focuses on a particular literary motif and its relationship to the larger message of the Gospel.

A BRIEF SURVEY OF PREVIOUS STUDIES
ON INGESTING THEMES IN THE GOSPEL OF JOHN

Although individual meals and many of the other "ingesting" passages in the Gospel of John have received a great deal of scholarly attention, the ingesting motif has not been explored in any comprehensive fashion. Interesting results have been achieved in the study of meal motifs in other New Testament literature, however. Dennis Smith, for example, has studied the socio-historical context of meals with a special focus on the Gospel of Luke and its relationship to the Greco-Roman symposium model.[105] The symposium was an established

---

[103] B. Malina and R. Rohrbaugh, *Social-Science Commentary on the Gospel of John* (Minneapolis: Fortress, 1998), 4–6.

[104] Ibid., 18–20.

[105] "Table Fellowship as a Literary Motif in the Gospel of Luke," *SBL* 106 (1987): 613–38. See also "The Historical Jesus at Table," in *SBL 1989 Seminar Papers* (ed. D. Lull; Atlanta: Scholars Press, 1979), 466–86; "Social Obligation in the Context of Communal Meals: A Study of the Christian Meal in the First Century in Comparison with Greco-Roman

social pattern in the first century C.E. and provided an opportunity for enlightened conversation as part of the meal. Smith points out the similarities between the Greco-Roman symposium genre and Luke—both include discussions on banquet etiquette and the roles of host and guest—and argues that Luke has clearly expanded these inherited traditions to evoke self-identification in his Greco-Roman readers.[106] Although John does not adopt the symposium genre in the same way that Luke does, Smith's study suggests that the relationship between the Johannine meal narratives and their associated discourses may have more significance than has previously been recognized.

Smith has also examined the concept of "messianic banquets" as the "interplay of mythological and literary motifs with allusions to ritualized versions of actual meals."[107] He divides the data in two ways: the motif of sacred food (fruit from the tree of life, water, fish, bread and wine) and the motif of the sacred banquet (victory over primordial enemies, eternal joyous celebration, abundance of food, the presence of the Messiah [assumed], judgment and the pilgrimage of nations). These two motifs are particularly prevalent in early Jewish and Christian literature such as the New Testament (especially the Gospels), 1QSa II, 11–22, *1 Enoch* 62:12–14 and *2 Bar.* 29. A variation of the messianic banquet is the wedding banquet (see, for example, Isa 54:5–55:5). This banquet motif is a "potent symbol for the joys of the afterlife or of the mythological world, since it carries with it the basic cultural imagery of the life-giving nature of food and the celebrative nature of the banquet."[108]

Communal Meals" (Th.D. diss., Harvard Divinity School, 1980); "Meals and Morality in Paul and His World," *SBL Seminar Papers* 20 (1981): 319–39. See also, X. De Meeûs, "Composition de Lc., xiv et Genre symposiaque," *ETL* 37 (1961): 847–70; E. S. Steele III, "Jesus' Table-Fellowship with Pharisees: An Editorial Analysis of Luke 7:36–50, 11:37–54, and 14:1–24" (Ph.D. diss., Notre Dame, Indiana, 1981); C. McMahan, "Meals as Type Scenes in the Gospel of Luke" (Ph.D. diss., Southern Baptist Theological Seminary, 1987); A. Just, *The Ongoing Feast: Table Fellowship and Eschatology at Emmaus* (Collegeville, Minn.: Liturgical, 1993); K. Corley, *Private Women, Public Meals: Social Conflict in the Synoptic Tradition* (Peabody, Mass.: Hendrickson, 1993) and "Jesus' Table Practice: 'Dining with Tax Collectors and Sinners,' Including Women," *SBL 1993 Seminar Papers* (ed. E. Lovering; Atlanta: Scholars Press, 1993), 444–59; J. Bolyki, "Die Tischgemeinschaften Jesu," *European Theological Journal* 3 (1994): 163–70; W. Braun, *Feasting and Social Rhetoric in Luke 14* (New York: Cambridge University Press, 1995). For other sociological approaches to this question in the Pauline corpus, see P. Gooch, *Dangerous Food: 1 Corinthians 8–10 in Its Context*, (Waterloo: WLU Press, 1993). For the table-fellowship motif in Qumran literature, see J. Dunn, "Jesus, Table-Fellowship and Qumran," in *Jesus and the Dead Sea Scrolls* (ed. J. Charlesworth; New York: Doubleday, 1992), 254–72.

[106] See for example, Luke 5:29–32; 6:24–25; 7:36–50; 10:38–42; 12:16–46; 14:1–24; 15:1–2; 16:19–31; 17:26–29; 21:34; 22:21–38.

[107] D. Smith, "The Messianic Banquet Reconsidered," *The Future of Early Christianity in Honor of Helmut Koester* (ed. B. Pearson; Minneapolis: Fortress, 1991), 64–73.

[108] Ibid., 69.

To suggest, as Smith does, that a literary motif reflects historical practice is problematic, however, for the Johannine meals are idealized. John 6:53–54, for example, is clearly a mythological ideal and does not provide details for ritualized expression. However, the Gospel of John does use the messianic banquet motif to express divine presence in the narrative world.

Judith McKinlay considers biblical invitations to eat and drink in wisdom literature and in the Gospel of John.[109] She argues that the shift from a female host in the wisdom literature to a male host—Jesus—in the Gospel of John has an effect on the perceived role of women in this Gospel. Using the Samaritan Woman narrative as a specific example, she points out the back-and-forth exchange of the roles of host and guest between Jesus and the woman. There are so many interpretive possibilities to this story, McKinlay argues, that it is unclear what the role of the woman is. Indeed, within the context of the whole Gospel, gender roles are so ambiguous that women have little ground to assert themselves and thus are unable to pose a threat to the patriarchal early church. Though McKinlay does not address ingesting language in a comprehensive fashion, she does consider the roles of host and guest in the Gospel.

Sharon Ringe reflects briefly on the significance of meals in John. She argues that the last three meals (12:1–8; 13:1–30; 21:1–14) "try again to prepare the community to understand and accept Jesus' death." They aid in the transition from "a time of memory of Jesus' time on earth into the new stage of the community's life."[110] In this way, meals serve a social function for the Johannine community.

The most comprehensive study of ingesting language and its symbolic interpretation has been conducted by Horace Jeffery Hodges in a dissertation titled, "Food as Synecdoche in John's Gospel and Gnostic Texts."[111] Hodges compares the synecdochical use of food (i.e., food as being part of and as signifying both the heavenly and earthly realms) in early Jewish and Christian texts, with a focus on the Gospel of John and Gnostic texts. He concludes that the Gnostic understanding of the heaven/earth dualism is quite distinct from that of the Gospel of John. The Gnostic texts represent the world as essentially evil; the dualism is ontological. The Gospel, however, reflects the Jewish ethical notion of a good-creation-gone-bad. By identifying Judaism as the principal source of background for the Gospel of John, Hodges argues that Jesus exists by doing the will of the Father (his "food," see 4:34) until he

---

[109] *Gendering Wisdom the Host: Biblical Invitations to Eat and Drink* (JSOTSup 216; Sheffield: Sheffield Academic Press, 1996). For similar arguments, see M. Scott, *Sophia and the Johannine Jesus* (JSNTSup, 71; Sheffield: JSOT Press, 1992).

[110] *Wisdom's Friends: Community and Christology in the Fourth Gospel* (Louisville, Ky.: Westminster John Knox, 1999), 76–77.

[111] Ph.D. diss., University of California, Berkeley, 1995.

consumes the vinegar on the cross. The vinegar represents the curse that the world took on with the fall from paradise. In this way, Jesus takes on the curse of the world in order to redeem it.[112] The real strength of Hodges' study is his thorough investigation into the development of ingesting images throughout various religious traditions.[113]

This dissertation will continue the work of Johannine literary and narrative criticism. Expanding on the work of Culpepper and Koester, it will focus on the presence and role of figurative language in the Gospel of John by examining, not a single symbol as Jones has done, but an entire literary motif drawn from the semantic domain of ingesting language. It will also fill a gap in the study of meal narratives in the Gospel tradition, a study that has proven to be very fruitful in other texts, as Smith has shown. Furthermore, this study will contribute to the discussion of soteriology in the Fourth Gospel by specifically exploring the relationship between the ingesting motif and salvation themes. Finally, this dissertation will reflect briefly on the possibility that Eucharistic language lies behind this ingesting motif.

In the pages that follow, I will examine in sequence the narratives that either feature ingesting language or take place during a meal. In each case, the focus will be firmly fixed on the way that ingesting language is used to convey the Gospel's soteriology. Chapter One discusses the title "Lamb of God" given to Jesus by John the Baptist in John 1. This title suggests that Jesus is identified with the Passover lamb. In the first century, the lamb was consumed to commemorate Israel's deliverance from Egypt and was associated in some ways with the idea of atonement for sin (1:29, 36). Chapter Two considers two passages in John 2: the Wedding in Cana during which Jesus turns water into wine (2:1–11), and the intriguing phrase, "zeal for your house will consume me" (2:17). Chapter Three explores the rich complex of ingesting language in the Samaritan narrative (4:4–42) and its related passage concerning living water in 7:37–39. Chapter Four studies the even more extensive ingesting theme presented in the Feeding of the Multitude and its explanatory Bread of Life Discourse (6:1–71). It also contrasts the notions of "eating life" in John 6 and "tasting death" in John 8:51–52. Chapter Five focuses on the supper in Bethany at which Mary anoints Jesus (12:1–8). Chapter Six examines the use of ingesting language in the Farewell Discourse, focusing specifically on the Last Supper (13:1–30) and the metaphor of the vine (15:1–17). Chapter Seven explores the enigmatic last actions of Jesus on the cross (19:28–37) and the

---

[112] Hodges, "Food," xii–xiii.
[113] For similar approaches see Borgen, Bread; E. Little, *Echoes of the New Testament in the Wine of Cana in Galilee (John 2:1–11) and the Multiplication of the Loaves and Fish (John 6:1–15): Towards an Appreciation* (Cahiers de la Revue Biblique 41; Paris: Gabalda, 1998).

related passage in 18:11 in which Jesus prepares to drink the cup his Father has given him. Chapter Eight discusses the story of the Miraculous Catch of Fish, the Resurrection Breakfast and Jesus' subsequent command to Peter to feed his sheep (21:1–25). Each chapter will include an introduction, an exegesis of the passage with particular attention paid to the way in which the roles of Jesus and the disciples are framed within the ingesting motif, and a conclusion that relates the ingesting motif to the larger soteriology of the Gospel. The dissertation will conclude with an examination of the effectiveness of the ingesting motif in the Gospel of John, based on the criteria of effectiveness established by Freedman. This ingesting motif is found to successfully communicate both the role of Jesus and the role of the disciples in Johannine soteriology. Finally, this dissertation will reflect on the possible relationship of the ingesting motif to Eucharist traditions.

Chapter 1

Lamb of God (1:29, 36)

In the opening chapters of the Gospel of John, various allusions to the ingesting motif begin to make their appearance. As they are developed and expanded throughout the course of the Gospel, their first mention is recognized and appreciated only in retrospect. Even then, this possible ingesting language may tease more than satisfy and suggest more than convince. Such is the case with the first example in this study that deals with the title given to Jesus by John the Baptist, "the Lamb of God."

John the Baptist is the first to testify to the physical presence of Jesus in the world. As one who is sent from God (1:6), John is neither the Messiah, nor Elijah, nor even "the prophet"; he is "a voice crying in the wilderness" (1:23, 25). He testifies "to the light"—Jesus—because the "world did not know him" (1:8–10). He says, "After me comes a man who ranks ahead of me because he was before me" (1:30, also 1:27). John's first recorded words when Jesus finally appears in the narrative are these: "Here is the Lamb of God who takes away the sin of the world!" (1:29). The next day, John the Baptist repeats this statement to two of his disciples in abbreviated form: "Look, here is the Lamb of God!" (1:36).

The expression "Lamb of God who takes away the sin of the world" appears nowhere in the New Testament but here. Its meaning poses a challenge for interpreters, who offer several interpretations. They argue that that the lamb refers to (1) the Passover lamb, (2) the Suffering Servant in Isaiah, (3) the Lamb who comes at the end of the world, (4) the replacement of Isaac who was willing to be sacrificed, or (5) the daily temple offering. Evidence from the Gospel of John points most strongly to the notion of the Passover lamb, but the other possibilities will be briefly considered first. If the Gospel understands Jesus to be the Passover lamb, a sacrifice that is to be eaten, then this may well be the first allusion to the ingesting motif.

The Suffering Servant in Isaiah has gained wide support as the background to the "Lamb of God" title in the Gospel of John.[1] This Suffering Servant figure

---

[1] O. Cullmann, *The Early Church* (London: SCM, 1956), 177–84; R. H. Lightfoot, *St. John's Gospel: A Commentary* (Oxford: Oxford Univeristy Press, 1957), 96–97; G. R. Beasley-Murray, *John* (WBC 36; Waco: Word, 1987), 25.

is described as one who

> was wounded for our transgressions, crushed for our iniquities; upon him was the
> punishment that made us whole, and by his bruises we are healed (Isa 53:5). . . . He
> was oppressed, and he was afflicted, yet he did not open his mouth; like a lamb that is
> led to the slaughter, and like a sheep that before his shearers is silent, so he did not
> open his mouth (Isa 53:7). . . . The righteous one, my Servant, shall make many
> righteous, and he shall bear their iniquities (Isa 53:11).

That the author of the Gospel of John knew Isaiah 53 is clear, for verse 1 is
cited in John 12:38.[2] Furthermore, according to John the Baptist, Jesus takes
away (ὁ αἴρων) the sin of the world (John 1:29) as the Servant bears
(φέρει/ἀνήνεγκεν) iniquities of many (Isa 53:11). Both are called lambs (ἀμνός
Isa 53:7; cf. John 1:29).[3] Although some textual variants in both Isaiah and John
raise doubts that a clear corelation does exist,[4] it is possible that the Gospel of
John draws on the imagery of Isaiah's Suffering Servant.[5]

Another possible referent for the "Lamb of God" title is the Lamb that,
according to some sources, would come at the end of the world. C. H. Dodd

---

[2] John the Baptist as "the voice crying in the wilderness" and all the references to the
Servant are found in Second Isaiah.

[3] Dodd (*Interpretation*, 235) acknowledges that Jesus is not consistently silent before his
accusers (see 18:8, 20–23, 34–37; 19:11) but sees the remnants of the Servant's silence (Isa
53:7) in John 19:9. It is likely that early Christians associated Jesus with the Suffering
Servant (see Acts 8:32 which cites Isa 53:7 as a fulfillment of Christ; Matt 8:17 = Isa 53:4;
Heb 9:28 = Isa 53:12; *1 Clem.* 1.16 applied Isa 53 in full to Jesus), but this does not
necessarily mean that John's "Lamb of God" title draws on this imagery. Brown, *Gospel*, 61.

[4] In the Hebrew text of Isa 53:7, the lamb is slaughtered and the sheep is shorn. In the
LXX, however, the lamb is shorn and the sheep is slaughtered. See C. K. Barrett, "The Old
Testament in the Fourth Gospel," *JTS* 48 (1947): 155; also D. B. Sandy, "John the Baptist's
'Lamb of God' Affirmation in its Canonical and Apocalyptic Milieu," *JETS* 34 (1991): 449;
A. Negoitsia and C. Daniel, "L'Agneau de Dieu est le Verbe de Dieu," *NT* 13 (1971): 24–37.
In another section of Isaiah that speaks of the Servant (but not as a lamb), the Servant is
called "my chosen one" (42:1; cf. a variant reading for "Son of God" in John 1:34), upon
whom God poured his spirit (42:1; cf. John 1:32). This assumes, however, that all references
to the Servant in Isaiah point to the same image, a proposition that is troubled by ambiguity.
See, for example, that the Servant is an individual in Isa 53 but a nation in 49:3. See C. K.
Barrett, "The Lamb of God," *NTS* 1 (1954–5): 214. R. Brown (*Death of the Messiah* [2 vols.;
New York: Doubleday, 1994], 1449, n. 10) notes that "we do not know the extent to which in
NT times these passages were seen as interrelated and/or distinguishable from the rest of
Isaiah."

[5] R. Bultmann (*The Gospel of John* [trans. G. Beasley-Murray, R. Hoare, and J. Riches;
Philadelphia: Westminster, 1964], 96) argues that it is not likely that the "Lamb of God" title
refers exclusively to Jesus as the Suffering Servant from Isaiah. There is no evidence that the
Suffering Servant had divine origins, whereas the Gospel emphasizes this aspect of Jesus
(1:1–18; 3:13, 31–32; 6:33, 38, 41, 51; 8:23–24). Nor is it clear that the Servant is raised
from the dead (cf. John 20:19–29; 21:1–23).

favors this position.[6] His argument hinges on the fact that "the Lamb of God who takes away the sin of the world" is understood by Andrew to be a messianic title. Because Nathanael later identified Jesus as "the King of Israel" (1:49), Dodd concludes that "Lamb of God," "Messiah," and "King of Israel" are synonymous.[7] Surprisingly, he does not address other titles for Jesus that do not suggest kingship, such as "Son of God" and "Rabbi" (1:49).[8]

Geza Vermes argues that the Johannine "Lamb of God" title reflects dependence on the Akedah tradition. By the first century C.E., he argues, there was a strong Jewish tradition that considered Isaac to be a willing sacrifice whose (non)death would atone for the sins of future generations. Thus, in the Gospel of John, Jesus is the new Isaac, "the Son of God" (John 1:34). As Abraham gave his son to be sacrificed, God "gave his only son in order that whoever believes in him will not perish but have everlasting life" (John 3:16). Like Isaac, Jesus carries his own wood (John 19:17). Vermes concludes that the "Lamb of God" title evokes the Akedah tradition, a conclusion that has met some resistance due to the nature of the textual evidence.[9] There are also significant differences between the Akedah and John's portrait of Jesus. For example, in the Akedah, the Lord provides an animal and the son is set free; in Christianity, the knife falls on the son. It is thus unlikely that the Akedah

---

[6] Dodd, *Interpretation*, 230–238; also Sandy, "Affirmation," 447–59. Brown (*Gospel*, 59) believes that this might have been what John the Baptist meant by the term.

[7] Dodd, *Interpretation*, 238. This lamb, according to Dodd, is expected to destroy evil in the world (Ezek 34; Dan 8; *T. Joseph* 19:8; *1 Enoch* 90:6–19; Rev 7:17; 17:14). See Barrett, *Gospel*, 176; Bultmann, *Gospel*, 95; Brown, *Gospel*, 59–60; cf. S. Smalley, "Salvation Proclaimed 8: John 1:29–34," *ET* 93 (1982): 326. Likewise, the Messiah will remove evil or sin (*T. Levi* 18:2, 3, 9; *Pss. Sol.* 17:27).

[8] The title "king" is used eighteen times, often ambiguously, to refer to Jesus (1:49; 6:15; 12:13, 15; 18:33, 36–39; 19:3; 12, 14–15, 19–21).

[9] G. Vermes, *Scripture and Tradition in Judaism* (Leiden: Brill, 1961), 204–25. See also B. Smith, "The Words of Institution: Jesus' Death as Eschatological Passover Sacrifice" (Ph.D. diss., McMaster University, 1988). For full discussion of the Akedah, see H. J. Schoeps, "The Sacrifice of Isaac in Paul's Theology," *JBL* (1946): 385–92; R. A. Rosenberg, "Jesus, Isaac and the Suffering Servant," *JBL* 84 (1965): 381–8; J. E. Wood, "Isaac Typology in the New Testament," *NTS* 14 (1968): 583–9; R. J. Daly, "The Soteriological Significance of the Sacrifice of Isaac," *CBQ* 39 (1977): 45–75; P. R. Davies and B. D. Chilton, "The Aqedah: A Revised Tradition History, " *CBQ* 40 (1978): 514–46; B. D. Chilton, "Isaac and the Second Night: A Consideration," *Bib* 61 (1980): 78–88; C. T. R. Hayward, "The Present State of Research into the Targumic Account of the Sacrifice of Isaac," *JJS* 32 (1981): 135–7 and "The Sacrifice of Isaac and Jewish Polemic against Christianity," *CBQ* 52 (1990): 292–306; R. M. Jensen, "The Binding or Sacrifice of Isaac: How Jews and Christians See Differently," *Bible Review* 9 (1993): 42–51; G. Vermes, "New Light on the Sacrifice of Isaac from 4Q225," *JJS* 47 (1996): 140–146.

tradition serves as the only background for the "Lamb of God" title.[10]

Another possible referent for the "Lamb of God" title is the Tamid offering.[11] Twice a day, an animal, usually a lamb, is offered as a burnt sacrifice in the temple.[12] These offerings are made to God in their entirety, and so a lamb that is sacrificed as a burnt offering is a "Lamb of God." While the Tamid offering may be given for the purpose of atonement (Lev 1:4; 12:6–7) and thus serves "to take away the sin of the world," the main purpose of the sacrifice is to "make a pleasing odor to the Lord."[13] What speaks most strongly against this explanation of the "Lamb of God" title is that Jesus is not a burnt offering, totally consumed by God. A better candidate is the lamb given for the Passover sacrifice.

The festival of the Passover commemorates the deliverance of Israel from slavery in Egypt, and in particular, from the destroyer who "passed over" them in the final plague (Exod 12:1–32). Each household was to take a yearling, male lamb (sheep or goat) without blemish, sacrifice it at twilight and wipe its blood on the doorposts and lintel of their house with a hyssop branch. They were to roast the lamb whole (breaking no bones) and eat it that night with unleavened bread and bitter herbs.[14] They were to eat hurriedly. Those within houses marked with the lamb's blood were passed over by "the destroyer," but in the houses not marked with blood, all first-born animals and humans were killed. Israel was to re-enact the sacrifice and meal every year on the fourteenth day of Nissan to "observe this rite as a perpetual ordinance" (Exod 12:24).[15] This

---

[10] G. L. Carey, "The Lamb of God and Atonement Theories," *Tyndale Bulletin* 32 (1981): 102–3.

[11] See Daly-Denton, *David*, 118–31.

[12] For the term, see Exod 29:42; Num 4:16; Dan 8:11. For a description, see Exod 29:38–42; Lev 1:3–17; Num 28:1–8. See also Josephus, *Ant.* 3.9.1. The word ἀμνός (lamb) is used in Exod 29:38–46.

[13] Exod 29:18, 25, 41; Lev 1:9, 13, 17, 2:2, 9, 12; 3:5, 16; 4:31; 6:15, 21; 8:21; 17:6; 23:13, 18; 26:31; Num 15:3, 7, 10, 13–14, 24; 18:17; 28:2, 6, 8, 13, 24, 27; 29:2, 6, 8, 13, 36. Carey ("Lamb," 102) denies that the Tamid is expiatory in any way. Brown (*Gospel*, 63) suggests that the sin offering would be a more likely candidate here, but he fails to note that the sin-offering sheep (πρόβατον) are to be female (Lev 4:32).

[14] See also *Jub.* 49:14. Compare Deut 16:1–8, where the smearing of blood is deleted and the ban on breaking bones is not mentioned. The commemorative nature of the sacrifice is thus emphasized over its apotropaic function. B. Bokser, "Feasts of Unleavened Bread and Passover," *ABD* 6:759.

[15] See also Exod 23:10–19; 34:18–26; Lev 23:4–8; Num 28:16–25; Deut 16:1–8; Ezek 45:21–24; Ezra 6:19–22. The festival was neglected after the period of the Judges but was re-instituted by Josiah (2 Kgs 5:10–15). Bokser notes that the Feast of Unleavened Bread and the Passover celebration became conflated in the post-biblical period. Those who were unable to travel to Jerusalem for Passover likely still observed the seven-day abstinence from leaven. "On their own they might gather to usher in the holiday with a special meal, instruct a child on the meaning of the event, offer praises to God, and drink wine" ("Feasts," 6:762).

Passover tradition is the most likely source for the phrase, "the Lamb of God who takes away the sin of the world."[16]

For one thing, the Gospel of John situates much of its narrative within the context of the Passover. Three separate Passover festivals are mentioned.[17] In the first, Jesus goes to Jerusalem for the festival where he cleanses the temple (2:13–22) and does many signs (2:23). In the second, Jesus feeds the multitude on the mountain (6:4). In the third, Jesus goes to Bethany where he is anointed by Mary (12:1), he has his last meal with the disciples (19:14), and he is arrested and executed.

Furthermore, the Gospel of John identifies the time of Jesus' death with the time of the Passover sacrifice. Unlike the Synoptic Gospels which situate the crucifixion on the day of Passover (Mark 14:12–17; Matt 26:17–19; Luke 22:7–13), the Gospel of John states that Jesus is crucified on the Day of Preparation (18:28; 19:14, 42), the day before Passover. Jesus' trial precedes the Passover, for the Jews refuse to enter Pilate's *praetorium* "so as to avoid ritual defilement and to be able to eat the Passover" (18:28). Moreover, the people demand Jesus' crucifixion at about noon on the Day of Preparation (19:13–16), the time that the lambs are slaughtered for the Passover celebration.[18] Finally, while Jesus is still on the cross, the Jews ask Pilate to remove the bodies of those who had been crucified in order to prepare for the imminent arrival of the "great day of solemnity" (19:31–38). In this way, the Gospel of John locates Jesus' crucifixion at the time when the lambs are slaughtered for the Passover festival, that is, on the Day of Preparation,[19] suggesting that Jesus is identified with the

---

[16] Scholars who support this position exclusively are Bokser, "Feasts," 6:763 and B. Lindars, *New Testament Apologetic: The Doctrinal Significance of the Old Testament Quotations* (London: SCM, 1961), 268; cf. Schnackenburg, *Gospel*, 3:15.

[17] Other festivals are mentioned in the Gospel. John 7 is set during the festival of Booths and John 10:22 mentions the festival of Dedication. Another unnamed festival is the context for the healing of a man in John 5:1–18. This last may or may not be Passover. See G. Yee, *Jewish Feasts and the Gospel of John* (Wilmington, Del.: Michael Glazier, 1989) and A. Guilding, *The Fourth Gospel and Jewish Worship* (Oxford: Clarendon, 1960).

[18] Brown, *Gospel*, 882–3.

[19] The Synoptic Gospels interchange the title of "The Festival of Unleavened Bread" with "Passover" (Matt 26:17; Mark 14:1, 12; Luke 22:1, 7), but the Gospel of John refers only to the "Passover," making the reference unambiguous. Dodd (*Interpretation*, 234) says the dating of the death of Jesus is too obscure and thus cannot be pinpointed to the hour of the paschal sacrifice. The three-fold emphasis on the date, however, suggests the opposite: the Gospel insists that Jesus died on the Day of Preparation. See Brown (*Death*, 1350–1378) for a discussion of the historical dating of the death of Jesus. See also J. Roberts, "The Lamb of God," in *The Christ of John: Essays on the Christology of the Fourth Gospel* (Potchefstroom, SA: Pro Rege, 1971), 42. J. Jeremias (*The Eucharistic Words of Jesus* [trans. N. Perrin; London: SCM, 1966]) argues that the emphasis on the Passover in the Gospels reflects an early Christian Passover liturgy.

paschal lamb.

Other images also point to the Gospel's interpretation of Jesus as the paschal lamb. Like the paschal lamb, none of Jesus' bones is broken "as a fulfillment of scripture" (19:33, 37; cf. Exod 12:46; Num 9:12; Ps 34:20). Hyssop is used to raise the sponge to Jesus' lips while he is on the cross (19:29), as it is used to smear the lintels and doorposts with blood (Exod 12:22). Jesus' blood is shed for the deliverance of the people (19:34; cf. 6:53), as also is the blood of the lamb shed for the deliverance of Israel.[20] Thus, the date of Jesus' crucifixion, the emphasis on the fact that none of his bones is broken, the use of hyssop, and the redemptive shedding of blood all suggest that the Gospel of John understands Jesus as the lamb of the Passover sacrifice.[21]

The difficulty with this argument for most scholars is that the Baptist calls Jesus "the Lamb of God *who takes away the sin of the world*" (1:29, 36, my emphasis). The Passover sacrifice is a commemorative ritual and not a sacrifice that is intended to atone for sin.[22] Rather, atonement for sin is made by means of the daily burnt offering or by sin and guilt offerings (Lev 1:4; 4:3–6:7). These atoning sacrifices are usually goats, bulls, or sheep (Lev 4:22–5:6; 16:6–10), not lambs. Nor are atoning sacrifices to be eaten by the worshiper; these are either burned completely (Lev 1:9) or eaten by the sacrificing priest (Lev 10:16–17, *Ant.* 3.9.3; 4.4.4).[23] The Passover lamb, in contrast, is to be eaten. Finally, the Greek LXX usually refers to the paschal lamb as πρόβατον ("sheep") and not ἀμνός ("lamb"), as we find in John, although Isaiah 53:7 has these two words in a parallel construction suggesting that the difference is insignificant.[24] G. Buchanan Gray points out that the proper word for the Passover sacrifice is πάσχα not ἀμνός and that "had the author of the Fourth Gospel intended this, he would, like St. Paul, have used the correct and unambiguous designation."[25] The Gospel of John's reference to Jesus as a "lamb" that "takes away the sin of the world" makes no sense, then, in this

---

[20] Caiaphas' remark that one would die for the sake of many does not clearly refer to redemption. The text itself states that Jesus' death would result in the "gathering into one the dispersed children of God" (11:45–53).

[21] Dodd (*Interpretation*, 233–4) mistakenly attributes dependence of these images on the Psalms without seeing that the Psalms themselves are dependent on the Passover tradition. See Roberts, "Lamb," 42; Lindars, *Apologetic*, 95; F. M. Young, *The Use of Sacrificial Ideas in Greek Christian Writers from the NT to John Chrysostom* (Cambridge: Patristic Foundation, 1979), 43–47.

[22] Dodd, *Interpretation*, 234.

[23] A portion of the sacrifice of well-being is to be consumed by the worshiper (Lev 7:15–18), but the Passover sacrifice is never called a sacrifice of well-being.

[24] Dodd, *Interpretation*, 234; Barrett, *JTS*, 155. 1 Peter 1:19 refers to the ἀμνός "without defect or blemish." See Brown, *Gospel*, 62.

[25] *Sacrifice in the OT* (Oxford: Clarendon, 1925), 397.

Levitical concept of sacrifice.

This may certainly be the case in the strict Levitical sense of the sacrifice, but the notion of the Passover sacrifice seems to have developed over time. After the cultic reforms of Josiah (621 B.C.E.), Passover was to be celebrated only in Jerusalem (Deut 16:5–7; 2 Kgs 23:21–23; 2 Chr 35:1; cf. *Jub.* 49:16–21). The slaughter and roasting of the lamb then became the duty of the priests and Levites (Ezra 6:19–22).[26] The blood was no longer spread on the doorposts and lintels but was dashed against the altar, as was the blood of other sacrifices (2 Chr 35:10–13; *Jub.* 49:20). The exact timing also became very important; *Jubilees* says that Passover must be observed

> on the fourteenth of the first month between the evenings from the third (part) of the day until the third (part) of the night because two parts of the day are given for light and one third for evening. This is what the LORD commanded you so that you might observe it between the evenings (49:10–12).

Philo refers to the Passover as a rite of purification; it is the purification of the soul in its "passing over from the body and its passions" (*Spec. Laws* 2, 17; see also *Alleg. Interp.* 3.165; *Moses* 2.41–43). It is quite possible, then, that the sacrifice of the lambs on Passover became associated with other offerings given at the temple, and thus became understood to be a form of atonement, but the evidence is more suggestive than conclusive.[27]

Be that as it may, the Gospel of John identifies Jesus as a "Lamb of God who takes away the sin of the world." That is, Jesus dies in order to save believers from the effect of sin. Motivated by love, Jesus is the "good shepherd who lays down his life for the sheep" (10:11; cf. 10:14–15). Those who believe in him will not die in their sins (8:24; cf. 9:41), but have eternal life (3:14–16, 36; 6:40, 47, 54; 10:28; 11:25–26; 20:31). They are sanctified (13:8; 15:3; 17:19). Though Dodd denies that John views Jesus' death as expiatory,[28] George Carey says,

---

[26] Likewise, the Gospel of John emphasizes the fact that the high priests were instrumental in the death of Jesus (especially 19:15; also 11:47–53, 57; 18:3, 13–14, 19–24; 19:21). Compare Luke 23:13–24 where "the chief priests, the leaders and the people" are all responsible.

[27] Brown (*Gospel*, 62) says that "the sacrificial aspect began to infiltrate the concept of the paschal lamb because the priests had arrogated to themselves the slaying of the lambs." While Jeremias argues that the notion of redemption was very prominent in the celebration of Passover during the first century (*TDNT* 5:902), B. Bokser ("Was the Last Supper a Passover Seder?" *BRev* [1987]: 31) argues convincingly that it was a notion that developed only after the fall of Jerusalem in 70 C.E. See Vermes, *Scripture*, 190–192.

[28] Dodd, *Interpretation*, 233. R. Brown (*Text and Interpretation* [Cambridge: University Press, 1979], 61) and Barrett (*Gospel*, 68) accept that there are allusions to the paschal sacrifice in Jesus' death but will not go so far as to say that Jesus' death is a redemptive sacrifice.

It is when we ask why it is that the public ministry in John is so directed towards Calvary, why the theme of his "hour" is so strong, why the gift of his body and blood (6:53–56) is so important, why Jesus believes that "love" drives him to the cross (15:12–13), why the power of Satan and evil is broken by the cross, that the views of those who deny the notion of vicarious sacrifice in John appear so unsatisfactory.[29]

Stephen Smalley says, "The Baptist's description of Jesus as God's lamb obviously alludes to the salvific activity of God's Son. It presupposes the entire OT pattern of sacrifice, especially that associated with a vicarious offering of sin."[30] As a "vicarious sacrifice," Jesus' death saves people from sin. Given the many references to the Passover and its imagery, the timing of Jesus' death and the possibility that atonement might be associated with the sacrifice, the "Lamb of God" title in the Gospel of John most likely refers to the paschal lamb. For this Gospel, which often suggests rather than explains, it may have seemed redundant to use the actual words "paschal sacrifice" (πάσχα). While the connection to the ingesting motif at this point is more allusive than obvious, it should be pointed out that the Passover sacrifice is the one sacrifice that is eaten by the worshiper in a celebratory context. As we shall see in the following study, Jesus invites those who believe in him to eat him.

THE RESPONSE OF THE DISCIPLES

After John the Baptist identifies Jesus as the "Lamb of God" (1:36), the disciples hear and follow Jesus (1:37). This is an active response signifying that they understand the importance of John the Baptist's declaration. (Andrew believes that they have found the Messiah, 1:41.) The result is that they stay with Jesus (1:39). Philip and Nathanael join them. All of these disciples are mentioned throughout the Gospel narrative and Peter and Nathanael are explicitly included in the final narrative (21:2).[31] Peter stays with Jesus until his own death (21:18–19; cf. 13:37). To stay with Jesus means to believe in Jesus, as we shall see, and to believe in Jesus means to eat his flesh and drink his blood (see Chapter 4). Furthermore, a pattern is established in which the disciples pass on their knowledge of Jesus to others. As Andrew comes to believe in Jesus as the Messiah, he tells Peter (1:42). In the same way, Philip comes to believe in Jesus ("the one about whom Moses in the law and also the prophets wrote," 1:45) and shares Jesus with Nathanael (1:46). This pattern of discipleship, in which the disciples pass Jesus on to others, is more developed

---

[29] "Lamb," 118.
[30] "Salvation," 326.
[31] Both Peter and Andrew are mentioned positively in John 6: Andrew brings the boy with bread and fish to Jesus (6:8), and Peter declares his confidence in Jesus on behalf of the faithful disciples (6:69). Andrew reappears in 12:22 and Philip in 12:21–22, 14:8–9.

in subsequent passages, especially in passages that use the ingesting motif. For example, in John 21, Jesus tells Peter to feed others. On the surface, John the Baptist's use of the title "Lamb of God" provokes the disciples to follow and to stay with Jesus.

CONCLUSION

The Gospel of John thus introduces the ingesting motif in a suggestive, hesitant way; its significance becomes apparent only in retrospect. Here it is seen that Jesus is introduced as "the Lamb of God who takes away the sin of the world," a title that is best understood as an allusion to the Passover lamb. As the Passover lamb must be slaughtered in order to give life, so too Jesus must die in order to give life. As the Passover lamb is understood to save people from death, so, too, Jesus saves people from death. The Gospel itself defines the "Lamb of God" image as primarily sacrificial by locating the death of Jesus at the time that the Passover sacrifice is offered. It is only after reflecting on John 6 and the Bread of Life discourse that the "Lamb of God" title emerges as an element of the ingesting motif. There, Jesus says that whoever wants eternal life must eat him (6:50–51). Then it is to be remembered that the Passover lamb is one of the few sacrifices that is eaten by the worshiper and that the eating of the lamb, in effect, "completes" the sacrifice. The ingesting motif is thus secondary to the sacrificial meaning in John 1:29, 36; it is only in retrospect that it becomes apparent.

Similarly, the response of the disciples to John the Baptist's identification of Jesus as the "Lamb of God" is not explicitly part of the ingesting motif, but themes introduced here will receive further development, again in John 6. There it says that those who believe in Jesus will eat him. In John 1, the first disciples believe John the Baptist's declaration, in effect, that Jesus must die to give life, and they follow Jesus and stay with him.

Chapter 2

Water to Wine and Consumed with Zeal (2:1–11, 13–25)

This chapter will address two events recounted in John 2. The first is the Wedding in Cana and is included in the ingesting motif because it is a meal narrative (that is, a gathering when people eat or drink) and because there is specific reference to wine. The second story, the Cleansing of the Temple, is less obviously included in the list of ingesting passages. It finds its way into this study because it uses a word that is drawn from the semantic field of ingesting: Jesus is understood by the disciples to "be consumed with zeal." Like the "Lamb of God" title discussed in Chapter One, this term, "consumed," does not appear at first glance to be directly relevant to the overall ingesting motif. It may be just an "innocent" word choice. Nevertheless, a return to this passage after further investigation of the ingesting motif reveals that many of the themes and images are consistent with other more developed passages invoking the ingesting motif. In order to preserve the Gospel order, however, the passage is presented here and will be tied to the ingesting motif in the conclusion.

THE WEDDING IN CANA (JOHN 2:1–11)

The Wedding in Cana story is the first meal narrative in which people gather and consume an edible substance, in this case, wine. In this narrative, Jesus, his mother (who is never named in this Gospel), and presumably his brothers (cf. 2:12) attend a wedding. When the wine runs out, the mother of Jesus tells him that "they have no wine." What she expects of Jesus is not clear, but his subsequent words and actions suggest that she is waiting for him to resolve the situation. Jesus' response in John 2:4 is confusing to commentators. He says, translated literally, "What to you and to me, Woman? My hour has not yet come" (Τί ἐμοὶ καὶ σοί, γύναι; οὔπω ἥκει ἡ ὥρα μου). The mother of Jesus tells the servants to do as Jesus asks. Jesus instructs them to fill with water six stone jars used for the Jewish rite of purification. When the servants draw some of the water-turned-into-wine and take it to the steward, the steward, who does not know where the wine has come from, calls the bridegroom and praises him for saving the good wine until now (2:10). The Gospel of John tells us that Jesus reveals his glory in this, the first of his signs, and that, because of it, the disciples believe in him (2:11).

Several elements suggest that this narrative should be understood as more than a straightforward account of a miracle. First, the narrative reflects a pattern that is repeated in other Johannine narratives: a suggestion is made; it receives an initial negative response but concludes with a positive outcome.[1] In this case, Jesus becomes aware of the need for wine (2:3), does not respond as expected (2:4), but eventually acts positively by turning water into wine. The frustrated expectation and surprise ending anticipate similar narrative patterns.

Secondly, the wedding takes place on the "third day." In the sequence of days in the Gospel to this point, there are more than two preceding days. The sequence begins on day one with the John the Baptist's conversation with the priests and Levites from Jerusalem (1:19–28). "The next day," day two, John points out Jesus (1:29–34), and "the next day," day three, he points Jesus out to his disciples, one of whom is Andrew (1:35–42). The "next day," day four, Jesus goes to Galilee and is joined by Philip and Nathanael (1:43–51). The Wedding in Cana follows but is referred to as "the third day" (2:1), though this would be day five according to the narrative.[2] Alternatively, "the third day" could refer to the third day after the last recorded event, that is, after the conversation with Nathanael. In any case, mention of the "third day" at this

---

[1] C. Giblin ("Suggestion, Negative Response, and Positive Action in St. John's Portrayal of Jesus," *NTS* 26 [1979–80]: 197–211) argues that the pattern of suggestion, negative response, and positive action found in this story (as well as 4:46–54, 7:2–13 and 11:1–44) "sets in relief Jesus' dissociation from the predominantly human concerns of those who, by merely human standards, would also seem to be rather close to him. . . . He never fails to attend to the situation presented to him, but in doing so he acts radically on his own terms" (210). The pattern is Christological: Jesus attends to human needs but acts independently. A. Reinhartz ("Great Expectations: A Reader-Oriented Approach to Johannine Christology and Eschatology," *JLT* 3 [1989]: 61–76) recognizes the same pattern in the death and resurrection of Jesus and thus in the Gospel as a whole. In this case, the pattern is eschatological: "the pattern affirms the eschatological expectations that ultimate salvation will come with Christ while at the same time replacing the future elements of that expectation with an emphasis on realized eschatology" (71).

[2] It is less likely that the sequence begins with the departure for Galilee (1:43) allowing two days for the journey from "Bethany, across the Jordan" (1:28; cf. 1:39), with the wedding on the third day of their journey. The range of interpretive options is impressive. Barrett (*Gospel*, 190) reckons the three days (i.e., the first 1:35–42, the second 1:43–51, and the third 2:1–11) and the days Jesus stays in Capernaum as the six-day period that leads up to the Passover (2:13). This six-day pattern is repeated in Jesus' last Passover (12:1). Brown (*Gospel*, 97) counts the days in the same way but does not make anything of the relationship to Passover. L. Morris (*The Gospel according to John: The English Text with Introduction, Exposition and Notes* [NICNT; Grand Rapids: Eerdmans, 1971], 129–130) reckons a full week (adding a day at 1:41) and relates the symbolism to the creation, a point that is sustained by the creation phrase "in the beginning," which starts the Gospel (John 1:1; cf. Gen 1:1). Most commentators will ascribe some symbolic power to the phrase, but they do not agree on what the meaning might be (Schnackenburg, *Gospel*, 1:325).

point seems to challenge the chronological sense of the narrative, and for this reason, it is more likely that the "third day" is used here figuratively to bring to mind the day of Jesus' resurrection. Though the Gospel of John generally makes little of this expression when compared to the Synoptic Gospels,[3] Jesus does refer to his resurrected body as the temple raised again after three days (2:19–22). The setting of the wedding within the temporal setting of the third day, therefore, anticipates the resurrection day of Jesus.[4]

The mysterious reference to Jesus' "hour" also points to his death and resurrection. In response to his mother's statement about the lack of wine, Jesus says, "My hour has not yet come" (2:4). In the Gospel of John, the "hour" generally refers to the expanse of time when Jesus was arrested (7:30; 8:20; 16:32) and when he died (12:23–24, 27; 13:1).[5] However, like the hour of childbirth that is forgotten after the arrival of a new life (16:21), Jesus' "hour" of agony results in joy (16:21). So Jesus' death will also be the hour of his glorification (12:23–24, 27; 17:1) and the hour when he returns to his Father (13:1). At that hour, "the dead will hear the voice of the Son of God, and those who hear will live" (5:25; also 5:28). The "hour" of Jesus therefore refers to the change wrought by Jesus' death and resurrection.[6] This change is anticipated in the miraculous transformation of water into wine, a miracle which proleptically "reveals his glory" (2:11).

The anticipation of Jesus' hour is set in the context of the wedding feast. Invitations are issued (2:2) and the guests arrive but there is not enough wine. Jesus' presence changes all that. Where once an invited guest, Jesus appears to take on the role of the bridegroom—the host—who, according to the steward, "saves the best wine until the last" (2:10). John the Baptist later refers to Jesus as the bridegroom and Messiah:

> You yourselves are my witnesses that I said, "I am not the Messiah, but I have been sent ahead of him." He who has the bride is the bridegroom. The friend of the bridegroom, who stands and hears him, rejoices greatly at the bridegroom's voice. For this reason my joy has been fulfilled (3:28–30; see also 1:41).

John the Baptist is obviously identifying Jesus as both the Messiah and the bridegroom (cf. John 1:20–23). This recalls the rich literary complex of

---

[3] Matt 12:40; 16:21; 17:23; 20:19; 26:61; 27: 40, 63–64; Mark 8:31; 9:31; 10:34; 14:58; 15:29; Luke 9:22; 13:32; 18:33; 24:7, 21, 46.

[4] Dodd, *Interpretation*, 300, 302.

[5] The enemies also have "their hour" when they will put the disciples out of the synagogue and put them to death. In so doing, they think that they are worshiping God (16:2).

[6] See Brown, *Gospel*, 99–100, 517–18; Barrett, *Gospel*, 159; F. Moloney, *Belief in the Word: Reading John 1–4* (Minneapolis: Fortress, 1993), 86–89; Koester, *Symbolism*, 81–82.

symbols used to describe the messianic age.[7]

The relationship between God and Israel is often depicted as a marriage. For example, the prophet Hosea reports this statement to Israel in the words of God: "And I will take you for my wife forever; I will take you for my wife in righteousness and in justice, in steadfast love, and in mercy. I will take you for my wife in faithfulness; and you shall know the LORD" (Hos 2:18–20; see also Isa 54:4–8). Jeremiah says this: "Go and proclaim in the hearing of Jerusalem, Thus says the LORD: I remember the devotion of your youth, your love as a bride, how you followed me in the wilderness, in a land not sown" (2:2). Antithetically, Israel is described as an unfaithful wife when she fails to keep the covenant (Jer 2:32; 3:1–13; 11:15; Ezek 16). Thus, the language of marriage is used to describe a future and idealized relationship between God and Israel; this language is used in a similar way to describe Jesus the Messiah as the bridegroom of the church (2 Cor 11:2; Eph 5:23–32).

The wedding banquet developed as an image that describes the beginning of this restored relationship between God and Israel. In Isaiah, for example, the divine marriage is followed by an extravagant banquet overflowing in abundance (Isa 54:5; 55:1–5). These images are picked up in the New Testament where they become a prominent motif with regard to the kingdom of God. Jesus tells parables of wedding feasts and banquets (Matt 22:1–14; 25:1–13; Mark 2:19–20; Luke 5:34–35; 14:7–11; 22:28–30) and refers to himself as a bridegroom (Matt 9:15; cf. John 3:29; cf. *Gos. Thom.* 104). This notion receives more developed expression in Revelation where Jesus the Lamb comes together with his bride, the church, for a marriage supper (Rev 19:7–9; see also 21:2, 9). With echoes of Isaiah 55, Revelation 22:17 says, "The Spirit and the bride say, 'Come.' And let everyone who hears say, 'Come.' And let everyone who is thirsty come. Let anyone who wishes take the water of life as a gift." The image of a marriage, with or without a banquet, thus often alludes to a restored relationship between God and the people.

Associated with these marriage and banquet themes is an abundance of food and drink. These foods usually include bread and fish, and the drinks usually include wine, water, and/or milk and honey. Wine, in particular, has significance as a beverage associated with the coming Messiah. In the book of Genesis, wine is a central image in Jacob's blessing of Judah (Gen 49:8–12). Based on these predictions about Judah's supremacy, the image of the grape and its products later become a symbol for the anticipated messianic age.[8] The vine

---

[7] For a summary of this concept, see D. Smith, "Messianic Banquet," *ABD* 4:788–91.

[8] The wine-cup, pitcher, grape leaf, and grape figure prominently in coins of the 66–73 C.E. and 132–5 C.E. uprisings. See Y. Meshorer, *Jewish Coins of the Second Temple Period* (Tel Aviv: Am Hassefer, 1967), 154–69, Plates 19-28; L. Mildenberg, *The Coinage of the Bar Kokhba War*, Typos, 6 (ed. and trans. P. E. Mottahedeh; Aarau: Sauerländer, 1984).

is also a symbol of the bounty of the Promised Land; its grape cluster are so large that they need to be carried on poles by two men (Num 13:23; see also Deut 33:27–28). Wine is served at the eschatological banquet that God prepares for Israel (Isa 25:6; 55:1).[9] The prophet Joel describes the abundance of wine this way: "The mountains shall drip sweet wine, the hills shall flow with milk, and all the stream beds of Judah shall flow with water; a fountain shall come forth from the house of the LORD and water the Wadi Shittim" (Joel 3:18).[10] The divine provision of wine is therefore understood to be a marker for the expected messianic age, especially when it is placed within the context of a wedding.[11]

Furthermore, wine is an important element in Jewish cultic practice. It is used in the temple cult as a drink offering to accompany the daily sacrifice, the Sabbath and New Moon sacrifices.[12] Strong wine is poured out in the sanctuary and contributes to the odor that is "pleasing to the LORD" (Num 28:8). According to Sirach, the drink offering is a significant moment in the order of the temple sacrifice. Sirach describes Simon coming to the altar, laying the

---

[9] This is understood to be eschatological because, on that day, there will be no more death (Isa 25:8).

[10] See also Joel 2:24–26; Amos 9:13; Prov 9:1–2, 5; Sir 15:3; 24:21.

[11] Jeremias (*Eucharistic*, 233–5) rightly notes that the provision of food and drink by God was not a notion limited to the messianic age, but also referred to such present notions as the will of God or "daily bread." The abundance of wine is used as a marker for the expected messianic age in early Jewish and Christian literature as well. For example, *2 Baruch* predicts that the day of the Anointed One will be accompanied by an incredible grape harvest (29:2–7). See also *Test Levi* 8:4–6; *Sib. Or.* 2:315–8; 8:211; 3:622. Cf. *Jos. Asen.* 8:5 and 15:5, where the "cup of immortality" refers to a beverage that guarantees eternal life to those who drink it (C. Burchard, "The Importance of Joseph and Aseneth for the Study of the New Testament: A General Survey and a Fresh Look at the Lord's Supper," *NTS* 33 [1987]: 109–17). Jesus was known for his unstinting consumption of wine in the Synoptic tradition (Luke 7:33–34; cf. Matt 11:19). Wine drinking is related to the theme of rejoicing in the "presence of the bridegroom" (Matt 9:14–17), to the inauguration of a new age (Matt 9:17; Mark 2:22; Luke 5:37–38; cf. *Gos. Thom.* 47), and to the institution of the Eucharist (Mark 14:24–25; Matt 26:29; Luke 22:14–23). Greeks would also appreciate the significance of the provision of abundant wine. For Philo's description of the Greco-Roman belief that Dionysus provides wine that has a "miraculous" effect on households, see *Embassy*, 83. During festivals dedicated to Dionysus, the god's presence would be signaled by the gift of abundant wine, sometimes flowing from a fountain or spring. For example, at Teos, a fountain of wine would surge spontaneously from the earth (Diodorus Siculus, *Library of History* 3.66.1–4). At Elis, three jars were placed in a sealed room and were found full of wine the next morning (Pausanias, *Description of Greece* 6.26.1–2). For Greeks, then, the miraculous provision of wine signaled the presence of a god.

[12] Exod 29:40, 41; Lev 23:13, 18, 37; Num 28:1–29:40; Josephus, *Ant.* 3.9.4. It was also used in the worship of the Baalim (Deut 32:38; Judg 9:26–27; Hos 2; Isa 57:11; Jer 7:18; 19:13; 32:29; 44:17–19, 25; Ezek 20:28), to seal contracts (Gen 26:26–31; Exod 24:11; 32:6), and to celebrate victory (1 Chr 12:38–40; 3 Macc 6:30–41).

sacrifice upon it, and pouring out a wine offering. He "held out his hand for the cup and poured a drink offering of the blood of the grape; he poured it out at the foot of the altar, a pleasing odor to the Most High, the king of all" (Sir 50:14–15).[13] In response to this last gesture, "the sons of Aaron" shout and blow their trumpets and all the people fall to the ground to worship. It appears then that the wine offering is associated with the blood of sacrifices.[14] Wine is also important in the celebration of Passover, as *Jubilees* attests: "And all Israel remained eating the flesh of the Passover and drinking wine and praising and blessing and glorifying the LORD the God of their fathers" (49:6).[15] So, in addition to the wedding banquet imagery, wine has cultic significance.

The Wedding in Cana narrative likely draws on this background of messianic and cultic imagery. Jesus, who has already been identified as the Messiah (1:41), attends a wedding banquet. In an ironic statement, the steward of the banquet attributes "the bridegroom" with providing more wine, when it is clear that Jesus has in fact provided the wine (3:7–10). Is Jesus, then, to be identified as the bridegroom? This is suggested in a later passage where John the Baptist refers to Jesus as the messianic bridegroom (3:23), as we have seen. Furthermore, recalling the prophetic visions of Isaiah and Joel, Jesus provides a great abundance of wine,[16] superior both in quantity and quality to what is known before (2:3, 10). He also replaces the cultic purification waters with choice wine that is to be consumed and enjoyed.[17] Though it does not go so far as to say that the wine symbolizes Jesus' blood poured out as a sacrifice, and is thus associated with Eucharistic wine, John 2:1–11 does suggest that traditional ritual practice (i.e., purification) is replaced in Jesus' presence. The focus is not on Jesus as the substance of the food or drink, as we shall see in later passages, but rather on Jesus as the provider of the wine.

---

[13] Goodenough, *Symbols*, 6:130.

[14] See also Gen 49:11; Deut 32:14; Sir 39:26; cf. Zech 9:15. Jesus' changing of water into wine may also allude to Moses' changing of water into blood (Exod 7:19). See Brown, *Gospel*, 100; Little, *Echoes*, 38.

[15] See also Philo, *Spec. Laws* 2, 17; Josephus, *Ant.* 4.8.7; Bokser, "Feasts," 6:760.

[16] Each of these jars held 2 or 3 measures. Since one measure equals about eight gallons, these jars held 16–24 gallons or the equivalent of 80–120 modern bottles of wine. J. Villescas, "John 2:6: The Capacity of the Six Jars," *Bible Translator* 28 (1977): 447.

[17] Many commentators see the replacement of water with wine as one example within a larger theme in which Jesus replaces Jewish tradition with something else. The law was given through Moses but grace and truth came through Jesus (1:17). The Jewish temple is replaced with Jesus' body (2:13–22). Jacob gives his descendants the well, but Jesus gives water that will quench thirst forever (4:4–42). Moses gives manna, but Jesus is bread that gives eternal life (6:32), etc. See O. Cullmann, *Early Christian Worship* (trans. A. Todd, J. Torrance; SBT 10; London: SCM, 1953), 70; Schnackenburg, *Gospel*, 1:339; Barrett, *Gospel*, 192; Little, *Echoes*, 41; Dodd, *Interpretation*, 297–300.

Finally, the text identifies this narrative as "the first of his signs" (2:11).[18] "Signs," in the Gospel of John, point not only to Jesus' power and divinity, but also to his death and resurrection, his ultimate sign. Belief follows. This trend is indeed identifiable in the Gospel as a whole. John 2:18–22 says that the sign of Jesus' death and resurrection results in the belief of the disciples. In what is called the "second sign," the royal official believes when he learns the "hour" of his son's deliverance from death (4:46–54). The sign of the multiplication of the loaves and fish connects the Passover, messianic expectations, and belief (6:1–14).[19] John 7:25–31 connects the signs, the hour of Jesus' impending death, his identity as Messiah, and the people's belief. Because many people see his signs and believe in Jesus (11:45–48; also 12:18–19), the chief priests and Pharisees decide that Jesus should be put to death. Just before we are told that "Jesus knew that his hour had come to depart from this world" (13:1), those who believe are contrasted with those who refuse to believe in Jesus based on the signs he had performed (12:36b–44). Clearly, the Wedding in Cana sign as "the first of his signs" introduces themes that recur whenever signs are mentioned in this Gospel; they include messianic expectations and identity, Jesus' impending death, and the response of belief.

THE ROLE OF THE DISCIPLES

Throughout the Wedding in Cana narrative, the disciples are silent observers. They are invited to the wedding with Jesus and his mother (2:2). They are not mentioned again until 2:11: "Jesus did this, the first of his signs, in Cana of Galilee, and revealed his glory; his disciples believed in him." This phrase, they "believed in him," does not immediately follow the miracle of the water being turned into wine. The narrative tells us that the disciples believe after Jesus "revealed his glory." The implication is that the disciples understand this sign as a manifestation of Jesus' glory, a glory that is fully manifest in his death.[20] This is the point of the Wedding in Cana narrative, according to

---

[18] Bultmann (*Gospel*, 113) argues that this formula indicates the use of a Signs Source. See also R. T. Fortna, *The Gospel of Signs: A Reconstruction of the Narrative Source Underlying the Fourth Gospel* (Cambridge: Cambridge University Press, 1970) and *The Fourth Gospel and Its Predecessor: From Narrative Source to Present Gospel* (Philadelphia: Fortress, 1988). R. Collins ("Cana [John 2:1–12]—the First of His Signs or the Key to His Signs?" *Irish Theological Quarterly* 47 [1980]: 89) argues that the interpretive framework is the replacement of Jewish tradition with the gifts of the messianic age brought by Jesus.

[19] The people's proclamation that Jesus was the "prophet who is come into the world" constitutes some form of belief that will be corrected in the Bread of Life discourse which follows in 6:22–71. See the section that deals with John 6 in detail.

[20] C. H. Dodd, *Historical Tradition in the Fourth Gospel* (Cambridge: University Press, 1965), 69. John 2 states that the disciples believe, but it does not specifically mention

Schnackenburg.[21] The disciples also stay (ἔμειναν) with Jesus. This, too, is understood by the Gospel to be an appropriate response to Jesus (1:39; 6:56; 8:31; 15:4–10).

The mother of Jesus is distinguished from the disciples. Her belief in Jesus is presumed: she expects that he will do what she asks (cf. 15:16; 16:23). She insists that the servants do as Jesus asks (2:5) and that the servants will comply with Jesus' requests (2:6–8). She is mentioned again briefly at the end of the narrative when we are told that she accompanies Jesus to Capernaum (2:12). In the Gospel, she reappears only at the crucifixion scene where, with the beloved disciple, she watches Jesus die. Her presence is noted in the narrative, therefore, only at the beginning and at the end of Jesus' time in the world;[22] she serves as a literary indicator, connecting both "his hour" anticipated at the Wedding in Cana (2:1–11) and "his hour" realized on the cross (19:25–27). Unlike most of the other disciples, however, she remains with Jesus through his death.

To summarize this first Johannine meal narrative, Jesus, a guest who takes the role of host, miraculously provides abundant delicious wine at a wedding banquet. The feast and the wine, with its strong allusions to the messianic banquet, point to Jesus as the Messiah. References to the third day and Jesus' hour and glory, however, suggest that this messianic wedding banquet is connected in some way to the death of Jesus. The wine itself replaces the water used for purification purposes, suggesting that Jesus provides an alternative to traditional Jewish ritual practice. The connection of wine with blood in the sacrificial cult also suggests that the death of Jesus has some kind of cultic

---

whether or not the brothers of Jesus believe. The brothers are not mentioned at the beginning of the narrative. Their presence is noted only at the conclusion: "After this he went down to Capernaum with his mother, his brothers, and his disciples" (2:12). Brown (*Gospel*, 112) notes that "and his brothers" was omitted in Codex Sinaiticus and the other early versions. Some have suggested that a copyist misunderstood and, thinking that "the brothers" referred to Jesus' relatives and not the disciples, added the "disciples" as a third party. This would explain the inclusion of the brothers so late in the narrative. I assume that the text distinguishes the brothers and the disciples intentionally. The implication is that the brothers were present at the wedding but, unlike the disciples, they did not believe. This contrast is noted again in John 7:3 where the brothers of Jesus do not include themselves among the disciples. The author intensifies this in an aside: "not even his brothers believed in him" (7:5). After his death and resurrection, however, Jesus tells Mary Magdalene to tell the "brothers" that he is ascending to the Father (20:17); the text tells us that she tells the "disciples" (20:18). Have the brothers progressed to the point where they also believe and so are now considered disciples? Was the death and resurrection of Jesus the turning point for their belief?

[21] *Gospel*, 323.

[22] The Jews know his mother and his father, and they use that as a reason to argue that Jesus did not "come down from heaven" (6:41–42); but Jesus speaks of another kind of birth, not from a mother's womb but "of water and Spirit" (3:5). So the mother of Jesus frames the narrative of Jesus' earthly life but is not central to his human identity.

significance. The role of the disciples in the wedding narrative, while very abbreviated, captures the essence of the Johannine soteriology: they believe and remain with Jesus.

The first meal narrative in the Gospel of John therefore introduces various themes that cluster around the ingesting motif. Jesus starts as a guest and becomes a host, providing miraculous drink. His drink is better than what is otherwise available. What Jesus provides is connected to his death in some way. The expected response of the disciples is also provided: they come to believe in Jesus and stay with him. These themes are developed throughout the course of the Gospel within the context of the ingesting motif.

CONSUMED WITH ZEAL (JOHN 2:13–25)

In the Cleansing of the Temple narrative, Jesus goes to Jerusalem at Passover (2:13). In the temple, he finds people selling cattle, sheep, and doves, with moneychangers seated at their tables (2:14). Making a whip of cords, he drives the sheep and cattle out of the temple. He pours out the coins of the moneychangers and overturns their tables (2:15). He tells those who were selling the doves, "Take these things out of here! Stop making my Father's house a marketplace!" (2:16). His disciples remembered that it was written in Ps 69:6, "Zeal for your house will consume me" (2:17). The Jews then ask Jesus why he has done this and ask for a sign (2:18). Jesus replies, "Destroy this temple and in three days I will raise it up" (2:19). The Jews respond that the temple has been under construction for forty-six years and ask how he would rebuild it in three days (2:20). The narrative ends there, but the Gospel tells us that the disciples remember what Jesus said after his death (2:22) and realized then that he referred to his body (2:21). They believe "the scripture and the word that he had spoken" (2:22).

This passage does not deal directly with food or drink. Nevertheless, it is relevant to this study because it uses a word drawn from the semantic field of ingesting language, namely κατεσθίω ("consume"); the disciples remember that it is written, "Zeal for my Father's house will consume me" (καταφάγεταί με). It is also closely connected to the Wedding in Cana story.[23] According to John 2:12, Jesus and his mother, disciples, and brothers stayed in Capernaum after the wedding for "a few days." The next sentence, joined to the last by a

---

[23] Koester (*Symbolism*, 77–85) refers to the Cleansing of the Temple as the "companion piece" (82) to the Wedding in Cana. They both feature conversations that disclose the significance of the symbolic actions. Both use Jewish institutions to reveal who Jesus is. Both foreshadow the passion and direct the readers "to reflect on their significance in light of Jesus' death and resurrection" (77).

καί ("and"), has Jesus "go up to Jerusalem" for the Passover (2:13).[24] These stories are meant to be read in sequence. Both stories also feature signs (2:11, 18) that lead the disciples to belief (2:11, 22), but whereas the sign ambiguously "reveals his glory" in Cana, the connection of the sign and Jesus' resurrection is more explicit in the temple scene (2:19–21).

Most exegetes focus on three main aspects of this passage.[25] The first is the troubling "displacement" of the Cleansing of the Temple from the end of Jesus' ministry, where it is found in the Synoptics (Matt 21:12–13, Mark 11:15–19; Luke 19:45–48), to the beginning of his ministry in the Gospel of John. The Synoptic placement of the story is usually deemed more plausible historically. The second aspect is the difference in details between the Synoptic and Johannine accounts; John adds the animals, a whip in the hands of Jesus, and the words he spoke. The third aspect is the biblical source for the quotation and other references. All of these concerns naturally raise questions of dependence of the Gospel of John on the Synoptic tradition. Different questions arise, however, when we focus on the language of ingesting.

John 2:13 is the first clear mention of the Passover, even though there are hints in John the Baptist's declaration that Jesus is "the Lamb of God" (1:29, 36), as we have seen.[26] Not only do references to this festival frame the narrative (2:13, 23), but the activities discussed reflect the events that are known to occur at Passover from other first-century sources.[27] For instance, Jesus makes the pilgrimage to Jerusalem for the festival and visits the temple (2:13). There he finds the animals—cattle (βόας), sheep (πρόβατα) and doves (περιστεράς)[28]—used for all types of sacrifices, including burnt, well being, sin, and guilt offerings. More sacrifices are made at Passover than at any other time, so extra animals are gathered. Again, the references to the festival and a description of the scene reinforce the importance of the Passover motif in the narrative.

The temporal setting—the Passover "was near" (ἐγγύς)—also sets the stage for the events that are about to occur. The imminence of the Passover suggests that the lambs would soon be slaughtered and the pilgrims would be preparing to feast on meat and wine. Anticipation is high. When Jesus drives out the

---

[24] Brown (*Gospel*, 113) disagrees because "Capernaum is a long detour from the road to Jerusalem." My point is that they are connected at a literary level.

[25] See, for example, Brown, *Gospel*, 116–7; Barrett, *Gospel*, 195–6; Schnackenburg, *Gospel*, 1:354–5.

[26] Barrett (*Gospel*, 197) and Jeremias (*Eucharistic*, 83) argue that the specific reference to the "Passover *of the Jews*" reflects a polemic against a *Christian* Passover. Moloney (*Belief*, 95), on the other hand, argues that it is intended to situate the narrative firmly in a Jewish context, rather than a Passover context.

[27] Josephus, *Ant.* 17.9.3; *J.W.* 6.9.3.

[28] Only the doves are mentioned in the Synoptics (Matt 21:12; Mark 11:15).

animals that are gathered for the sacrifice (2:15), the expected feast is put into jeopardy. When he overturns the tables of the moneychangers (2:15b), he "pours out" (ἐξέχεεν) coins, possibly in a parody of the sacrificial blood being poured out on the altar.[29] By driving out the sacrificial animals, he challenges both the sacrifice and the subsequent Passover feasting.

In the place of the Passover sacrifice, the Gospel seems to substitute Jesus.[30] Jesus says, "Stop making my Father's house a marketplace" (2:16). In a sense, this statement suggests that the marketplace in the temple is no longer necessary, for Jesus provides the only appropriate sacrifice.[31] Indeed, he is himself the "Lamb of God" who "takes away the sin of the world" (1:29, 36). Furthermore, the disciples remember what had been written: "Zeal for your house *will consume me*" (καταφάγεταί με; 2:17, emphasis added). While it appears that it is Jesus' own zeal that consumes him in this instance,[32] the one who is zealous is not strictly identified. Some scholars suggest that the religious authorities are zealous in their protection of the temple and, because Jesus threatened it, they put him to death.[33] When this passage is read in the light of the greater ingesting motif, however, it is more likely that those who are zealous are those who seek true worship (see 4:23–24), thereby "consuming Jesus."

This notion is supported by the future tense of the verb κατεσθίω. The closest parallel to "Zeal for your house will consume me" (ὁ ζῆλος τοῦ οἴκου σου καταφάγεταί με; 2:17) is found in Ps 69:9 (LXX 68:10), which says, "It is zeal for your house that has consumed me" (ὁ ζῆλος τοῦ οἴκου σου κατέφαγέν με). The verb here is in the aorist tense (κατέφαγεν), but in its citation in John

---

[29] The same word, ἐξέχεεν, is used in LXX Lev 4:7, 18, 25, 30, etc.

[30] Barrett (*Gospel*, 198) and J. C. Fenton (*The Gospel according to John* [Oxford: Clarendon, 1970], 50) also accept this as a possibility.

[31] Alternatively, this statement may be understood to claim that the temple is not the appropriate location for a marketplace. Many commentators see allusions here to the final words of Zechariah's apocalypse: "There shall no longer be traders (*or* Canaanites) in the house of the Lord on that day" (14:21). The vision is for a holy Jerusalem restored under the provision and protection of God when the temple would be sanctified. While the Gospel of John speaks out against the *misuse* of the temple only here, it does refer to the replacement of the *need* for the temple in John 4:21. Jesus says to the Samaritan woman, "Woman, believe me, the hour is coming when you will worship the Father neither on this mountain nor in Jerusalem." See Barrett, *Gospel*, 198; Dodd, *Interpretation*, 300; Moloney, *Belief*, 96. An allusion to Zechariah is more likely than Jer 7:11 or Isa 56:7, which depends too heavily on the Synoptic reference for the connections (i.e., "den of robbers" and "house of prayer").

[32] Barrett (*Gospel*, 199) suggests that Jesus is "eaten up" by zeal for the temple, that is, he is emotionally consumed.

[33] See Brown, *Gospel*, 124; Dodd, *Interpretation*, 301; Schnackenburg, *Gospel*, 1:347; Bultmann, *Gospel*, 124.

2:17, it is in the future tense (καταφάγεται).[34] The verb tense thus points to an event that will occur in the relative future of the narrative: Jesus is "yet to be consumed," a concept that the disciples understand only in retrospect. The importance of this citation to the disciples is emphasized in John 2:22: the disciples "believed the *scripture* and the word that Jesus had spoken" (emphasis added).

In response to Jesus overturning the tables and driving the animals out of the temple, the Jews ask Jesus for a sign to justify his actions. They ask him, "What sign can you show us for doing this?" (2:18). Jesus responds, "Destroy this temple, and in three days I will raise it up" (2:19).[35] Now the restoration of the temple, like the provision of heavenly bread and abundant wine, is understood to be an eschatological sign that will occur on "the day of the LORD," either (1) through the rebuilding of an earthly or a heavenly sanctuary or (2) through purification of the present structure.[36] The restoration itself is often tied to the coming of the Messiah.[37] For example, Malachi 3:1 predicts that "the LORD whom you seek will suddenly come to his temple." Zechariah 14:21 says that "in that day [i.e., the day of the LORD] there shall be no more traders in the house of the LORD of Hosts."[38] Hence, Brown says that the historical witnesses of the scene likely understood Jesus' actions as a "protest like that of the

---

[34] For John 2:17, some authorities have the aorist κατέφαγέν, likely in an attempt to bring the citation into conformity with the LXX. The future tense is more likely the original and indicates that the evangelist understood the Psalms to be prophecies about Jesus. See Bultmann, *Gospel*, 124, n. 3. Daly-Denton (*David*, 118–31) argues that this Psalm is chosen because the word κατεσθίω is frequently used to show God's acceptance of a sacrifice (see Lev 9:24; 2 Chr 7:1; 1 Kgs 18:38; Sir 48:3). For this reason, she argues that John 2:17 is one of the more significant "outcroppings of sacrificial imagery" used to interpret the death of Jesus (see p.127). This conclusion leads her to understand that the "Lamb of God" title in John 1:29 refers to the daily burnt offering. She does not take into account, however, the larger ingesting motif that requires believers to "eat Jesus" (see John 6). Believers do not eat the daily sacrifice; it is entirely consumed by fire.

[35] Compare 11:48, where the priests fear the destruction of the temple by the Romans because of Jesus. O. Cullmann ("Significance of the Qumran Texts," *JBL* 74 [1955]: 222–4) argues that an anti-temple polemic is common among the Hellenists, the Qumran sect, and the Johannine community. Dodd (*Interpretation*, 301) suggests that the sign has already occurred in the Cleansing of the Temple but the observers do not recognize it as a sign. Compare a similar pattern in John 6:30.

[36] Ezek 40–44; Hag 2:7–9; Zech 2:5–9; Tob 13:10; 14:5; Sir 36:19; *T Benj.* 9:2; *Sib. Or.* 3:294; 702–20, 772–4; 5:422; *1 Enoch* 90:29; *Jub.* 1:15–17; 11QT XXIX, 8–10.

[37] Targums on Zech 6:12 and Isa 53:5; *Sib.Or.* 5.422.

[38] The Gospel sees Jesus as the fulfillment of other prophecies in Zechariah: John 12:15 = Zech 9:9; John 19:37 = Zech 12:10; John 7:38 has echoes of Zech 14:8 (cf. John 7:10, Zech 14:18). Psalm 69, cited in John 2:17, was also thought to be messianic. See also John 15:25; 19:29. This is a common trend in the early church. See Mark 15:36 par.; Matt 27:34; Acts 1:20; Rom 11:9f; 15:3; Lindars, *Apologetic*, 104; Schnackenburg, *Gospel*, 1:347; Dodd, *Tradition*, 159, and *Interpretation*, 301.

prophets of old against the profanation of God's house and a sign that the messianic purification of the temple was at hand."[39] According to the Gospel, however, the Jews are sceptical that Jesus can do this; they say, "This temple has been under construction for forty-six years, and will *you* raise it up in three days?"[40] They take Jesus' words literally and think Jesus is referring to the stone edifice of the temple. The Gospel makes it clear, however, that Jesus' prediction does not refer to the stone edifice of the temple but, rather, to Jesus' own body (2:21). Jesus predicts that he will be destroyed and raised again in three days. That means that Jesus' death and resurrection serve, for the Gospel, as a sign that establishes the legitimacy of his actions.

By equating the temple and Jesus' body, the Gospel establishes a new locus of worship.[41] Jesus as the locus of worship has already been suggested in John 1:14 where it says that Jesus "tabernacled (ἐσκήνωσεν) among us" (referring to the portable tent used for worship in the wilderness, Exod 25:8–9). In John 1:51, Jesus tells Nathanael that he will see "heaven opened and the angels of God ascending and descending upon the Son of Man." Here, Jesus is associated with the ancient place of worship in Bethel (see Gen 28:10–22). Even more explicitly, Jesus tells the Samaritan woman that true worship is neither "on this mountain nor in Jerusalem," but in spirit and in truth (4:21–23).[42] The spirit of truth comes from Jesus to the believers only after his ascent to the Father

---

[39] *Gospel*, 121. See also Léon-Dufour, "Le signe du temple selon Saint Jean," *RSR* 39 (1951): 155–75; Dodd, *Interpretation*, 300. In contrast, Schnackenburg (*Gospel*, 1:347) says that this allusion is not specific enough to make a messianic connection: the words arise naturally for the context; the emphasis is on the fact that Jesus calls God his father.

[40] The second singular pronoun "you" is grammatically emphasized. Léon-Dufour ("Symbolic," 448–9) argues that the Jews were expecting God himself to take the place of the temple. Jesus, in making a similar claim to take the place of the temple, identifies himself with God.

[41] See also Daly-Denton, *David*, 122; Brown, *Gospel*, 90. John 2:14 refers to the temple as τό ἱερόν, likely referring to both the temple precincts and the inner sanctuary, where Jesus teaches, walks, and heals (see 5:14; 7:14, 28; 8:2, 20, 59; 10:23; 11:56; 18:20). John 2:19, 20 and 21, however, use ναός to refer to the inner sanctuary of the temple. See Barrett, *Gospel*, 199. In this case, therefore, "the human body of Jesus was the place where a unique manifestation of God took place and consequently became the only true Temple, the only center of true worship" (Barrett, *Gospel*, 201).

[42] This type of worship is a rather vague notion in the Gospel of John but most likely refers to what happens when those who love Jesus and keep his commandments experience the divine presence (14:15–24) and are taught by the Spirit (14:25–26). It may also include a meal and footwashing, as we will see. It is unlikely that the body of Jesus as a locus of worship refers to the church, as Paul would imagine (Rom 12:5; 1 Cor 12:12–27; cf. Origen, *Comm. In Jn.*10.35.20), for it is first destroyed and then rebuilt (John 2:19). See also Schnackenburg, *Gospel*, 1:357; X. Léon-Dufour, "Signe," 171. Attempting to combine these two notions, Barrett (*Gospel*, 201) says, "It was his own body, killed on the cross, that Christ raised up, but in doing so he brought the church into being."

(14:16; 16:7). It is thus *through* his death and resurrection that Jesus inaugurates true worship. The Gospel thus substitutes Jesus' body both for the sacrifice and for the place of worship.

Although the interpretation of Jesus' death may well find its beginning in the imagery of the Passover sacrifice, the Gospel of John extends the imagery to introduce a new kind of paschal sacrifice. In this new Passover, God offers the sacrifice, not the worshipers. "For God so loved the world that he gave his only son, so that anyone who believes in him may not perish but have eternal life" (3:16). The sacrifice of Jesus thus replaces the offering of sacrificial animals.[43] Furthermore, the place where worship is conducted becomes more abstract: Jesus' body is now the temple (2:21). In this way, through his death, Jesus inaugurates true worship. What remains is the full participation of the worshiper in the consumption—or consummation—of the sacrifice, namely, believing in the necessity of Jesus' death.

THE ROLE OF THE DISCIPLES

This narrative describes different levels of response to Jesus' words. The Jews directly question Jesus and his actions, but their consequent reaction to his answers are not recorded. The narrative suspends the record of their response. Many others "believed in his name because they saw the signs that he was doing" (2:23), but Jesus "does not entrust himself" (οὐκ ἐπίστευεν αὐτὸν) to them, because he "knows them all" (2:24).[44] They are prepared to accept Jesus on the basis of his signs alone, without the knowledge of his death and resurrection. In contrast, the disciples do believe. Their belief focuses on two main concepts. First, they believe the scripture. This refers to the scriptural citation that they remembered, "Zeal for your house will consume me." Second, the disciples believe in the word that Jesus speaks. This refers to the claim that Jesus will rebuild the temple in three days. The word is not straightforward, however; it requires interpretation that is made possible only in light of the death and resurrection of Jesus (2:22). Thus, according to the narrator (2:22), the disciples come to realize only after his death and resurrection that Jesus replaces the temple as a place of worship.[45] For the Gospel of John, therefore, only believers who "read the signs" through the lens of his death and resurrection will receive ("be entrusted with") Jesus (see also 1:12).

---

[43] Daly-Denton, *David*, 130; J. D. M. Derrett, "The Zeal of the House and the Cleansing of the Temple," *Downside Review* 95 (1977): 90; Carey, "Lamb," 100.

[44] The same word, πιστεύω, is used in the positive sense to refer to the disciples' belief, and in the negative sense to refer to Jesus' "disbelief" or "distrust" of the others.

[45] Schnackenburg, *Gospel*, 1:352, 356; Dodd, *Interpretation*, 301; Barrett, *Gospel*, 164; Lightfoot, *John*, 114; Brown, *Gospel*, 122–5; Cullmann, *Worship*, 72.

CONCLUSION

This passage develops the ingesting motif by emphasizing the necessity of Jesus' death and the response of believers in accepting his death as efficacious. Whereas the Wedding in Cana narrative demonstrates that Jesus provides consumable material (i.e., wine), the Cleansing of the Temple narrative demonstrates that Jesus is, in fact, the very substance of the food. Jesus is more than a miracle worker who can rebuild a temple in three days; he expels the animals from the temple and becomes himself a more appropriate sacrifice, the "Lamb of God who takes away the sin of the world," assuring deliverance. Those who acknowledge the necessity of the death of Jesus respond with belief.

Chapter 3

Living Water and Dying Food (4:4–42; 7:37–39; 12:24)

The narrative of Jesus in Samaria weaves two stories together. The first story features a dialogue between Jesus and a Samaritan woman at the well of Jacob: Jesus asks for a drink of water; when she demurs, he teaches her about living water and true worship (4:1–26); she goes to her compatriots and brings them to Jesus (4:39–42). While she is gone, another story moves to center stage: the disciples bring food for Jesus; he refuses it but teaches them about a different kind of food and a different kind of harvest (4:27–38). These two stories address parallel misunderstandings, one about drink and the other about food.

LIVING WATER (JOHN 4:4–42; 7:37–39)

In the story of Jesus and the woman at the well, a contrast is established between the water that the Samaritan woman can provide and the water that Jesus offers. The woman's water, on the one hand, is predominantly associated with the well of Jacob (4:6, 12). This well was "given" by the patriarch and was the source of water for his many sons and abundant flocks (τὰ θρέμματα; 4:12).[1] It is a source of fertility and life.[2] As a gift of Jacob, it also serves as a

---

[1] Τὰ θρέμματα occurs nowhere else in the Greek bible and likely includes all those for whom Jacob provided nourishment. See J. H. Bernard, *A Critical and Exegetical Commentary on the Gospel according to St. John* Vol. 1 (ICC; Edinburgh: T&T Clark, 1928).

[2] Water serves as an implicit reference to semen in the subsequent sexual repartee between Jesus and the woman, according to L. Eslinger, "The Wooing of the Woman at the Well: Jesus, the Reader and Reader-Response Criticism," *JLT* 1 (1987): 167–83. In John 2:1–12, the steward in Cana refers ambiguously to Jesus as the bridegroom (2:10). The connection of Jesus with the bridegroom is made explicit by John the Baptist, who says, "I am not the Messiah, but I have been sent ahead of him. He who has the bride is the bridegroom. The friend of the bridegroom who stands and hears him, rejoices greatly at the bridegroom's voice" (3:28–29). John 4 completes this narrative development by depicting Jesus as the bridegroom and Messiah. First, the encounter of Jesus and the woman at the well evokes significant betrothal scenes in the biblical tradition: Isaac's servant and Rebecca (Gen 24:10–54), Jacob and Rachel (Gen 29:2–19), and Moses and Zipporah (Exod 2:15–22; see also *Ant.* 2.11.2). In these various stories we see recurring patterns of a man who experiences conflict and travels to a foreign country. There, he meets a woman at a well and they have some kind of conversation about water. After she tells her people about him, the man and woman become betrothed and they celebrate the wedding with a meal. Jesus may thus be

reminder of the Samaritans' heritage and as a unifying symbol of their communal identity as his children.[3] But access to this water is limited: the well is deep and a bucket is required (4:11); it is fixed in one location so they must go there each day to draw water (4:15).[4] Moreover, giving out this water is a problem because Samaritans and Jews do not "share things in common" (4:9).[5] Though the water from this well is undoubtedly exceptional, especially to the Samaritans, those who drink of it "will be thirsty again" (4:13). It is "earthly water" that does not satisfy.

The water that Jesus offers, on the other hand, does satisfy. Given as a gift from God, this is "living water" (4:10, 11).[6] It is available to whoever asks for it (4:10). It quenches thirst forever (4:10, 14) and need never be drawn again (4:15; also suggested when the woman leaves her jar behind, 4:28[7]). It is not

---

understood as the bridegroom to the Samaritan woman; in this case, however, their "union" is spiritual and its fruit is a harvest of many believers. Some would say that the woman calls Jesus κύριε, not meaning "Lord" but rather "husband." For a full treatment of this subject, see N. Bonneau, "The Woman at the Well: John 4 and Genesis 24," *The Bible Today* 67 (1973): 1252–9. C. Carmichael, "Marriage and the Samaritan Woman," *NTS* 26 (1980): 332–46; Eslinger, "Wooing," 167–83.

[3] According to Gen 33:19 and 48:22, Josh 24:32 and Acts 7:15, Jacob purchased the land from Shechem, pitched his tent there, and built an altar called El-Elohe-Israel ("The God of Israel"). He gave this land to his son Joseph. It was there that Jacob's bones were buried. Shechem is a center for cultic activity (see Gen 12:6–7; 33:18–20; Josh 24:26, 32; Deut 11:29; Judg 9:6; *Ant.* 11.8.6). B. Olsson (*Structure and Meaning in the Fourth Gospel: A Text-Linguistic Analysis of John 2:1–11 and 4:1–42* [trans. Jean Gray; Lund: C. W. K. Gleerup, 1974], 162–73) suggests that the tradition of a primordial well lies behind John 4. This well "traveled" with the Hebrews throughout their sojourn in the wilderness and rose up again at opportune moments (see, for example, *L.A.B.*11:15). God also gave them water at a place called "Matttanah," which means "gift" (Num 21:18; cf. John 4:10). See also Koester, *Symbolism*, 170.

[4] Note the numerous references to the location of this well in 4:4–6. Some Jewish sources suggest that Jacob made the water "spring up" in this place. See Olsson, *Structure*, 169–70. Later Samaritan sources focus attention on the water that Moses gave (*Memar Marqah* 4:4, 8; 5:3; 6:3).

[5] D. Daube, "Jesus and the Samaritan Woman: The Meaning of συγχράομαι," *JBL* (1950): 137–47. The distinction between Samaritan and Jew is also reflected in the discussion of true worship in John 4:20–24.

[6] While this passage is not explicitly about purification, Koester (*Symbolism*, 168) notes that "living water," in contrast to water in a cistern, was used by both Jews and Samaritans to purify themselves from defilement such as skin disease (Lev 14: 5–6, 50–52), bodily discharges (15:13), and corpse defilement (Num 19:17).

[7] This detail has engendered many interpretations depending on the focus of the commentator. For example, Bultmann (*Gospel*, 193) says that the woman leaves the jar because of her zeal. Barrett (*Gospel*, 240) suggests that the woman left it there so that Jesus can help himself to a drink, thus disregarding Levitical regulations and incurring impurity. Fenton (*Gospel*, 62) argues that the jars in John 2:6–7 stand for the Law; that the woman left

fixed to one location. No bucket is needed (4:11). It becomes "a spring of water gushing up to eternal life" from those who drink of it (4:14) and supplies living water to others. Thus, the water that Jesus offers is far superior to the water that the Samaritan offers,[8] and his role shifts from a guest who asks for inferior water to a host who gives living water.

In biblical and Jewish tradition, "living water" is salvific. Exodus 17:1–7 tells of the miraculous provision of water from a rock upon which God stands (see also Num 20:2–13). Ezekiel 47 speaks of the rivers that arise from the temple precinct and flow out to all nations, nourishing trees which "bear fruit every month" and which bring healing in their leaves (47:12; see also Zech 14:8; Joel 3:18). Likely dependent on these images in Ezekiel, the *Odes of Solomon* speak of the living water that comes from God as a great river which restores the earth (6:8–18; cf. 11:7–8; 30:1–7).[9] God is the source of water in these cases. Jeremiah says that God is the "fountain of living waters" (2:13; 17:13; cf. Ps 36:9).[10] Similarly, in John, God is the source of the gift of living water (4:10).

Another cluster of traditional images associates water, wells, and fountains with Wisdom and the Law.[11] For example, Prov 13:14 says, "the teaching of the wise is a fountain of life" (cf. Prov 14:27; Ps 36:9).[12] Sirach describes "the water of wisdom to drink" which is offered by Wisdom (15:1–3); this water will arouse thirst rather than quench it, for "those who drink of [Wisdom] will thirst for more" (24:21). Sirach explicitly identifies Wisdom, i.e., this drink, as the Law (24:23); anyone who "drinks in" the Law, therefore, will never be satisfied. This is an admirable quality of the Law, according to Sirach, for its value is known and appreciated only through consumption.

At first glance, there appear to be similarities between the Gospel of John and these traditional images involving living water as the Wisdom of God. Jesus is depicted as Wisdom incarnate. Like the personified Wisdom of Proverbs, Baruch, Sirach, and the Wisdom of Solomon, Jesus speaks words of

---

her jar in 4:28 might mean, therefore, that she left the Law in order to follow Jesus. See also Chrysostom, *Hom.*, 34,1: *PG* 59, col. 193.

[8] We might also conclude that Jesus is also superior to Jacob (4:12). The theme of replacement is evident here again. Jesus replaces the water on which the Samaritans flourish, and true worship replaces worship on Gerazim and in Jerusalem (4:23). See Dodd, *Interpretation*, 314.

[9] Revelation 22:1–2 and 17–19 have a similar image (see also 7:17; 21:6).

[10] See also Philo, *Spec. Laws* 1. 303; *Flight* 197–9.

[11] Brown, *Gospel*, 178–9; Koester, *Symbolism*, 170–1; M. Scott, *Sophia and the Johannine Jesus* (Sheffield: Journal for the Study of the Old Testament Press, 1992); Barrett, *Gospel*, 233–5; Schnackenburg, *Gospel*, 1:426–32.

[12] Philo calls the water from Moses' well "incomparable wisdom" (*Drunkenness* 112; also *Dreams* 2.271). See also CD VI, 4; III, 13–17; XIX, 32–35.

wisdom, dwells with Israel, makes people friends with God, and invites people to drink living water. Like Wisdom, Jesus is understood to be this living water and is to be ingested. Furthermore, Wisdom is depicted as the savior of Israel in ways that echo the Samaritans' declaration that Jesus is the savior of the world (Wis 9:18; 10:4; John 4:42). However, unlike the notion of Wisdom, Jesus is not identified with the Law. In fact, a clear distinction is made between Jesus and the Law: "The law indeed was given through Moses; grace and truth came through Jesus Christ" (1:17). As Wisdom is both the provider and substance, so too is Jesus both the provider and the substance of living water.

The notion that Jesus is the provider and substance of living water is further developed as the Gospel progresses. In a later passage, we find this proclamation by Jesus:

> On the last day of the festival, the great day, while Jesus was standing there, he cried out, "Let anyone who is thirsty come to me, and let the one who believes in me drink. As the scripture has said, 'Out of his belly shall flow rivers of living water.'" Now he said this about the spirit, which believers in him were to receive; for as yet there was no spirit, because Jesus was not yet glorified. (7:37–39)

Jesus again invites people to come to him and to drink. He again indicates that whoever drinks of him will become a source for flowing water.[13] But here, the flowing water is identified as the spirit given to believers after Jesus' death, that is, "when he is glorified." Indeed, when Jesus dies, he "gives up the spirit" (19:30), and when his side is pierced, "blood and water come out" (19:34).[14] Although this flow of water/spirit in 19:30 appears to anticipate the moment when Jesus gives the Holy Spirit to his disciples after his resurrection (20:22), Jesus' body is identified as the source of water at his death. So when Jesus says to the woman, "If you knew the gift of God and who it is speaking to you" (4:10), he is referring not only to the water that he has to offer but also to his spirit made available only after his death.[15]

Why then does the Gospel present this water as a gift that is available to the woman before Jesus' death? According to J. Louis Martyn,[16] the Gospel of John functions within two temporal settings. On the one hand, the Gospel tells the narrative of Jesus and the events of his life from the beginning of his ministry to

---

[13] The word αὐτοῦ in 7:38 may refer to either Jesus (i.e., "Jesus' belly") or to a believer (i.e., "a believer's belly"). Both referents are possible in this context. See Schnackenburg, *Gospel*, 2:153–4; Daly-Denton, *David*, 147; cf. Brown, *Gospel*, 321.

[14] The word "spirit" is used in a number of ways in the Gospel of John. These will be discussed in Chapters 4 and 7.

[15] Daly-Denton (*David*, 144–61) argues that John 7:38 cites Psalm 77 (78) (with resonances from Zech 14:8 and Ezek 47:1–2) and refers simultaneously to the rock struck by Moses and to the temple.

[16] J. L. Martyn, *History and Theology in the Fourth Gospel* (2d ed.; Nashville: Abingdon, 1979), 143–51.

his death and resurrection. In this sense, the narrator carries the reader into a sequential unfolding of the revelation, hopefully to result in the reader's belief (20:31). On the other hand, the Gospel also tells the story of Jesus from the post-resurrection perspective (see, for example, 2:22) and affirms that Jesus did all that he promised to do. So, while the characters in the narrative do not know that Jesus will be raised from the dead, the Gospel knows the resurrection as a thing of the past. The death and resurrection of Jesus are thus read both as "not yet" and as "already accomplished"; we see this in such phrases as "the hour is coming and now is" (4:23; 5:25; 16:32). Therefore, the Gospel presents the gift of water as available only after the death of Jesus but also as available for the Samaritan woman before his death and, by extension, for the reader.

"Living water" is a "gift from God" (4:10); likewise, Jesus is understood to be a "gift from God." We read, "For God so loved the world that he gave his only Son, so that everyone who believes in him will not perish but have eternal life" (3:16). Thus, when Jesus says to the woman, "If you knew the gift of God and who it is that is speaking to you" (4:10), he refers not only to the living water that he offers but also to himself as the provider of this water. This underscores Jesus' two-fold function in the Gospel of John: he is both the giver of the gift and the gift itself,[17] the messenger and the message, the source and the substance.

How then can we understand Jesus as the provider of living water and the essence of living water at the same time? In this story, the substance of the water is conceived, not so much as a material element, but as Jesus' self-revelation. The woman asks Jesus for the water he offers and rather than explicitly giving it to her—in the narrative sense anyway—he asks her about her husband. Denials and correction lead to proclamations that gather strength throughout the discourse. The woman calls him a prophet and asks for more information, this time about proper worship. His answer leads her to the tentative conclusion that he is the Messiah. So, what Jesus actually gives her is not "living water" *per se*, but rather a glimpse of himself (by giving her a glimpse of *herself*) and then full disclosure in the words, "I am he [i.e., the Messiah], the one speaking to you."[18] Living water that satisfies thirst forever is therefore understood to be the knowledge that Jesus is the Messiah. Satisfied,

---

[17] Koester, *Symbolism*, 168.

[18] Bultmann, *Gospel*, 188. The statement ("I am the one speaking to you") joins a series of statements with the "I am" formula. Bultmann (*Gospel*, 225–6) differentiates these statements as formulae of presentation, qualification, identification, or recognition. Though the differences are somewhat arbitrary and the distinction between a sacred and non-sacred "I am" statement is not made clear, Bultmann dismisses 4:26 as a non-sacred formula (224). Regardless, it is clear that both Jesus' supernatural knowledge of her and his confirmation that he is the Messiah motivate her declaration to the rest of the Samaritans.

the woman leaves her water jar, but takes this water (read "revelation") to the Samaritans, and they too come to know him and are satisfied. Thus, Jesus is the substance of the revelation. Alternatively, the living water could be understood to be Jesus' words, where Jesus is the source of the revelation. Jesus speaks the words of God to the woman, and she speaks his words to others. They first believe because of her word and then believe because of Jesus' word. To distinguish the revelation of Jesus' identity from the word that Jesus speaks, however, introduces a dichotomy that is not present in the Gospel. Jesus is the Word, "the one who speaks" (4:26). Accepting Jesus' words, or Jesus as the Word, and passing them/him to others constitutes the call of the Gospel on the reader. By using ingesting language, however, the Gospel emphasizes that the words/Word must be internalized.

The means for salvation, according to this story, is knowledge of or belief in Jesus. Jesus tells the woman that if she *knew* (ᾔδει) the gift of God and who was speaking to her, she would ask and receive living water. We are never told that she is certain of Jesus' identity. She asks if Jesus could possibly be greater than Jacob (4:12). She "sees" (θεωρέω) that he is a prophet (4:19). She knows (οἶδα) that a Messiah is coming who will proclaim all things (4:25). In John 4:29, she anticipates a negative response when she questions the other Samaritans: "He cannot be the Messiah, can he?" (μήτι οὗτός ἐστιν ὁ Χριστός;). Her questions are framed in such a way as to indicate doubt. However, we are told that her testimony, which is based on the knowledge that Jesus has of her (4:29, 39), is convincing enough to bring the Samaritans to believe in Jesus (4:39, 41). They express their belief in terms of knowledge. They say, "We know (οἴδαμεν) that this is truly the savior of the world" (4:42). Knowledge and belief are thus synonymous in this story and are understood to be saving.

The consequence of receiving Jesus' living water is twofold. First, the water that Jesus gives "will become a spring of water gushing up to eternal life" (4:14). The expression "to eternal life" (εἰς ζωὴν αἰώνιον) articulates the kind of salvation envisioned in the Gospel of John. Those who believe in him "will have eternal life" (3:15, 16, 36; 5:24, 28–29, 39–43; 6:47, 68; 17:2–3) or be "raised on the last day" (6:40, 54). The second consequence of receiving Jesus' living water is the responsibility of the recipient to pass along the benefits. This pattern is described throughout the discourses in the Gospel: God gives to Jesus, Jesus gives to the disciples, and the disciples give to others. In this case, God gives the gift of Jesus who, in turn, gives God's gifts of "living water"—

and himself—to those who ask, and they in turn give him to others.[19] They provide "a spring of water gushing up to eternal life" (4:14; cf. 7:37). Similarly, God gives the gift of Jesus to the Samaritan woman, and she "gives him" to her compatriots.

To summarize the first story, then, Jesus shifts roles from guest to host when he offers living water to the Samaritan woman. His water is greater than anything else she has ever had, because it satisfies thirst forever. Jesus is both the provider and the substance of this living water and it is available at his death to those who ask for it. Received, or "ingested," this water gives eternal life, and, when shared with others, gives them eternal life (4:14). The Samaritan woman is a model for one who shares for the benefit of others. She asks for this water, which in this case is Jesus' self-revelation as the Messiah, and takes it in the form of a testimony to the other Samaritans who, in turn, first receive it and then go to the source themselves. They "ingest" his word, believe, and receive salvation. But, as we will see in the Bread of Life discourse and other passages, knowledge of Jesus as the messianic provider of good things (bread, wine, and even revelation) is not enough for salvation. This knowledge must be coupled with the acceptance of the efficacy of Jesus' death.

DYING FOOD (JOHN 4:31–38; 12:24)

The Gospel establishes another contrast in a story that winds throughout the encounter of Jesus and the Samaritan woman. The contrast, in this case, is between the food that the disciples have and the food that Jesus has. Like the water that must be drawn everyday, the food that the disciples offer must be purchased from time to time (4:8). It comes from the city, and it is recognizable as food (by implication in 4:32). In contrast, the food that Jesus has does not need to be purchased. Its source is unknown to the disciples (4:33). It is not recognized as food (4:32). Jesus' words in 4:32 underline this difference with the use of the emphatic pronouns: "*I* have food to eat that *you* do not know about" (ἐγὼ βρῶσιν ἔχω φαγεῖν ἣν ὑμεῖς οὐκ οἴδατε). His apparent refusal of the disciples' food suggests that his food is superior. As in the living water story where Jesus first asks for water and then offers himself as water, in this story, Jesus is offered something to eat by his disciples but then speaks of a different kind of food altogether.

In John 4:34, Jesus identifies this food explicitly as "doing the will" of the

---

[19] A similar pattern is established with the words of God: the Father gives the words to the Son, the Son gives the words to the disciples, and they give the words to others (17:7–8, 20; cf. 12:49–50).

one who sent him and as "completing his work" (ἐμὸν βρῶμά ἐστιν ἵνα ποιήσω τὸ θέλημα τοῦ πέμψαντός με καὶ τελειώσω αὐτοῦ τὸ ἔργον). To do the will (τὸ θέλημα) of the one who sent him (that is, the Father) is "to raise up [all those who believe] on the last day" (6:38–39).[20] In order to accomplish this task, Jesus must "complete his work." Now, the Father's work that Jesus is doing (5:36) may be understood in two different ways. First, his work refers to the teaching (7:14, 21) and miracles (9:3) that serve as a testimony to both Jesus and the Father (5:20, 36; 10:25–30, 37–38; 14:11) and that lead to belief (10:25–30). Second, Jesus "completes" this work at his death.[21] "When Jesus knew that all was finished (πάντα τετέλεσται), . . . he said, 'It is finished' (Τετέλεσται). Then he bowed his head and gave up the spirit" (19:28–30; see also 17:4). When Jesus refers to his food, then, as doing the will of the one who sent him and completing his work, he is saying that his food is both to bring others to belief and to go to his death.[22] His death paradoxically leads to his resurrection and eternal life for those who believe in him (3:16; 4:36; 5:24; 6:47, etc.). This is the food that sustains Jesus (4:34).[23]

At the same time, Jesus himself is also understood to be the food that is to be eaten. The harvest image in John 4:35–38 develops this notion in five ways. First, it introduces the idea that Jesus is a consumable substance. In conjunction with a later passage, Jesus says at the "hour of his glorification" that, "unless a grain of wheat falls into the earth and dies, it remains just a single grain; but if it dies, it bears much fruit" (12:24). An analogy is established between what happens to the grain of wheat and what will happen to Jesus at his death. Jesus is thus understood to be the seed that is sown and that later must be harvested. Second, the harvest image underlines the imminent completion of Jesus' work, and thus, the availability of "food." Like a field ready for harvest, Jesus' work

---

[20] Jesus does not seek his own will but the will of the Father (5:30; 6:38–40; 14:31).

[21] Jesus' works, whether the healing and miracles or his death, lead to belief. They come from the Father (10:32; 14:10) and show that Jesus and the Father are one (10:38; 14:11). They testify to the fact that he is the Messiah (10:24–25). Those who believe in Jesus' works belong to his "sheep" (10:25) and follow him (10:27). This results in eternal life (10:28). Those who do not believe sin (15:24) and do not have eternal life (10:25–27). While Dodd (*Interpretation*, 316) interprets the "completion of God's work" to be the replacement of the earthly life with the spiritual one and elsewhere connects the inauguration of this new order with Jesus' death (302), he does not make this connection here.

[22] Note that the Samaritan story is linked to Jesus' crucifixion at five points. It occurs at noon (4:6; 19:14); Jesus thirsts (4:7; 19:28); he is a source of water (4:13; 19:34); a witness' testimony leads others to belief (4:39; 19:35); and Jesus stays in Samaria and "in death" for two days (4:40; 19:42–20:1).

[23] E. Cothenet ("La nourriture du Christ et la mission," in *Nourriture et repas dans les milieux Juifs et Chrétiens de l'Antiqité* [ed. M. Quesnel, Y.-M. Blanchard, C. Tassin; Paris: Cerf, 1999], 181–91) argues that the metaphor of food indicates that Jesus was internally motivated to complete his Father's will.

has already begun and is nearing completion. Even though it appears that the harvest is four months hence, Jesus points out that the fields are already ripe (4:35) and the food that appeared to be available only in the distant future is soon, or even now, available at Jesus' death.[24] (Recall the same two temporal levels in the living water story.) Third, the harvest motif is also associated with an eschatological age. Amos 9:13 says, "The time is surely coming, says the LORD, when the one who plows shall overtake the one who reaps, and the treader of grapes the one who sows the seed."[25] Fourth, this picture of the harvest indicates that Jesus looks forward to a new world where the sowing and reaping are not separated by time but are simultaneous: "Sower and reaper will rejoice together" (4:36).[26] Fifth, the fruit of the harvest is understood as "eternal life," recalling the water that "gushes up to eternal life" and all its benefits. The image therefore introduces the theme that the Messiah Jesus will even now inaugurate a new age through his work and his death.

The interpretation of the harvest image depends on the identity of that which is sown. In the context of the harvest metaphor, as the source of the food, Jesus' work as teaching and miracles comes to the fore. The one who sows is likely Jesus.[27] Jesus "sows the seed" of his word in the Samaritan woman.[28] She in turn passes "the word" (τὸν λόγον) to the people in the city (4:29–30). (Jesus and the woman thus constitute the "others" of 4:38.[29]) Many come to believe in

---

[24] The fields have not yet been harvested, but the harvester is already receiving his wages. Jesus says that "his time has not yet come" to do his works (7:6, see also 2:4), but he is already doing them (7:3; also 5:20, 36; 7:21; 9:4). See also 4:23; 5:25; 16:32. See Brown, *Gospel*, 182.

[25] See also Lev 26:5. Amos 9 also refers to mountains dripping with sweet wine. Cf. John 2:1–11. Bernard (*Gospel*, 1:158–9) points out that the servants usually sow the fields and the master takes the produce. In this passage, however, the image is reversed and the produce goes to the servants. This is the cause for rejoicing.

[26] Bultmann (*Gospel*, 196) limits this new world-order to the work that the disciples are able to perform, namely the work of sowing and reaping. Clearly the harvest image refers to an age when the harvest itself overtakes the sowing, not just the harvesters. This speaks of a new kind of creation (cf. 1:1).

[27] In John 4:6, Jesus is described literally as "having labored (κεκοπιακώς) out of the journey." See Bauer, *Lexicon*, 443. The word in 4:6 and 4:38 forms an *inclusio* around the Samaritan narrative.

[28] Brown, *Gospel*, 183. See my "Transcending Alterity: Strange Woman to Samaritan Woman," in *Feminist Companion to the Johannine Literature* (ed. A.-J. Levine; Sheffield: Sheffield Academic Press, forthcoming), where I argue that a spiritual "union" between Jesus and the Samaritan woman results in many spiritual children.

[29] It might be posited that the "others" also include the Father, for Jesus is "completing [the Father's] work" (4:34; cf. 5:19, 36; 6:44–46, 65; 8:16; 10:32, 38; 14:6–16, 31; 16:32). This is problematic because Jesus, and not the Father, completes the work through his death. Bultmann, *Gospel*, 199; Bernard, *Gospel*, 1:159. If we depend strictly on the Samaritan context for this saying (and not the later Johannine community), we can eliminate the

Jesus because of her word (4:39). They say to her, "It is no longer because of what you said that we believe, for we have heard for ourselves, and we know that this is truly the savior of the world" (4:42). So both Jesus and the woman sow the seed of Jesus' word in Samaria, and the harvest—that is, the response to Jesus' word—is both dramatic and immediate. The disciples, whom Jesus sends as reapers (and later as "messengers," 13:16, also 13:20; 17:18; 20:21), are presumably involved in the "reaping" of the Samaritans during their two-day stay in Samaria. Furthermore, if Jesus' work is to perform deeds that bring people to belief, then so are the disciples to perform deeds that bring others to belief (3:21; 6:29; 9:4; 14:12).

When the seed is understood as Jesus' body, the harvest image assumes a more profound interpretation. Jesus is the "grain of wheat that falls into the earth and dies . . . [and] bears much fruit" (12:24). His death results in the fruit of eternal life, that is, the availability of life for those who believe in him (cf. John 6: 40). The harvest approaches quickly as, within the chronology of the narrative, Jesus' death is imminent; from the perspective of the believing community, however, the harvest has already been inaugurated by Jesus' death and resurrection.

The nature of the harvest is plain: the disciples are sent to gather up those who believe in Jesus because of his word and deeds and, more importantly, who believe in his death and resurrection. As we will see in John 6 with the gathering of the bread fragments, the conditions are such that the disciples need only complete the work, for many are ready to believe (i.e., the fields are ripe for the harvesting, 4:35). The reward for those who do believe, including the disciples, is eternal life (4:36; cf. 6:12). We see the same idea at work in the living water story of John 4.

The second story about Jesus' food makes several points. In doing the will of God, Jesus provides food (teaching and miracles) to give others life. In this way, he nourishes himself. Jesus is also the substance of the food in that it is through his physical death and resurrection that others have eternal life. He is

---

Hebrew prophets who prepared the way for Jesus, because the Samaritans accepted only the Pentateuch. Brown, *Gospel*, 183. We might also eliminate John the Baptist and his disciples. This possibility is suggested by J. A. T. Robinson, "The 'Others' of John 4.38," in *Twelve New Testament Studies* (SBT 34; London: SCM, 1962), 61–66. Although we know that John had preached at Aenon near Salim (see 3:23), it is not certain that Aenon is in Samaria. See J. Pattengale, "Aenon," *ABD* 1:87; Brown, *Gospel*, 183–4. Compare Brown (*Gospel*, 183–4) who suggests that 4:38 refers to the combined work of Jesus and John the Baptist. It has also been suggested that the "others" might include those who spread the seeds of the Gospel in Samaria (such as Philip) before others came to reap the harvest (Peter and John) (see Acts 8, Rom 1:13). See Cullmann, *Early Church*, 185–92. While a compelling case may be made for these various suggestions, suffice it to say that, on a narrative level, Jesus expects the disciples to carry on the work (κόπον) that he has started (4:38).

the "grain that dies and falls to earth" that "even now" produces a miraculous harvest. He is the "dying food."

A COMPARISON OF LIVING WATER AND DYING FOOD

These two stories in the narrative of Jesus in Samaria explicitly develop the ingesting motif, and in many ways, they complement one another. They both point to God as the initiator in salvation: Jesus, as God's gift, does his will. Both portray Jesus as the provider and substance of food and drink of a different kind, and the means through which people are given eternal life. Both indicate the expected role of the one who receives Jesus: they are to pass Jesus on to others and thus provide the means for others to come to belief.

In both stories, the narrative action and the discourse are at odds. The Samaritan woman is asked for a drink, but we are not told that she provides it. She, in turn, asks Jesus for living water, but we are not told whether she receives it, though her testimony to the Samaritans suggests that she does. The disciples bring Jesus food, but we are not told that he eats it.[30] This suggests that earthly food and drink are of no use to Jesus; his appetite is to do the will of the Father and thus provide food for others. As well, roles are reversed, not unlike those in the Wedding in Cana story, in that Jesus moves from being a potential guest who is offered food and drink to becoming the host who provides a new and improved version of this food and drink. Those who receive his food and drink are then asked to serve others; they become the hosts of a new kind of food and drink.

THE ROLE OF THE DISCIPLES

The Samaria passage compares the response to Jesus of the woman and of the disciples. In the first story, the woman vigorously questions Jesus on many issues: the appropriateness of a Jew asking a Samaritan woman for water (4:9), the ability of Jesus to provide living water (4:11), his status in relation to Jacob (4:12), the proper place to worship (4:20), and his identity as the Messiah (though it is not a direct question here) (4:25, also 4:29). Jesus honors her questions. In turn, the woman tells others what she has learned, and they believe in Jesus because of her word (4:39).[31] She takes them to Jesus, and they believe because they hear for themselves (4:42). In contrast, the disciples do not ask (4:27) but are astonished (ἐθαύμαζον, 4:27), an attitude viewed negatively

---

[30] The only time in the Gospel we are told that Jesus does drink is when he is on the cross (19:28–30).

[31] Similarly, Andrew brings Peter (1:41) and Philip brings Nathanael (1:45) to Jesus.

in the rest of the Gospel (3:7; 7:21; 9:30).[32] The woman thus serves as an example to the disciples (and the reader, of course) on how to disseminate the seeds that produce a harvest for eternal life. This contrast is further extended to the Samaritans as a whole. Like the Jews who "know" what to worship (4:22), the disciples "know" Jesus, but not as they should. In contrast, the woman did not know "the gift of God" at first, but she passed the gift on to her compatriots. Though the Samaritans "do not know what they worship" (4:22), they also ask and come to know that Jesus is the "savior of the world" (4:42).

At the same time, it is not clear that the Samaritans understand that Jesus must die in order to provide eternal life. Like the multitude who is fed to satisfaction on the mountain and who declares Jesus to be "the prophet who is to come into the world" (6:14), the Samaritans are satisfied by the words of Jesus and declare him to be the Savior of the World (4:42). In contrast to the recipients of the bread and fish, however, the Samaritans are not rebuked (4:42; cf. 6:26–34). Indeed, the text is silent about the validity of their response. Hence, they may understand Jesus only as the provider of living water, or as the fount of revelation. The disciples, in contrast, receive the information that Jesus' food is "to do the will" of God, and whether they understand this or not, they are given directions for future action. In this way, they are exposed to a more profound expression of the Gospel's soteriology, a soteriology that will be made more explicit throughout the remainder of the Gospel.

CONCLUSION

The interwoven stories of the Samaritan woman, the disciples, and the Samaritans combine for the first time the notion that Jesus is both the provider and the substance of food and drink. He offers living water. By doing the will of God and completing his work, he is the "grain of wheat that falls to the ground" producing a great harvest; he is the substance of sacrifice providing life for others. The corresponding response to Jesus is varied: the Samaritan woman brings others to Jesus through her testimony; the Samaritans believe that Jesus is the savior of the world; and the disciples engage in the work that Jesus has started. While each response is viewed positively in its own way, none is complete. Yet when all three responses are combined—belief, testimony, and action—a complete picture of discipleship begins to emerge.

---

[32] Schnackenburg (*Gospel*, 443) assumes that the disciples do not ask because they respect Jesus too much to ask.

Chapter 4

Tasting Life and Tasting Death (6:1–71; 8:51–52)

This chapter will look at two opposing ideas. The first section will examine the extensive passage in John 6 that describes Jesus as the bread of life that must be eaten: to taste Jesus is to taste life. The much shorter second section deals with the idea of tasting death in John 8. While John 6 develops the ingesting motif positively and substantially, John 8 mentions tasting death without further amplification. Certainly, the idea needs little development: no one would choose death when life is an option.

TASTING LIFE (JOHN 6:1–71)

The most extensive development of the ingesting motif in the Gospel of John is found in chapter 6. John 6:1–15 describes the journey of Jesus and his disciples to the other side of the Sea of Galilee where Jesus turns a few loaves and fish into enough for more than five thousand men. When the people want to make him king, Jesus withdraws up the mountain alone. John 6:16–25 tells the story of Jesus walking on the water to meet his disciples who have already started out in their boat. John 6:26–71, set in Capernaum on the following day, presents a series of dialogues about bread. Each of these narratives is separated by changes in time (day to night to day), changes in setting (from the mountain, to the sea, to the synagogue in Capernaum), changes in perspective (Jesus to the crowds, to the disciples, and back to the crowds), and changes in plot. At the same time, the two narratives and the following discourse are united by continuity in time and space (though the setting changes, the reader is always informed), by the constancy of characters, and by the return in the discourse to issues introduced in the feeding miracle. They are also united by structural elements. John Dominic Crossan points out that a precise inclusion in the handling of the disciples and the Twelve frames the narrative.[1]

The Disciples (6:1–15)   *The Twelve (6:67–71)*
The Disciples (6:3)   The Twelve (6:67)

---

[1] J. D. Crossan, "It Is Written: A Structuralist Analysis of John 6," *Semeia* 26 (1983): 4.

Philip (6:5, 7)   Simon Peter (6:68)
Andrew (6:8)   Judas (6:71a)
The Disciples (6:12)   The Twelve (6:70, 71b)

There is also a general parallel within the chapter. The encounter flips back and forth between the crowds and Jesus:

(a) Jesus and Crowds   6:1–15   6:22–59
(b) Jesus and the Disciples   6:16–21   6:60–71

Gary Phillips argues that all of John 6 is a literary unit because the various discourse levels evoke a response from the reader parallel to the response expected of the narrative characters.[2] These two narratives and the following discourse are thus drawn together into one unified piece.

Since the second section, Walking on the Water, is not directly relevant for this study on ingesting language, it will not be treated in detail here.[3] Suffice it to say that this scene serves to separate the crowd from Jesus and the disciples, it enables a change in setting, and it provokes questions upon which the discourse will build. Exegesis will be limited to the first and third sections of John 6: the Feeding of the Multitude and the Bread of Life Discourse.

Feeding the Multitude (John 6:1–15)

The Feeding of the Multitude is a miracle story. Around the time of Passover, Jesus goes to the other side of the Sea of Galilee with his disciples.

---

[2] G. Phillips, "'This Is a Hard Saying. Who Can Be a Listener to It?': Creating a Reader in John 6," *Semeia* 26 (1983): 23–56. See also Crossan, "Written," 4.

[3] Because the Walking on the Water narrative follows the Feeding of the Multitude in Mark 6:45–52 and Matthew 14:22–33, it is commonly assumed that the shape of the inherited literary tradition restrains the arrangement of material in the Gospel of John. Brown (*Gospel*, 252), for example, argues that, in the Synoptic tradition, the Walking on the Water narrative concludes the feeding miracle. The Gospel of John does not use the Walking on the Water narrative to conclude the feeding miracle; in fact, it would make more sense to follow the feeding miracle with the Bread of Life discourse. Because the Walking on the Water narrative is included here, it appears that the Gospel was "controlled by an earlier tradition." While this might certainly be the case, it seems odd that tradition would rule the arrangement in this case when it has not ruled elsewhere in the Gospel. For example, the Gospel of John places the Cleansing of the Temple at the beginning of Jesus' ministry (John 2:13–25), but the Synoptics place it just prior to the passion narrative (Mark 11:15–18; Matt 21:12–13; Luke 19:45–47). See Schnackenburg, *Gospel*, 2:10–12; Borgen, *Bread*, 180. Barrett (*Gospel*, 279) agrees that John is dependent on Mark but adds that the Walking on the Water story serves as a bridge to bring Jesus and the disciples back to Capernaum. Guilding (*Fourth Gospel*, 58–59) points out that the Passover *haphtarah* Isaiah 51:6–16 corresponds to the crossing of the Red Sea (Exodus 15).

He is followed by a large group of people who have seen the "signs that he was doing for the sick" (6:2). When he sees the crowd, Jesus asks Philip where they can buy some bread to feed them all. Philip tells him that "Six months wages would not buy enough bread for each of them to get a little" (6:7). Andrew, however, points out that a boy has five barley loaves and two fish. Jesus takes the offered food, thanks God, and distributes it to the people. When everyone eats their fill, the disciples gather the leftover pieces and fill twelve baskets. As a result, the people are sure that Jesus is a prophet, but because Jesus knows that they will try to force him to be king, he withdraws to the mountain by himself. The central accomplishment of the story is the miraculous multiplication of the bread and fish by Jesus.

The Feeding of the Multitude narrative opens with the retrospective phrase, "after these things" (μετὰ ταῦτα).[4] Immediately preceding the Feeding of the Multitude story, Jesus heals a lame man on the Sabbath and then rebukes the Jews who are persecuting him because he "broke the Sabbath and called God his own Father, thereby making himself equal to God" (5:18). Jesus concludes his rebuke by claiming that Moses had testified to him and they had not accepted even this authoritative testimony (5:45). The account of the Feeding of the Multitude and the following discourse will demonstrate that Jesus is similar to Moses in many ways but that, unlike Moses, Jesus is "equal to God" (5:18).

The Feeding of the Multitude narrative takes place at the time of Passover: "Now the Passover, the festival of the Jews, was near" (6:4).[5] Several other markers also point to this festival. For example, "Jesus went up the mountain" (6:3) at the same time that the pilgrims would be climbing up towards Jerusalem on the eve of this pilgrimage feast. He sits down there, perhaps as a prelude to sharing the Passover meal with his disciples (6:3).[6] The people gather and eat together as they do for the pilgrimage festival. Their national

---

[4] See also 3:22; 5:1, 14; 6:1; 7:1; 13:7; 21:1. Brown (*Gospel*, 232) says that μετὰ ταῦτα is "a vague sequential reference," especially given that Jesus is in Jerusalem in chapter 5 and in Galilee in chapter 6. For a discussion of the ordering of these chapters, see Brown, *Gospel*, 235–6.

[5] Unlike other Johannine narratives that are set in the context of festivals (1:29, 35, 43; 2:1, 13, 23; 5:1; 6:16, 22; 7:37; 12:1, 12; 13:1; 20:1, 19, 26), this story begins with the fact that Jesus travels and that he is followed by a crowd who want to see signs. Only then is the chronological marker given. For the similar use of a delayed chronological marker, see 3:2 and 7:2. Crossan ("Written," 5) also notes that this phrase is displaced. This delay and the explanation "festival of the Jews" syntactically emphasize the setting. This is the "second Passover" in the Gospel's chronology (cf. Jesus goes to Jerusalem for Passover, 2:13; he returns to Galilee, 4:43, then back to Jerusalem for a "festival" (Passover?), 5:1; back in Galilee at Passover time, 6:4).

[6] Jesus sits down to teach in Luke 4:20, but this does not seem to be his intention here. See Barrett, *Gospel*, 273.

identity as the twelve tribes is recalled in the mention of the twelve baskets, and national aspirations are suggested in the people's recognition of Jesus as a prophet and possible king (6:14). Allusions to the Passover festival are cut short, however, because the people go to Jesus rather than to Jerusalem. The prophecies that Jesus' resurrected body will be the new locus of worship (2:19–22) and that true worship will be "neither on this mountain [that is, Gerazim] nor in Jerusalem" (4:21) anticipate this shift in devotional focus.

Similarly, allusions to the Passover and wilderness stories in Exodus 12–17 are evident in John 6:1–15. For example, instead of leading the people into the wilderness, as Moses does, Jesus goes alone (6:15).[7] Instead of leading the people across the (dry) sea, Jesus abandons them on the shore (6:24). However, like Moses, Jesus does provide food for people in the wilderness (cf. Exod 16–17). Thus, allusions to the Exodus focus on Jesus as one who provides food for the people. Jesus delivers the people by feeding them.

The geographical setting is specifically referred to as "the mountain" (6:3, 15) and evokes various narrative tropes in the biblical tradition.[8] On a mountain, Moses encounters God in a burning bush (Exod 3:1–4:17), receives the law (Exod 24:15–18; 32:15–16), looks over to the Promised Land, and goes to his death (Deut 34:1–6). On a mountain, Elijah hears the still small voice of God (1 Kgs 19:8–18). Mount Zion is the dwelling place of God (e.g., Ps 2:6; 78:69). On a mountain, Isaiah envisions a feast as the quintessential restoration of the relationship between God and all people.

> On this mountain the LORD of hosts will make for all peoples a feast of rich food, a feast of well-aged wines, of rich food filled with marrow, of well-aged wines strained clear. He will destroy on this mountain the shroud that is cast over all peoples, the sheet that is spread over all nations; he will swallow up death forever. Then the LORD GOD will wipe away the tears from all faces, and the disgrace of his people he will take away from all the earth, for the LORD has spoken. (Isa 25:6–8)

In Matthew, a mountain is the setting for the Sermon on the Mount (Matt 5–7), the transfiguration (Matt 17:1–8, par.), and the final ascent of Jesus (Matt 28:16). By situating this narrative on a mountain, the Gospel sets up the expectation of some kind of theophany; in this case, Jesus' divine nature is manifested in the miraculous provision of food.

Bread is an important symbol in the biblical tradition and is associated with divine rescue. The provision of manna in the wilderness is associated both with salvation and with the Passover-Exodus event. David and his men are saved when they are given five loaves of the "bread of the presence" (1 Sam 21:3–6)

---

[7] The fact that he goes alone is emphasized by the use of the personal pronoun and adjective μόνος.

[8] Barrett (*Gospel*, 273) only concedes that there might be "an allusion to Moses and Mount Sinai" in this verse.

and Elijah is fed bread and meat by the ravens (1 Kgs 17:9). In these passages, bread is provided by God or his agents, and this provision is understood to be a saving action.

The miraculous provision of bread is also associated with the messianic age or the last days. Sitting down to eat with the Messiah is a recurring theme throughout the literature of the Second Temple period. For example, *First Enoch* 62:12–14 says that after the final victory the righteous and elect "will eat and rest and rise with that Son of Man forever and ever." *First Enoch* 48A:10 says that "the kingdom of Israel, gathered from the four quarters of the world, shall eat with the Messiah." The food at this banquet is often bread, sometimes referred to as manna or as "heavenly food." The *Syriac Apocalypse, 2 Baruch,* prophesies that "it will happen at that time that the treasury of manna will come again from on high, and they will eat of it in those years because these are they who have arrived at the consummation of time" (29:8). These texts suggest that eating bread was understood both as an activity of the present world and as an activity in the world to come. The multiplication of bread in John 6, therefore, evokes God's provision both in the wilderness in the past, on this mountain in the present, and at the messianic banquet in the future.

The eating of fish near the Sea of Galilee need refer to no more than the simple fact that fish is a food staple for people in that place. But because fish are a part of both this miracle and the closing story of the Gospel (John 21), it is likely that traditional images are again being called into service. One possibility is found in the Numbers account of the feeding miracles, where Moses complains that it is not feasible to gather enough fish for the hungry multitude in the wilderness.[9] Another possibility is the primordial chaos monster Leviathan found in Job 41 and Ps 104:26 (cf. Rev 12:3–9; 21:1). Leviathan is a sea creature who will be killed in the age of the Messiah and will be cut up and served as an unending supply of food. Isaiah 27:1 describes the events on the day when the LORD comes: "On that day the LORD with his cruel and great and strong sword will punish Leviathan the fleeing serpent, Leviathan the twisting serpent, and he will kill the dragon that is in the sea." In Ps 74:13, the Psalmist describes how God divides Leviathan and distributes him for food: "You divided the sea by your might; you broke the heads of the dragons in the waters. You crushed the heads of Leviathan; you gave him as food for the creatures of the wilderness." *Second Baruch* 29:2–41 envisions the consumption of sea monsters as part of the eschatological banquet (see also *1 Enoch* 10:7–10, 24; *4 Ezra* 6:49–52). Ezekiel 47:1–12 envisions a river flowing out of the heavenly temple that is filled with a multitude of fish, a theme that recalls the living

---

[9] The same words are used for gathering (συνάγω, Num 11:22; John 6:9) and the fish (ὄψον, Num 11:22), although the diminutive ὀψάριον is used in John 6:9,11.

water theme in John 4:4–14 and 7:37–39. Fish, like the bread, are thus biblical symbols of God's providence in the past, present, and future.

As in the Wedding in Cana and Jesus in Samaria stories, a contrast is made between the food that is available to the people and the food that Jesus offers. In John 2:1–11, the primary contrast is in the *quality* of the wine that has run out and the wine that Jesus provides. In John 4, the contrast is in the *source* of the water (Jacob or Jesus). In John 6:1–15, the contrast is in the *quantity* of the available food and the need. The size of the crowd is mentioned four times: it is a "large crowd" (6:2, 5), five thousand men in number (6:10),[10] and "so many" (6:9). With apparent despair, Philip declares that "six months wages (i.e., 200 denarii) would not buy enough bread for each of them to get a little" (6:7). Andrew, however, tells Jesus of a boy who has some food; he is a small boy child with five barley loaves and two fish (6:9). This meagre offering is pitiful in light of the great need. Nevertheless, Jesus takes this meagre offering and distributes it to the people, and they eat until they are satisfied. Jesus transforms a small amount of food into enough for many people with plenty leftover. No comment is made about the quality or the nature of the food. We are not told that the food was the "best bread and fish" (cf. 2:10) nor that the bread and fish were spiritual, abstract elements (cf. 4:10, 14, 34). The distinguishing feature of the food in John 6:1–15 is its quantity.

The story also establishes a contrast among the disciples. Jesus asks Philip where they might buy some food for the people who come. According to the narrator, Jesus "tests" him (6:6).[11] Philip seems to think that feeding this multitude is impossible: "Six months wages would not be enough," he says (6:7). On the other hand, Andrew does attempt to find a solution by drawing Jesus' attention to the boy with the fish and loaves, but he too thinks that this offering is not enough (6:9). On the surface, it seems that neither of the two "passed the test" that Jesus had set up, because they, unlike Jesus, did not know what he was about to do (6:6).

Although Jesus himself distributes the food,[12] the disciples do have an active role in this miracle, and they see the sign with their own eyes.[13] Jesus tells the

---

[10] The term used is ἄνδρες, which usually refers to men in distinction from women. It is unclear if this term is used in a generic sense here; if so, the number would include both men and women. If not, the number could be easily doubled or tripled to account for the presence of women and children.

[11] Brown (*Gospel*, 233) states that this parenthetical comment by the narrator is "an editorial attempt to forestall any implication of ignorance on Jesus' part." K. Quast (*Reading the Gospel of John: An Introduction* [New York: Paulist, 1991], 50) suggests a parallel with Exodus 16:4 where God tests Israel with manna.

[12] Compare Matt 14:19; Mark 6:41; Luke 9:16.

[13] The steward and servants observe the changing of water into wine (2:9); the official's servants witness the healing of the child (4:51); only the lame man is a witness to his own

disciples to "make the people sit down" (6:10). The word ἀναπίπτω, translated by the NRSV as "sit down," is more accurately rendered "recline," an action that describes the first-century posture for eating.[14] Its modern equivalent would be something like "sit down at the table to eat" or "find your place at the table." Obviously, there are no tables on the mountain; the disciples have the people take their place on the "grass" or χόρτος, a word that usually refers to a feeding place, akin to a pasture, a meadow, or a hay field (6:10).[15] The disciples thus prepare the people to eat the food that Jesus offers. This is emphasized by the comment that Jesus distributes food "to those who are *seated*" (τοῖς ἀνακειμένοις; 6:11).[16]

The disciples are also responsible for gathering the fragments of leftover bread. When the people are satisfied, Jesus tells his disciples, "Gather (Συναγάγετε) up the fragments leftover, so that nothing may be lost." So the disciples "gathered (συνήγαγον) them up, and from the fragments of the five barley loaves, left by those who had eaten, they filled twelve baskets" (6:12–13). The word "gather" (συνάγω) is used twice in these two verses and recalls several traditional images. First, "gathering" (συνάγω, לקט) is often used simply to describe bringing in the harvest (Exod 23:10; 34:22). More particularly, it is used to describe the "harvest" of manna in the wilderness, an image evoked by the context of the feeding narrative and emphasized in the following passage from Exodus.

> Moses said to them, "It is the bread that the LORD has given you to eat. This is what the LORD has commanded: 'Gather (συναγάγετε, לקטו) as much of it as each of you needs, an omer to a person according to the number of persons, all providing for those in their own tents.'" The Israelites did so, some gathering (וילקטו) more, some less. . . . they gathered (לקטו) as much as each of them needed. . . . Morning by morning they gathered it (וילקטו), as much as each needed. (Exod 16:15–21)

Second, the word "gather" is used to describe the action of God in bringing all of Israel back to the land, either after the exile or in the eschaton. Deuteronomy says this:

> When all these things have happened to you, the blessings and the curses that I have

---

healing (5:13). The disciples are not featured as direct eye-witnesses to the miracles of Jesus up to this point.

[14] Tob 2:1; 7:9; Jdt 12:16; Sir 32:2; Luke 11:37; 17:7; 22:14; John 12:2; 13:12. According to Jeremias (*Eucharistic*, 49), Jews reclined at meals only on Passover; he does not account for John 12:4, in which Jesus and Lazarus recline to eat at a meal that is definitely not a Passover meal.

[15] Bauer, *Lexicon*, 884. This image evokes Psalm 23.

[16] According to Bauer (*Lexicon*, 55, 59), there is no significant difference in the meaning of ἀνάκειμαι (6:11) and ἀναπίπτω (6:10). They both mean "recline" or "lie." It might also be noted here that, after Jesus and the disciples leave the place where Jesus performed this miracle, the crowd is again left "standing" (ἑστηκώς) on the shore (6:22).

set before you, if you call them to mind among all the nations where the LORD your God has driven you, and return to the LORD your God, and you and your children obey him with all your heart and with all your soul, just as I am commanding you today, then the LORD your God will restore your fortunes and have compassion on you, gathering (συνάξει) you again from all the peoples among whom the LORD your God has scattered you. Even if you are exiled to the ends of the world, from there the LORD your God will gather (συνάξει) you, and from there he will bring you back. (Deut 30:1–4; cf. Ps 50:3–5; 107:2–9)

Isaiah 11 speaks of an eschatological vision of a renewed creation in which God will gather (συνάξει) all the people of Israel and return them to the land.[17] A reference to gathering, therefore, solicits traditional notions of the harvest, not just as a harvest of grains, but as the eschatological gathering of the people by God. The Gospel of John uses the word συνάγω in similar ways. It refers both to the harvest of grains (4:36) and to the eschatological gathering of the dispersed children of God (11:52; cf. 15:5–6).

In the Feeding of the Multitude story, the disciples gather the pieces of broken bread "so that none would be lost" (ἵνα μή τι ἀπόλλυμι).[18] On the surface of the narrative, the collection of fragments is evidence of the miracle; after all, five loaves and two fish could never fill twelve baskets in a natural way. But the collection of the fragments into twelve baskets also suggests the gathering of the twelve tribes of Israel by God and the harvest of the disciples mentioned in John 4:36–38. The disciples' role, then, is first to prepare people to eat and then to gather believers into eternal life, that not one "might be lost" (6:12; cf. 3:16; 10:28; 12:25; 17:12; 18:9).

The reaction of the crowd is also of particular interest in this narrative. First, the people follow Jesus because they see the signs that he has done for the sick (6:2) and (presumably) hope to see more signs (see 6:30). They do not express their hunger but are asked to sit on the grass. Jesus then gives them food. They eat and are satisfied (6:12); they are willing participants in the feast. The dramatic reaction, however, follows the gathering of the fragments into twelve baskets (6:13); it is at this moment that the people refer to the actions of Jesus as "a sign" and identify him specifically as "the prophet who has come into the world" (6:14).

Several biblical prophets are associated with food multiplication miracles. Moses is a prime example of this: he brings water from a rock (Exod 17:1–7), manna from heaven, and quail from the wind (Exod 16:1–36). Elijah also multiplies meal and oil for the widow of Zarephath (1 Kgs 17:8–24). Elisha

---

[17] See also Ezek 11:17; 28:25; 36:24; Jer 23:2–4; 31:8; 32:37; Mic 2:12; Zeph 3:20; Matt 24:31; 25:32–33.

[18] F. Moloney (*Signs and Shadows: Reading John 5–12* [Minneapolis: Fortress, 1996], 36) suggests that the preservation of these fragments would reassure the early readers of the Gospel that Jesus' bread is still available.

multiplies barley loaves to feed a hundred men and purifies a pot of contaminated food (2 Kgs 4:38–44).[19] It is not surprising, therefore, that the people identify Jesus as a prophet after he multiplies the loaves and fish (6:14; cf. 7:40, 52; 9:17).

The expression "the prophet who has come into the world" most likely refers to the prophet who Moses says will come, a prophet who will be like him (Deut 18:15–18).[20] This "prophet like Moses" communicates God's words, words that are verified because they are later fulfilled (Deut 18:18–22). First Maccabees also expects a prophet who would lead the people (1 Macc 4:46; 14:41–43). Until this prophet comes, the high priest Simon and his descendants would fill this role (1 Macc 14:41–43). Philo refers to Moses as both a prophet and a king (*Moses* 1.158). A passage in 4Q175 connects the anticipated prophet like Moses and some kind of leader described as "a scepter [that] has arisen from Israel," though the precise relationship between the two is unclear (cf. 1QS IX, 11). This connection between prophet and leader provides the likely background for John 6:14 in which the people call Jesus a prophet and then want to make him king.[21]

The Gospel portrays Jesus as a prophet. Various characters identify him as a prophet, such as the Samaritan woman (4:19) and those who see his actions (7:40, 9:17; 12:38;[22] cf. 7:52). The narrator supports Jesus' own testimony that he is a prophet (4:44). Jesus "comes into the world" (1:9; cf. 7:27, 41–42) and is the "one who is coming" (1:15, 27, 29, 30; 3:31; 11:27). Like a prophet, Jesus predicts events that are fulfilled, both explicitly within the time frame of the narrative (such as the denials of Peter, the betrayal of Judas, and the resurrection of Lazarus) and implicitly beyond the Gospel's time frame (such as the promise of the Paraclete).[23]

The Gospel also portrays Jesus as a king. When Nathanael responds to

---

[19] See Brown (*Gospel*, 246) for a list of the similarities between John 6:1–12 and 2 Kgs 4:42–5:19. Brown also suggests Ruth 2:14 as a possible source: Boaz gives Ruth some grain; she eats her fill and has some leftover.

[20] A prophet (4:19) or "one who is coming" (4:25) was expected by the Samaritans, according to the woman at the well. John the Baptist refers to Jesus as "the one who is to come into the world" (John 1:27). In Acts 3:22, Peter identifies Jesus as the prophet expected by Moses. See H. Teeple, *The Mosaic Eschatological Prophet* (Philadelphia: SBL, 1957), 84–94; D. Hill, *New Testament Prophecy* (Atlanta: John Knox, 1979), 36, 57; T. F. Glasson, *Moses in the Fourth Gospel* (London: SCM, 1963), 27–31.

[21] See Barrett, *Gospel*, 277; Meeks, *Prophet-King*, 91–98; Brown, *Gospel*, 235; Daly-Denton, *David*, 138–44.

[22] In John 12:38, the narrator equates Jesus and the prophet Isaiah in a citation of Isaiah 53:1.

[23] For a full discussion of the predictions of Jesus, see A. Reinhartz, "Jesus as Prophet: Predictive Prolepses in the Fourth Gospel," *JSNT* 36 (1989): 3–16.

Jesus' foreknowledge with the words, "Rabbi! You are the Son of God! You are the King of Israel!," Jesus does not correct him but promises to show him even greater things (1:47–51). A great crowd calls Jesus the "King of Israel" when he enters Jerusalem on a donkey (12:13). According to the Gospel, this action fulfills the prophecy that a king would come to them "sitting on a donkey's colt" (12:12–15; cf. Zech 9:9). When questioned by Pilate, Jesus answers Pilate, "*You* say that I am a king" (18:37).[24] The emphasis on the personal pronoun, "you," suggests that others including Jesus might not agree, so this answer is ambiguous. To Pilate and the soldiers, Jesus is indeed the "king of the Jews" (18:39; 19:3, 14, 15; 19:21–22), but, ironically, in the wake of the triumphal entry (12:12–15), the Jews refuse to acknowledge him as king (19:12, 15, 21). Jesus clarifies his role as king in the following declaration: "My kingdom is not from this world. If my kingdom were from this world, my followers would be fighting to keep me from being handed over to the Jews. But as it is, my kingdom is not from here" (18:36). He is not a king in the way that most people would expect, for his kingdom is "not of this world." The Gospel of John therefore suggests that king (if understood correctly) and prophet are plausible titles for Jesus. Jesus withdraws at the close of the narrative because, as "a prophet," he knows that the people want to make him king, although they do not know what kind of king he really is.[25]

The Feeding of the Multitude story thus focuses on two main aspects. First, Jesus takes a small amount of food from a young boy and multiplies it to satisfy over 5,000 people. Jesus provides the food. The setting on the mountain pastures at Passover and the use of bread and fish as food point to an eschatological feast resembling prophetic miracles in the biblical tradition.[26] Second, for the first time in the Gospel narrative, the disciples participate in the miracle; they are to prepare the people to eat and to gather up the leftover fragments so that "none will be lost."

The Bread of Life Discourse (John 6:26–71)

The Feeding of the Multitude story sets the context for the discourse on the Bread of Life that follows. After Jesus feeds the multitude, he goes into the mountains. During the night, his disciples leave for the other side of the Sea of Galilee and Jesus follows them by walking on the water. They arrive in Capernaum (6:17, 24, 59). The next day, the crowd finds Jesus on the other side of the Sea, although they do not know how he arrived there. They say to him, "Rabbi, when did you come here?" (6:25). Jesus does not answer this question

---

[24] The use of the personal pronoun σύ indicates that the word "you" is emphasized.

[25] See Schnackenburg, *Gospel*, 2:19.

[26] Ibid., 2:16.

directly but responds, "You seek me, not because you saw signs but because you ate your fill of the loaves." The Gospel then provides a long discourse to explain that the sign means more than the people realize and that it will require a response from them.

Four sets of dialogues may be discerned within the larger structure of the discourse. They are demarcated by changes in the terms used to describe the conversation partners. The first dialogue is between Jesus and the crowd who eats the bread and follow him from the other side of the Sea (6:22–40). The second is between Jesus and the Jews (Ἰουδαιοι) in the synagogue in Capernaum (6:41–59).[27] We might note here that the crowd in the first discourse and the Jews in the second might be the same group, but the term Ἰουδαιοι is not used in the first discourse. The third is between Jesus and his disciples (6:60–66). The fourth is between Jesus and the "Twelve" (6:67–71) and includes one direct exchange between Jesus and Simon Peter (6:68–69). The four conversations flow from one to the other, and each one draws on themes that precede it, while at the same time they add new and more complex dimensions to each theme.

The unity of the Bread of Life discourse has been the subject of debate and needs to be addressed here briefly. Source critics note the repetition of phrases and segments that use one selection of words in contrast to others. For example, Bultmann argues that 6:51c–6:58 is a Eucharistic supplement inserted by the "ecclesiastical redactor." This section uses τρώγω instead of ἐσθίω for "eating" and identifies the bread with the flesh of Jesus, a connection made in other accounts of the Eucharist (Mark 14:23; Matt 26:27; Luke 22:17; 1 Cor 11:24). Furthermore, argues Bultmann, this section can be excised from the text without destroying the narrative flow.[28] Other commentators, however, argue that the Bread of Life discourse is a unified whole.[29] Borgen, for example, demonstrates that 6:27–58 is a Midrash on the scripture citation "He gave them bread from heaven to eat" (6:30; cf. Exod 16:15); the first section of the discourse deals with the nature of the bread from heaven; the second section

---

[27] Crossan, "Written," 7.

[28] Bultmann, *Gospel*, 234–7. In a similar vein, Brown (*Gospel*, 286) argues that 6:35–58 represents the juxtaposition of two different forms of the discourse stemming from two different stages of Johannine preaching. The first section of the discourse (6:35–50) "refers primarily to revelation and secondarily to the Eucharist; and the second part (6:51–58) refers only to the Eucharist" (272). For a survey of the various positions, see Schnackenburg, *Gospel*, 2:58–59; Brown, *Gospel*, 293–4.

[29] Schnackenburg (*Gospel*, 2:31–32) is a strong proponent of a unified John 6, and challenges the various theories that attempt to divide it according to formal criteria (by theme, formulaic words, Midrash models, etc.), for the whole discourse is dependent on the wilderness account. Barrett agrees, but on the basis of a common Son of Man theme. See "The Flesh of the Son of Man," *Essays on John* (Philadelphia: Westminster, 1982), 37–49.

addresses the way in which this bread is given.[30] Meeks points out the literary *inclusio* of 6:27 and 6:58 that holds the discourse together.[31] Most convincing is the fact that the discourse as a whole is "the elucidation of themes by progressive repetition"[32] and, as such, requires increasing belief from the reader.

Jesus and the Crowd (John 6:25–40)

The first part of the discourse is a conversation between Jesus and the crowd who first eats the loaves on the other side of the Sea and then later tracks Jesus down in Capernaum. While John 6:2 says that the people originally follow Jesus because they see the signs that he does for the sick, it now states that the people follow him because they have eaten. Jesus says, "You are looking for me not because you saw signs, but because you ate your fill of the loaves" (6:26). The people recognize that Jesus' multiplication is a "sign" (6:14) but now ask Jesus for another sign so they may "see it and believe" (6:30). They look for a sign like that given by Moses in the wilderness: manna provided on a daily basis. They cite scripture as both their authority and their precedent (6:31; cf. Ps 77:24; Exod 16:15). Jesus provides bread on the mountain, but only once; they seek further confirmation that he is a prophet like Moses. In the discourse that follows, Jesus addresses their interpretation of the sign and offers them something more than Moses could give.

In the biblical tradition, the manna that Moses provides in the wilderness only satisfies the people temporarily. Every night, the manna falls from heaven with the dew, and the people collect it and prepare it for eating. If the people attempt to collect more than they can eat in one day, the manna putrefies and they cannot eat it (except on the Sabbath when special provision is made).[33] The people live on this bread for forty years (Exod 16:35; Neh 9:20). Once they eat the produce of the Promised Land (at the time of Passover, Josh 5:10–11), the

---

[30] Borgen (*Bread*) notes that John 6:31–58 is a Midrash based on haggadic and halakhic traditions in the sense that it follows exegetical methods, patterns, and terminology. D. M. Swancutt ("Hungers Assuaged by the Bread from Heaven: 'Eating Jesus' an Isaian Call to Belief: The Confluence of Isaiah 55 and Psalm 78 [77] in John 6:22–71," in *Early Christian Interpretation of the Scriptures of Israel: Investigations and Proposals* [ed. Craig A. Evans and James A. Sanders; JSNTSup 148; Sheffield: Sheffield Academic Press, 1997], 219–20) argues that it is a Midrash on Ps 78 (LXX 70) in light of Isa 54–55. See also Daly-Denton, *David*, 134–44.

[31] Meeks, "Man from Heaven," 58. Meeks uses the idea of "living forever" to form the *inclusio*, but other, equally convincing, *inclusiones* may be identified on the basis of "living bread" or "bread that comes down from heaven."

[32] Meeks, "Man from Heaven," 55; see E. Hoskyns, *The Fourth Gospel* (2d ed.; London: Faber & Faber, 1947), 67.

[33] See Exod 16:4–8; Num 11:8–9.

manna ceases to fall (Exod 16:35; Josh 5:12). This manna is unlike any other food that they have ever seen or tasted (Deut 8:3, 16). It is variously described as the "grain of heaven" and the "bread of angels" (Ps 78:23–25; Wis 16:20; *4 Ezra* 1:19). It comes from heaven (Ps 78:23; 105:40; Neh 9:15). It is abundant (Ps 78:23). It is such a mark of God's providence that a jar of manna is retained in the Ark of the Covenant (Exod 16:33; Heb 9:3–4).[34] The Feeding of the Multitude story explicitly recalls the miraculous provision of manna in the wilderness and the life it gives to Israel.

Like the Samaritan story, the Bread of Life discourse establishes a contrast between earthly and heavenly food and drink. The well in Sychar is founded by one of the patriarchs, Jacob. It is the source of water for Jacob's large family and his flocks for many, many generations (4:12). It is a life-giving well. Nevertheless, the water from the well must be drawn daily, according to the woman (4:15), and the well is deep, the water difficult to acquire. The water does not quench the thirst forever, just one day at a time. Jesus offers a different kind of water: water that provides eternal life and that satisfies thirst forever. In the Feeding of the Multitude story, the people "eat their fill" but they are hungry again the next day and must return to the source on a daily basis. The bread and fish supplied by a small boy, although multiplied by Jesus, has its origins in earthly food and does not satisfy the people in perpetuity. This is food that perishes (6:27). Neither Moses and his manna, nor Jacob and his well, nor even Jesus and his bread and fish will satisfy forever.

Jesus offers a new kind of food that does satisfy forever. Like the water that Jesus gives which quenches thirst forever and gives eternal life (4:14), the food he gives does not perish but "endures for eternal life" (6:27). This food, like the living water (4:10), also comes from the Father through the agency of Jesus

---

[34] By the first centuries of the common era, manna was also associated with the revelation of God (Rev 2:17; *Jos. Asen.* 16:8; 14–16). *Jos. Asen.*16.14 identifies the "bread of life" with manna. Burchard ("Joseph and Aseneth," 129, n.40) says that despite similarities in John 6 and *Jos. Asen.* 16 such as "living bread," food that gives eternal life, its heavenly origin and universal destination, differences emerge. For example, Jesus *is* the bread of life, where the bread of life is *like* Aseneth's honeycomb, not part of it. Jesus' words are the spirit of life (6:63) and not the honey (16:14). Aseneth understands the angel's test and recognizes the heavenly food while the Jews do not recognize Jesus' food. Jesus deals with hostile recipients, the angel deals with repentant Aseneth. "Bread of life" for Burchard, does not necessarily mean "manna." Philo interprets manna to be a type of the *Logos*, or word and wisdom of God, which nourishes the soul (*Alleg. Interp.* 2.86; 1.166–70). Paul refers to the manna and water from the rock as "spiritual food" and "spiritual drink" (1 Cor 10:3–4). The Synoptic Jesus also spiritualizes bread when he cites Deut 8:3 that a person "does not live by bread alone, but by every word that comes from the mouth of the LORD" (Matt 4:4; Luke 4:4). See Barrett, *Gospel*, 288.

(6:27, 32).[35] It is "true bread" (6:32); its source is heavenly, not earthly, and it gives life to the world (6:33). This new kind of bread is what the people want from Jesus (6:34).

Jesus explicitly identifies himself as the substance of the food that he offers, for he says, "I am the bread of life" (6:34). Jesus *provides* the food that comes down from heaven and *is* the food. As his food gives life forever, so also his being gives life forever. This idea has already been suggested throughout the Gospel narrative in several ways. He is the paschal "Lamb of God who takes away the sin of the world" (1:29), the "gift of God" that satisfies thirst forever (4:14), and the grain that must fall to the ground before it produces a harvest (4:36; cf. 12:24). What has only been suggested in the Gospel up to this point, now becomes explicit: Jesus is both the provider and the substance of the food that God gives.

The connection with the Passover is significant. In the biblical narrative, the Passover remembers Israel's deliverance from Egypt and the manna provided in the wilderness. At a Passover forty years later, the manna ceases (Josh 5:10–11). At the time of Passover, Jesus drives the animals out of the temple (2:17). He is the Passover lamb that takes away the sin of the world (1:29). Here again, Passover is the temporal setting for the Feeding of the Multitude, as it will be for Jesus' death. Jesus is the new manna that will provide deliverance from hunger and death, not in the short term, but for eternity.

The mechanism for receiving Jesus as "food" includes coming to Jesus and believing in him. Those who come to Jesus (6:35)[36] will never be driven away (6:37).[37] Sometimes, they must actively search for him (6:24–26).[38] Though they see Jesus and the signs that he does (6:36, 40), they do not always believe in Jesus (6:29, 35, 40). When they do come to Jesus and believe in him, however, they will never be hungry or thirsty again (6:35; cf. 7:37–39; 11:45).

---

[35] Barrett (*Gospel*, 286–7) notes that the Son of Man title in the Synoptics usually has an eschatological meaning. John uses it here however, not to refer to the eschaton, but to the glorification of Jesus (his death) when his gifts would be made available. The present indicative δίδωσιν (in contrast to the perfect δέδωκεν of Moses' gift) makes it clear that God's gift has not been completed in the past but continues through the present. See Schnackenburg, *Gospel*, 2:42.

[36] For examples of those who come to Jesus, see 1:39, 46; 3:20–21; 4:29; 7:37; 11:43. Some refuse to come to Jesus (5:40). Others, who want to come to Jesus, are unable to do so. See 7:34–36; 8:21; 13:33.

[37] In contrast, the Jews drive the blind man out of the synagogue (ἐξέβαλον αὐτὸν ἔξω; 9:34–35). Jesus drives out the ruler of this world (ἐκβληθήσεται ἔξω; 12:31) and the animals out of the temple (ἐξέβαλεν; 2:15), replacing both.

[38] The two disciples of John also seek Jesus (1:38–39), and Mary seeks Jesus in the garden (20:15–16). Not everyone who seeks Jesus will find him, though. See 7:1, 11, 34–36; 8:21; 11:55; 13:33.

But their belief must endure.[39] Barrett rightly says that believing in Jesus is "not an *act* of faith, but a *life* of faith."[40]

Belief in Jesus results in eternal life (6:40; see also 3:15–16, 36; 5:24; 6:47; 20:31), synonymous with the phrase, being "raised up on the last day" (6:39, 40, 44, 54).[41] The repetition of this phrase, "raised on the last day," underscores both the benefit of God's gift in Jesus and the penalty for not believing in Jesus, that is, those who do not believe will *not* be raised on the last day but will be lost (6:39; 10:28; 12:25).[42] In the language of eating and drinking, the people should "not work for food that perishes" but for the "food that endures for eternal life" (6:27); they do this through believing.[43]

In the first part of the Bread of Life discourse, therefore, the Gospel makes explicit the fact that Jesus both provides and is the substance of the food that God gives. The people who look for Jesus think that he is merely the provider of the food, as Moses has been the provider of the food in the wilderness. The Gospel corrects this misunderstanding. The Father, not Moses, provides manna from heaven (6:32). In the same way, the Father provides bread through the agency of Jesus on the mountain. Nevertheless, neither the manna nor the multiplied loaves and fish satisfy hunger forever, for they are material food; whoever comes to Jesus and believes in him, however, will never be hungry or thirsty again. Although Jesus is the provider of miraculous bread on the mountain, the Gospel insists that he also be understood as the substance of the food itself: he *is* the bread of heaven.

Jesus and the Jews (John 6:41–59)

The second part of the discourse on the Bread of Life begins with a more precise description of Jesus' dialogue partners: Jesus talks to "the Jews." In this

---

[39] The present subjunctive of πιστεύω is used by Jesus in 6:29 and has a durative meaning suggesting the translation, "that you continue to believe." Constructed with the preposition εἰς, the sense is "continuously believing in" or "trusting in." In contrast, the aorist subjunctive is used by the people in 6:30 and has no such durative sense. Their belief is temporary.

[40] *Gospel*, 287–8.

[41] I see no reason to concur with Barrett (*Gospel*, 294–5) that, on the basis of a preceding ἵνα, ἀναστήσω be read as subjunctive ("that I might raise up") instead of future ("I will raise up") in 6:39. The repetition of the same form of the verb in the identical phrase in 6:40, 44, and 54 is unambiguously in the future tense. D. Moody Smith (*John* [Nashville: Abingdon, 1999], 155) points out that the Gospel presents eternal life as a present reality (5:24) and a future hope (11:24; cf. Isa 26:1; Dan 12:2).

[42] That none shall be lost is the motive of God's action in sending Jesus into the world (3:16; 6:39; 17:12; 18:9; cf. 6:12). At the same time, however, no one can come to the Son unless the Father "gives" him to the Son (6:37, 44, 45, 65; 17:12; 18:9).

[43] Moloney (*Signs*, 45) suggests that the people's question, "What must we do to do the works of God?" is an attempt to bypass the Law (see 1:17).

dialogue, Jesus clearly states that he is the bread that has come down from heaven and that whoever eats him will live. In this way, he surpasses Moses.

To say that Jesus engages in a dialogue with the Jews is somewhat inaccurate, for the Jews do not directly address Jesus. It is reported that they "were complaining" (ἐγόγγυζον) about Jesus (6:41), a verb given in the imperfect, indicating a continuous action in the past. Their words are not directed at Jesus because they speak of him in the third person singular, and they speak among themselves using the first person plural "we" (6:42).[44] John 6:52 says that the Jews "disputed among themselves" (ἐμάχοντο πρὸς ἀλλήλους), again in the imperfect, continuous past. However, Jesus speaks to the Jews directly (according to the Gospel) in the present imperative: "Do not complain among yourselves" (Μὴ γογγύζετε μετ' ἀλλήλων). In contrast to the first section of the discourse where the people ask Jesus a question and he answers, in this section of the discourse, the Jews do not come to ask Jesus questions directly but instead they ask each other. From the reported reaction of the Jews, however, it is clear that they know what Jesus says.[45]

The identity of the Jews is obscure in the narrative.[46] It is possible, according to the narrative, that the title "Jews" more specifically defines the entire crowd that eats the multiplied loaves and fish. It is also possible that the Jews formed a sub-group of the larger crowd who eats the bread and fish; this sub-group is now being identified in 6:41. Or, it is possible that the Jews are not a part of the crowd who eat the bread and fish; they could be responding to reports that they hear but do not experience. Whatever the historical or narrative relationship between the crowd and the Jews, there is a change in the discourse structure with the introduction of the Jews as dialogue partners in 6:41.

Phillips points out that this distinction separates the first part (6:22–40) of the discourse from the second (6:41–59), and that these two parts reflect

---

[44] See Phillips, "Hard Saying," 31.

[45] Very likely, this literary construction reflects a later conversation between the historical Johannine community and a more abstract group called "the Jews."

[46] The Gospel of John uses the term "Jews" in many different ways. Sometimes, the term is used in a positive way. For example, Jesus says, "Salvation comes from the Jews" (4:22). Jesus is identified as a Jew (4:9) and comes to his own (1:11). Jews weep with Mary at the loss of her brother, Lazarus (11:33). Nicodemus, a leader of the Jews (3:1), buries Jesus' body (19:39). Many Jews believed in Jesus (12:11). Sometimes the term is used in a negative way. For instance, the parents of the blind man are afraid of the Jews (9:22; cf. 12:42; 19:38; 20:19). The Jews arrest Jesus (18:12) and demand that Jesus be put to death (19:7, 14–15). Sometimes the term is used in a neutral fashion, as when Jewish festivals or practices are mentioned (2:13; 4:9; 5:1; 6:4; 7:2; 11:55; 19:40, 42). The Gospel does not always distinguish the different groups of Jews (such as the Pharisees, the Jewish police, or the Sanhedrin) but, in many cases, mixes them all together. Although most references to the Jews are negative in nature, care must be exercised against assuming the Jews are always opponents of Jesus.

different levels of misunderstanding.[47] Unlike the crowd who follows Jesus from one side of the Sea to the other and who call him "Lord" (6:34), the Jews do not come to Jesus. They are not willing dialogue partners, nor are they willing recipients of bread from heaven when compared to the "crowd" who says, "Give us this bread always" (6:34). Jesus compares the Jews to their ancestors (literally "your fathers")—note that Jesus does not say "our fathers"[48]—who wandered in the wilderness; their fathers ate the manna (bread that came down from heaven) but they still died. Now these Jews have an opportunity to eat Jesus as the bread that comes down from heaven and to live (6:50–51), but they refuse. Indeed, they are defined by their rejection.

Their rejection centers on two issues. Primarily, they challenge Jesus' origin with its ensuing authority. They complain because Jesus said, "I am the bread that came down from heaven" (6:41). They argue that Jesus could not have come down from heaven because they know his father, Joseph, and his mother (6:42). They know from whence he has come; they know his origins (cf. 7:41–42). Jesus responds to this charge with two rebuttals. First, because the Jews have not learned from God through the prophets nor have they come to Jesus directly, they do not know who his Father is, in spite of their claim to the contrary (6:45). In contrast, Jesus does know the scriptures and cites them here against his opponents. Second, only Jesus knows where he comes from because only he has seen the Father (6:46; cf. 1:18; 14:8–10). According to the Gospel, Jesus originates in heaven (6:35, 38, 48, 51; repeated for literary emphasis in the mouths of the Jews in 6:41–42) and speaks with the authority given to him by his Father (6:27). The "I am" (ἐγώ εἰμι) formula is repeated here (see 6:20), and while it may have no other meaning than the words of self-identification (that is, Jesus, not some other thing/person, is the bread of life[49]), it drives home the connection between Jesus and his divine origin.

The second issue that causes dissent among the Jews is the notion that Jesus tells them to eat his flesh, a notion that has been developing throughout the discourse. In the Feeding of the Multitude story, the bread that Jesus takes up and distributes is concrete, for it originates from the earth and satisfies people on a day-to-day basis. A comparison is started in the first section of the Bread of Life discourse that speaks of a more abstract substance: Jesus is the "true

---

[47] Phillips, "Hard Saying," 38–43. Crossan ("Written," 7–8) also agrees that the Jews are set off against the rest of the crowd.

[48] In any case, Jesus exists before the patriarchs according to John (see 8:58).

[49] Bultmann (*Gospel*, 225–6, n.3) identifies this "I am" statement as a "recognition formula" answering the question, "Who is the one who is expected, asked for, spoken to?" The question assumes that there might be more than one contender for the title. John asserts that Jesus is the true bread (6:41, 48, 51), the true shepherd (10:7, 9, 11, 14), true vine (15:1, 5), etc.

bread" that originates from heaven and satisfies forever (6:32–33). Those who believe in him will live forever (6:40). In this second section of the discourse, the notion of the bread of life that has come down from heaven is made more concrete: the bread of heaven is Jesus' flesh, his person. Jesus gives his life as a gift to the world (6:51; cf. 3:16). The Gospel calls his flesh "true food" and his blood "true drink" (6:55). Whoever eats his flesh and drinks his blood will have eternal life (6:51, 54, 58). For the Jews who were listening, this was a problem.

Consequently, the Jews challenge Jesus' ability to give them his flesh to eat (6:52), asking "How can this man give us his (αὐτοῦ) flesh to eat?" (6:52). A textual variant that omits the word αὐτοῦ ("his") would render this translation: "How can this man give us flesh to eat?"[50] This question, together with other words in John 6 such as "gathering" (συνάγω), the "bread" (ἄρτος), according to their "number" (ἀριθμός), bread that "the Lord had given them to eat," eating their "fill" (πίμπρημι) and the "sons of Israel complaining" (γογγύζω), recalls Exod 16:10–20 (LXX) and the need for meat in the wilderness.[51] God provided quails for the hungry crowd. Like their ancestors who resent leaving the "fleshpots" where they have eaten "their fill of bread" in Egypt (Exod 16:3) and who have to trust God's provision of food in the wilderness, the Jews in John 6 are not sure that Jesus can provide them with meat. When the text is read with the αὐτοῦ, providing the translation, "How can this man give us *his* flesh to eat," the question takes on a different significance. The Jews challenge Jesus' ability to give them his flesh to eat. Like the Samaritan woman (4:11), they misunderstand what he is talking about.[52] This is the more likely reading of the text, for the following sentences sharpen the notion that Jesus gives his flesh as food.

Eating the flesh and drinking the blood of Jesus are made a condition for eternal life: "Unless you eat (ἐὰν μὴ φάγητε) the flesh of the Son of Man and

---

[50] According to the *Greek New Testament* (UBS 2d ed., 347), there is considerable doubt about the superior reading. Mss including αὐτοῦ are p^66 B T 892 1079 (1216 1253 1646 τὴν ἑαυτοῦ σάρκα) it^a, aur, b, c, e, f, q, rl vg syr^c, s, p, h, pal cop^sa, bo, ach2 arm eth geo Diatessaron^a, i, n Origen^lat Chrysostom Cyril Ammonius-Alexandria. It is omitted in ℵ C D K L W Δ Θ Π Ψ *f*1 *f*13 28 33 565 700 1009 1010 1071 1195 1230 1241 1242 1344 1365 1546 2148 *Byz Lect* ^itd, ff2 goth Origen Cyril.

[51] For other parallels, see Num 11:1–22 which tells a variation of the same story: people grumbling (Num 11:1; John 6:41, 43), references to the manna (Num 11:7–9; John 6:31) and to the flesh (the LXX of Num 11:13 uses the word κρέα rather than the Johannine term σάρξ in 6:51–63); the notion of gathering (συνάγω, Num 11:22; John 6:9) and the fish (ὄψον, Num 11:22; the diminutive ὀψάριον, John 6:9,11). As Little (*Echoes*, 139) points out, the people ask for "flesh" to eat in the desert and then remind Moses of the abundant fish they had in Egypt (Num 11:4–5); fish (ὄψον) therefore ranks as meat (cf. Num 11:22). See also Schnackenburg, *Gospel*, 2:60.

[52] Schnackenburg, *Gospel*, 2:60.

drink his blood, you have no life in you" (6:53). John 6:54 sharpens the language of eating even further: the flesh of Jesus must be "crunched" (τρώγω).[53] "Crunching" does not imply passive reception but active manducation of Jesus' flesh, and is necessary in order to have eternal life. Bultmann points out that "it is a matter of real eating and not simply of some sort of spiritual participation" for it is *real* food and drink.[54] The unusual position of the genitive pronoun μου ("of me") immediately following the verb of eating suggests two things. First, the object of consumption is Jesus (6:54, 56, cf. 13:18),[55] a conclusion that is supported by 6:57, "The one eating *me* will live because of me." Second, emphasis is placed on the provider of the bread, that is, Jesus. The climax of the theme comes in the following verse: "Those who 'crunch' (τρώγων) my flesh and drink my blood abide (μένει) in me and I in them" (6:56). The act of eating Jesus' flesh and drinking his blood internalizes Jesus so that his flesh and blood become a part of the consumer and the consumer becomes a part of Jesus.

The critical aspect of consuming Jesus is not so much the role of the one eating Jesus but the fact that Jesus must first die. Like an animal that cannot be eaten alive, Jesus must die before he is available as the substance of food. He thus gives his flesh "for the life of the world."[56]

The discourse also adds "and drinks his blood" as a criterion of receiving

---

[53] The word τρώγω is used in the LXX only twice and refers to painful destruction (Prov 24:22; Mic 7:4). Outside of John 6 and 13:18, the word is used in the New Testament only in Matt 24:38–39. For its translation, see Bauer, *Lexicon*, 829. C. Spicq ("ΤΡΩΓΕΙΝ: est-il synonyme de ΦΑΓΕΙΝ et d'ΕΣΘΙΕΙΝ dans le Nouveau Testament?" *NTS* 26 [1979–80]: 414–9) argues that τρώγω is interchangable with φάγον and ἐσθίω, but it is not synonymous. Τρώγω has the sense "d'abord celle de 'croquer,' puis celle de manger de bonnes choses, un dessert, enfin celle d'avaler et de se gorger. C'est le contexte [Jean 6] qui permet de discerner l'accent, qui porte soit sur la qualité, soit sur la qualité de la nourriture, soit même sur la façon de goûter la nourriture et de se repaître" (418–9). See Bultmann, *Gospel*, 236 n.3; Schnackenburg, *Gospel*, 2:62. J. J. O'Rourke ("Two Notes on John's Gospel: Jn 19:13 *eis ton topon; phagein* and *pinein* in John," *CBQ* 25 [1963]: 126–8) argues that a change in the grammatical structure of the object of the verb (either τρώγω or ἐσθίω) from the accusative (6:23) to ἐκ plus the genitive (6:26, 50, 51) indicates a "different kind of eating," i.e., the Eucharist. Furthermore, the μου ("of me") indicates that they were to eat "the whole of Jesus." Barrett (*Gospel*, 299) claims that τρώγω is used here in the present tense instead of ἐσθίω, which is not found in John; it thus carries no extraordinary significance

[54] *Gospel*, 236.

[55] Verbs of eating and drinking are often followed by the partitive genitive (sometimes preceded by ἐκ) or the accusative of the thing consumed. In these cases in John 6, the genitive pronouns likely modify the following noun, but their position at the head of the phrase leads to some ambiguity. The same ambiguity is found in 6:50 (ἵνα τις ἐξ αὐτοῦ φάγῃ) where αὐτοῦ may be translated as "of it" referring to the bread or "of him" referring to Jesus. See O'Rourke, "Notes," 126.

[56] John 6:51. See Léon-Dufour, "Symbolic," 452.

eternal life (6:53, 54, 55, 56). Drinking blood is strictly forbidden in the law (Lev 17:10–14); it is an action that would be repugnant both to the Jews and the Hellenistic public.[57] Most commentators agree that this refers to the consumption of wine (the "blood") in the Eucharist (Mark 14:22–25 par.; 1 Cor 11:22–23).[58] The conjoined expression "flesh and blood" is used elsewhere, however, to mean simply "humanity" (see 1 Cor 15:50; Matt 16:17; Sir 14:18; 17:31).[59] In other words, the Eucharist tradition does not necessarily determine the meaning.[60] The blood may also refer in general to the life force that is shed by Jesus at his death (19:34) which, when "consumed" through belief, gives life to others.[61]

It is within the context of the dialogue with the Jews that the subject of Jesus as the substance of food is clearly defined, and it is the conflict with the Jews that forces the clarification. The Jews challenge the fact that Jesus comes "down from heaven" because they know his earthly parents. They also challenge the fact that Jesus, like Moses, can provide meat for them to eat or that Jesus is the meat that they are to eat. The Gospel's response to these challenges is clear and is repeated over and over again: Jesus is the only one who has seen the Father. He is sent by God from heaven. Available only because of his death, his flesh is the bread of life (true food), and his blood is true drink. If people have been drawn (or taught) by the Father, they will come to Jesus and believe in him.[62] This is described as eating and drinking Jesus. If people do this, Jesus will do the will of God and raise them up on the last day, give them eternal life and abide with them. In contrast, those who are not drawn by the Father, do not believe in Jesus, do not eat his flesh and drink his blood, will die. They are compared to "the fathers" who eat the food (both bread and meat) in the wilderness and die.

---

[57] See Dodd, *Interpretation*, 341; Barrett, *Gospel*, 303.

[58] See, for example, Barrett, *Gospel*, 299; Schnackenburg, *Gospel*, 2:61; Brown, *Gospel*, 284–5; Bultmann, *Gospel*, 234–7; R. Alan Culpepper, *The Gospel and Letters of John* (Nashville: Abingdon, 1998), 163.

[59] See Léon-Dufour, "Symbolic," 453; Smith, *John*, 158. John 6:56 "whoever eats my flesh and drinks my blood" is balanced with John 6:57 "whoever eats me," supporting the notion that "flesh and blood" refers to Jesus' humanity. See Barrett, *Gospel*, 300. Lightfoot (*John*, 162) disagrees that "flesh and blood" refers to Jesus' humanity because that would imply that Jesus was separate from God, "apart from the divine"; this separation is inconceivable.

[60] The conclusion explores the Eucharist theme more thoroughly.

[61] Cf. Barrett, *Gospel*, 299.

[62] The initiative and pre-destination of the Father in this process are emphasized by Barrett (*Gospel*, 295) and Lightfoot (*John*, 160–1). Schnackenburg (*Gospel*, 2:52) rightly sees John's construction of a "bipolarity" in which both the initiation of God and the response of humans are factors inherent in the word "believe." The same bipolarity may be seen in 1QS III, 15–IV, 6.

Jesus and the Disciples (John 6:60–66)

The third dialogue within the larger context of the Bread of Life discourse is between Jesus and "many of the disciples" (6:60). The "many disciples" speak (6:60) but, it would seem, not directly to Jesus, because he "knows" (εἰδώς), as he "knows" other things unspoken (e.g., 6:6, 64), that they are complaining (γογγύζουσιν). Although they are called disciples here, they are more like the Jews in the previous passage who hear his words, but do not come to him. These "disciples" find his word "hard" (σκληρός) and wonder (literally) "who is able to hear it." (The sense is that the disciples find his word unacceptable.)[63] For them, his word is a stumbling block, an impediment or offence. It literally "scandalized" (σκανδαλίζει, 6:61) them.[64]

The singular use of the term "word" (λόγος) in 6:60 refers back to the collective teaching of the discourse thus far, that is, that Jesus has come down from heaven and that, in order to have eternal life, disciples have to eat his flesh and drink his blood.[65] The term λόγος recalls the prologue in John 1. There, Jesus is the "Word" (λόγος) who was "with God" and "was God" (1:1). He brought life (1:4; cf. 6:53, 54, 57–58, etc.). There too, his word is enfleshed (ὁ λόγος σάρξ ἐγένετο, 1:14; 6:51) and "he came to his own and his own people did not accept him" (1:11; 6:60). In the Bread of Life discourse, Jesus' teaching is the λόγος but this teaching refers to his flesh and blood as elements that must be ingested in order to give eternal life. Jesus is thus not only the provider of the λόγος (teaching), but he is the substance—the flesh and blood—of the λόγος (the Word).

Jesus says, "Does this offend you? Then what if you were to see the Son of Man ascending to where he was before?" (6:61–62). The discourse addresses the disciples' offence in one of two ways. First, those who do not accept the fact that Jesus has come down from heaven in the first place will be more offended if he claims that he will return there.[66] Alternatively, those who do accept that he has come down from heaven and must die in order to give life to others will

---

[63] Barrett (*Gospel*, 303) notes that ἀκούω is close to the meaning of "obey" here. Cf. Schnackenburg, *Gospel*, 2:451, n.137.

[64] Compare 16:1. Schnackenburg (*Gospel*, 2:70) argues that the "many disciples" are the contemporaries of the evangelist who are pulling away from the community because they find Jesus' words unacceptable.

[65] K. Matsunaga ("Is John's Gospel Anti-Sacramental: A New Solution in Light of the Evangelistic Milieu," *NTS* 27 [1981]: 516–24) argues that the "word" refers to the *kerygma* of the church that Jesus was ascending to the Father and sending the Spirit.

[66] Meeks, "Man from Heaven," 59. Moloney (*Signs*, 61) argues that the disciples expect Jesus to ascend into heaven as others have done in the past, such as Moses, Enoch, Elijah, and Isaiah. Yet the emphasis in John 6:62 is not that Jesus ascends to receive the revelation of God for the first time, but that he ascends *to where he was before*. Moloney does not consider, however, that in order to do this, Jesus must be "lifted up" on the cross, i.e., die.

no longer be offended to learn that he will return to heaven.[67] Quast points out that "the reader is forced to make a decision: if Jesus ascended back into heaven, would it be easier or harder to accept?"[68]

Jesus continues with the lines: "It is the spirit that gives life, the flesh is useless" (6:63). Until now, that which gives life has been identified as belief in Jesus (3:15, 16, 36; 5:40; 6:40, 47; see also 11:25; 17:3; 20:31), and in John 6, believing is equated with the act of ingesting his flesh (6:40, 47, 48, 51, 53, 54). For the first time in this discourse, the life-giving principle is identified as the spirit.[69] The use of the term "spirit" ($\pi\nu\epsilon\hat{\upsilon}\mu\alpha$) in the Gospel of John is very complex.[70] First, the term is used to distinguish that which is of the heavenly realm from that which is "of the world." So, for example, Jesus tells Nicodemus that he must be born of the spirit or "from above" (3:3–8). When $\pi\nu\epsilon\hat{\upsilon}\mu\alpha$ is understood in this sense, John 6:63 claims that that which comes from the earth does not give life, but that which comes from heaven (bread = Jesus) does give life (cf. 6:48–50).[71] "Spirit" also refers to the life force that animates Jesus' flesh. Thus, when Jesus "gives up the spirit," he dies (19:30). His flesh "is useless" without the presence of this animating spirit. Finally, "spirit" refers to the life-giving Holy Spirit that Jesus imparts to believers after his death (7:39; 17:2; 20:22).[72] In this way, 6:63 can claim that "it is the [Holy] spirit that gives life [to believers], the flesh is useless." Because the Gospel often combines various references in one image or word, it is possible that all three of these aspects of the Spirit are at play here.

The idea that the spirit gives life is extended in the next sentence. Jesus' *words* are "spirit and life" (6:63).[73] He both speaks the word and is the Word

---

[67] See Schnackenburg, *Gospel*, 2:71; Crossan, "Written," 16.

[68] Quast, *Reading*, 56.

[69] But see John 3:5. See Brown, *Gospel*, 1135–44.

[70] The term is also used in 11:33 and 13:21, where it refers to emotional status, such as "he was disturbed in spirit." It is used in a word play in 3:8; the wind and the spirit are compared, but the word for both wind and spirit is $\pi\nu\epsilon\hat{\upsilon}\mu\alpha$. The Gospel continually plays with words, and so encourages the reader to appreciate multiple meanings concomitantly.

[71] According to Brown (*Gospel*, 300), the contradictory reference to the flesh (i.e., that it is "useless," 6:63) reflects the spirit/flesh dichotomy introduced in 3:6 (cf. Matt 16:17); the spirit or "the divine principal from above" gives life, not "the natural principle in man." Smith (*John*, 162) makes a similar argument. Barrett (*Gospel*, 304–5) states that this phrase makes it clear that faith, and not the Eucharist, is necessary for salvation; this faith is made possible only by God's initiation.

[72] Schnackenburg (*Gospel*, 2:71) argues that the Holy Spirit is in mind here. The "Spirit" or "Holy Spirit" (3:34; 20:22) has a more personified sense when it aligned with the "Paraclete" (14:26) and the "Spirit of Truth" (14:16–17; 15:26; 16:13). It descends on Jesus (1:32–33), baptizes (1:33), and "gives birth" (3:5–6, 8).

[73] The emphatic personal pronoun is used here to underscore that fact that only the words that *Jesus* has spoken will give eternal life. In contrast, the law of Moses, which is also

(1:1), as he both provides bread and is bread. He embodies that which comes down from heaven.

A contrast is established between those who believe what Jesus says and those who do not (Jesus knows who they are from the beginning, 6:64). There are those who follow Jesus looking for signs and wanting to eat their fill of bread (6:26). There are those who never come to Jesus in the first place; these are identified as the Jews (6:41–59). There are the "many disciples" who heard his words but found them too difficult to accept; these are the ones who "turned back and no longer went about with them" (6:66). Finally, there are the remaining disciples, introduced here for the first time as the "Twelve" (6:67).[74]

Jesus and the Twelve (John 6:67–71)

The fourth and final dialogue occurs between Jesus and the Twelve (6:67). The discourse reaffirms the election of the Twelve while maintaining that Jesus knew from the first that one of them would betray him (6:64, 70–71). Peter's declaration sums up neatly the content of the Bread of Life discourse: "Lord, to whom can we go? You have the words of eternal life. We have come to believe and know that you are the Holy One of God." Addressed as a group with the second person plural "you" (θέλετε), and answering as a group with the first person plural emphatic "we" (ἡμεῖς), the Twelve claim "in one voice" that Jesus "has the words of eternal life" (6:68).[75] They recognize that Jesus is both the only provider of the words (where else could they go?) and the very Word itself. They appreciate that his words are more valuable than the signs.[76] They understand that they must receive both Jesus and his words and internalize him/them and that they will receive life. As a collective, they have believed (ἐπιστεύκαμεν) and they have known (ἐγνώκαμεν, 6:69).[77] They say to Jesus, "You are the Holy One of God" (6:69). Included in this sentence is the disciples' positive affirmation that Jesus is indeed the "I am"; they say the equivalent in the emphatic second person singular, "you are." They address him as "Lord" (κύριε). They also affirm Jesus' claim that he comes down from

---

referred to as "manna" or the bread of heaven in the Wisdom literature, will not give life (see Borgen, *Bread*, 148–64).

[74] The disciples in the Gospel of John are not listed as they are in the Synoptic Gospels (Matt 10:1–4; Mark 3:13–19; Luke 6:12–16; cf. 1 Cor 15:5).

[75] Barrett (*Gospel*, 306) points out that the phrase "words of eternal life" is not preceded by an article and is thus not formulaic.

[76] Smith, *John*, 163.

[77] Both verbs are in the perfect tense signifying actions completed in the past but continuing into the present. According to J. Gaffney's extensive study, "Believing and Knowing in the Fourth Gospel," *TS* 26 (1965): 215–41, believing and knowing are used synonymously. See 11:42; 17:8, 21 with 17:3; 16:27–30 with 7:17; 11:27 and 20:31 with 6:69, and especially 17:8. See Barrett, *Gospel*, 307.

heaven for he is "of God" (τοῦ θεοῦ); he is the Holy One of God (σὺ εἶ ὁ ἅγιος τοῦ θεοῦ; cf. Mark 1:24), the one "set apart for God."[78] The Twelve are those who understand the words of Jesus and recognize that there is life in him alone.

The final words of the discourse drive home the meaning of "abiding in Jesus." Though Judas is counted among the Twelve, is chosen from the beginning to believe in Jesus (6:64), and says with Peter that Jesus has the words of eternal life, he betrays Jesus at the hour of death (13:27). His motive to betray Jesus is unclear in the Gospel of John (but see 12:6). We learn only that he is a devil (διάβολος) and that "Satan enters him" when he eats the physical bread and wine that Jesus gives him (13:27) but also that, all along, Jesus knows that he is a betrayer. Judas does not remain with Jesus but leaves at the critical hour (13:1, 30). He does not abide with Jesus unto death.

Conclusion to John 6

With each development of the Bread of Life theme, the circle around Jesus becomes smaller and smaller. The crowd on the mountain numbers over 5,000. They recognize Jesus as the provider of food: they eat their fill of the bread and want to make him a king who will provide daily bread. When Jesus withdraws from them, some of them actively seek out Jesus. When they find Jesus, they ask for the bread that he has to offer, but they do not understand what that means. When they learn that it is spiritual, not physical bread, many leave. The Jews, meeting in a synagogue (seating capacity unknown, but certainly less than 5,000), reject Jesus because he claims to have come from heaven and offers them (his) flesh to eat. "Many disciples" turn back because they cannot accept that Jesus will ascend to where he was before or that his words are life giving. In the end, there are only Twelve, and, of these, Simon Peter stands out as the one who is able to put into words the significance of Jesus' teaching. The Twelve will remain ("abide") with Jesus because they believe and know that he has the words of eternal life. Judas, however, will not abide with Jesus until the end, or so it is foretold. The gradual narrowing of the circle around Jesus functions in this discourse as a way to delineate true disciples from the crowd, the Jews, "the many disciples," and those who do not remain with Jesus. But let the reader be warned: even having once believed, betrayal is still possible.

The Bread of Life discourse proceeds from the narrative setting and concerns of the Feeding of the Multitude story. The crowd hungers for food and Jesus offers them a different kind of food: spiritual food. In fact, Jesus himself is the food and he must die so that they may eat. If people accept that Jesus comes down from heaven and that he must die to give them life, they metaphorically "eat" him; if they do not believe, they die. While it has been

---

[78] Smith, *John*, 164.

argued that John emphasizes the will of the Father in the economy of salvation, that is, unless the Father draws them, they cannot come,[79] the language of ingesting makes it clear that reception of Jesus is not passive. To the contrary, human acceptance and *ingestion* of Jesus is necessary for life. To taste Jesus is to taste life.

TASTING DEATH (JOHN 8:51–52)

The Gospel of John usually refers to ingesting substances that provide life. In one passing statement, however, it also refers to death as an "edible" substance. That is, if people do not keep Jesus' word, they will "taste death" (8:52). This phrase occurs in the midst of an accusatory dialogue between Jesus and the Jews in which the identity and actions of both are put to the test. On the one hand, Jesus accuses the Jews of knowing neither his origins (8:14) nor his Father (8:19). Although they call God their own (8:54) and they are descendants of Abraham (8:37), they act as though they are the children of the devil, for they lie and kill (8:39–44, 55). In short, they do not accept Jesus' word (8:43). The Jews, on the other hand, accuse Jesus of being a Samaritan and one who has a demon (8:48, 52). They challenge Jesus' claim that his word gives eternal life; they accuse him of making himself out to be more than he is (8:53). When Jesus says that Abraham rejoiced to see his day and that he, in fact, existed before Abraham as "I am," the Jews attempt to stone him (8:56–59).

The phrase that draws our attention as ingesting language—"will not taste death"—is found in the mouths of the Jews. Jesus first says, "Very truly I tell you, whoever keeps my word will never see death" (8:51). The Jews retort, "Now we know that you have a demon. Abraham died, and so did the prophets; yet you say, 'Whoever keeps my word will never taste death'" (8:52). There is a change from "see death" (θεωρέω θάνατον) in the mouth of Jesus to "taste death" (γεύομαι θανάτου) in the mouth of the Jews.[80]

It is unclear whether the change in terminology is significant. On the one hand, this could be another instance of misunderstanding. Jesus refers to spiritual death, that is, the death of the soul (cf. 3:3, 36), but the Jews think that he means the death of the body, and so they cite the physical deaths of Abraham

---

[79] See Barrett, *Gospel*, 295; Lightfoot, *John*, 160–161.

[80] To "taste death" is also found in *L.A.B.* 48:1; *4 Ezra* 6:26; Matt 16:28; Mark 9:1; Luke 14:24; Heb 2:9; *Gos. Thom.* 1, 18, 19, 85 (The *Gospel of Thomas is* likely dependent on John, according to R. Brown, "The Gospel of Thomas and St. John's Gospel," *NTS* 9 [1962] 159). To "see death" is found in Psalm 88:49 (LXX), Luke 2:26, and Heb 11:5, but in these cases the verb ὁράω is used instead of θεωρέω.

and the prophets as proof against Jesus' claim (8:53).[81] On the other hand, it may be that the two phrases are virtually synonymous and are altered only for the purpose of style.

CONCLUSION

The way to avoid "tasting death," according to the Gospel, is to keep Jesus' word (8:51). As Jesus keeps the word of God (8:55), the disciples are to keep Jesus' word (his commandments) out of love for Jesus (14:15–23; 15:10). In this way, they too keep the Father's word (17:6). This is extended to those who come after the disciples (the readers); they keep the disciples' words and hence the words of Jesus as well as the Father (15:20). Just as the disciples keep the word that Jesus provides by obeying his commandments, they are also to eat Jesus as the Word incarnate. He is the bread of life and whoever eats him will live forever (6:51). In this way, the one who keeps Jesus' word tastes life, not death.

---

[81] This is the position taken by Barrett (*Gospel*, 350) and H. Odeberg, *The Fourth Gospel: Interpreted in Its Relation to Contemporaneous Religious Currents in Palestine and the Hellenistic-Oriental World* (Amsterdam: Grüner, 1968), 305. Bultmann (*Gospel*, 325) thinks the distinction is "overly subtle."

Chapter 5

Supper in Bethany (12:1–8)

The motif of Johannine ingesting language includes John 12:1–8, an account of the narrative of a supper given in Jesus' honor by Lazarus, Mary, and Martha. While Lazarus reclines with Jesus, Martha serves and Mary anoints Jesus' feet with ointment and dries them with her hair. Judas, identified as a thief with designs on the proceeds, says the costly ointment should have been sold and given to the poor. Jesus rebukes Judas and says that Mary has kept the ointment for the day of his burial. He says further, "You always have the poor with you, but you do not always have me." While the Gospel states explicitly that this event occurs during a meal, there are very few details about the meal itself. In other words, there is no mention of eating or drinking. The food and drink are not described. No one talks about the food or drink and no one offers food or drink. The meal serves only as a setting for the narrative. It is important to note, however, the themes of the narrative that emerge while the meal is in the background.

The temporal context of the narrative is again identified with respect to the Passover, specifically, "six days before the Passover" (12:1).[1] This follows a note that the people had already started to go up to Jerusalem to purify themselves (11:55; cf. Josephus, *J.W.* 1.11.6; 6.5.3) and were looking for Jesus (11:56), but Jesus was in the district of Ephraim with his disciples, hiding (11:54). The chief priests and the Pharisees had given the order that the whereabouts of Jesus should be reported so that they could arrest him (11:57). The plot gathers momentum around the upcoming Passover, and unlike the paschal reference in John 6 that emphasizes the provision of food in the wilderness, this temporal reference, with the one in John 2:13, is identified primarily with Jesus' death.

The occasion for the narrative is a supper (δεῖπνον) that Lazarus, Mary and

---

[1] This is the third Passover mentioned in the Gospel of John, or the fourth, if the unnamed festival in 5:1 refers to a Passover. See Brown, *Gospel*, 447. Y.-M. Blanchard ("Le repas de Béthanie [John 12,1–11] au regard de l'ecclésiologie Johannique," in *Nourriture et repas dans les milieux Juifs et Chrétiens de l'Antiquité* [ed. M. Quesnel, Y.- M. Blanchard, C. Tassin; Paris: Cerf, 1999], 227–37) argues that the anointing at Bethany echoes the Johannine ecclesial memorial meal practice because it recalls the resurrection of Lazarus and looks forward to the resurrection of Jesus.

Martha "make" (ἐποίησαν) for Jesus (John 12:2). Lazarus is the man that Jesus has loved and has raised from the dead (11:28–44); Mary and Martha are his sisters (11:1–2). They are the hosts of a meal, presumably.[2] Jesus is the guest and reclines with Lazarus and is served by Martha (12:2). While they are at the table, Mary anoints Jesus.

There are three ways that we might interpret the significance of Mary's gesture. First, given the setting of a meal, it is likely that Mary anoints Jesus as a host (or the host's servant) anoints a guest. That is, Mary honors and adorns Jesus as a guest in the house (see Luke 7:46).[3] This manner of anointing occurs to celebrate special events such as festivals and banquets or, conversely, to mark the end of mourning.[4] Jesus' words to Judas—"You always have the poor with you, but *you do not always have me*" (12:8, emphasis added)—and the fact that they prepare a supper for him (12:2) suggest that the presence of Jesus at the supper was an event to celebrate. Furthermore, the fact that Mary wipes Jesus' feet with her hair suggests that, in mopping up the excess ointment (a pound of ointment is much more than most feet can absorb!), she also anoints herself as part of the celebratory ritual (12:3; cf. Ruth 3:3; Cant 1:3; Jdt 10:3).[5] The comment by Theodore of Mopsuestia may not be far wrong:

---

[2] Noting that the subject of the verb ἐποίησαν is not explicit, Brown (*Gospel*, 448) argues that other unnamed persons provide the supper and that Lazarus is a fellow guest with Jesus, not the host. To presume a different subject, however, seems to deny a straightforward reading of the text. See Smith, *John*, 233; A. Reinhartz, "The Gospel of John," in *Searching the Scriptures: A Feminist Commentary* Vol. 2 (ed. E. Schüssler Fiorenza with A. Brock and S. Matthews; New York: Crossroads, 1994), 582.

[3] See Matt 26:7; Luke 7:38.

[4] Guests are anointed in Ruth 3:3; 2 Sam 12:20; 14:2; 2 Chr 28:15; Ps 23:5; Ezek 16:9; Dan 10:3; Amos 6:6; Mic 6:15; Jdt 10:3; 16:8; Matt 6:17. Brown (*Gospel*, 451) claims that the anointing of feet is "really unparalleled." However, the following passages do describe such anointing, usually in the context of greeting an honored visitor: Homer, *Odyssey* 19.503–7; Aristophanes, *Wasps* 606–9; Athenaeus, *Diepnosophists* 12.553; Pliny, *Natural History* 13.22; Petronius, *Satyricon* 70; Curtius, *History of Alexander* 8.9.27; Tosepta *Sabbat* 3:16; *Sipre* on Deut 33:24. See J. Coakley, "Anointing at Bethany and the Priority of John," *JBL* 107 (1988): 246–8.

[5] Based on Num 5:18 (and its corresponding citation in Philo, *Spec. Laws* 3.56), in which the priest messes up or uncovers the hair of a woman who is suspected of adultery, some commentators suggest that Mary was a woman of loose morals (or that she had no respect for public opinion) because her hair was loose in public. See Morris, *Gospel*, 577; Barrett, *Gospel*, 412; Brown, *Gospel*, 451. B. P. Robinson ("Anointing by Mary of Bethany," *Downside Review* 115 [1997], 102) argues that Mary is a courtesan, well practised in the role of washing and anointing feet, yet as he himself admits, "we know too little about the social mores of first-century Palestine." As nothing else in the Gospel suggests that Mary is either adulterous or promiscuous or that the dinner was indeed public, these conclusions should not form the basis of the interpretation. See Coakley, "Anointing," 250.

For it was as if the woman planned this so as to attach the fragrance of our Lord's flesh to her body. For she took care that she should always be with him: she did this in her love so that if she should come to be separated from him, by this she could suppose he was with her still.[6]

Looking back, Mary's grief at the death of her brother in 11:33 is so profound that she weeps at Jesus' feet. Now, she casts off her mourning, again at the feet of Jesus, by anointing her own hair with the excess ointment (12:3).[7] Her act of anointing is thus a celebration that casts off mourning and celebrates the presence of Jesus.

Second, the text explicitly states that Mary anoints Jesus for the day of his burial (12:7).[8] The Gospel tells us, however, that Nicodemus and Joseph are the ones who prepare the body of Jesus after his death by wrapping it in spices and linen cloths (John 19:40); Mary does not do it. Thus, Mary's pre-death anointing would serve merely to anticipate Jesus' post-death anointing.[9] But the anointing scene in John 12 also anticipates the narrative of Jesus washing the feet of the disciples in John 13:1–30.[10] As Mary demonstrates her servanthood at the feet of Jesus, Jesus demonstrates his servanthood at the feet of the disciples. As Mary's hair is used to dry Jesus' feet, so too Jesus lays down his

---

[6] Syriac version ed. J.-M. Vosté (CSCO 115; Louvain: CSCO, 1940), 233, cited in Coakley, "Anointing," 252.

[7] Both the narrative of the raising of Lazarus and the anointing of Bethany refer to each other (11:1–2; 12:1–2), suggesting that the dinner may have been motivated by gratitude. Robinson ("Anointing," 99–111) argues that Mary's anointing with oil in the house reverses the account in John 11:28–37 in which Mary stays in her house until she is called and anoints Jesus' feet with her tears, demonstrating her lack of trust in Jesus' ability. G. O'Day ("John," in *Women's Bible Commentary: Expanded Edition* [ed. C. Newsom and S. Ringe: Louisville, Ky.: Westminster John Knox, 1998], 388) adds that Mary demonstrates her love for Jesus in her extravagant gift. However, John 12 says nothing about Mary's love for Jesus. Based on John's dependence on Luke 7:47, Bultmann (*Gospel*, 415) also draws the conclusion that Mary was motivated by love.

[8] Mark 16:1. Oil was also applied to the ill for healing (Mark 6:13; Jas 5:14; Rev 3:18; cf. Tob 6:8; 11:8).

[9] In 12:7, "Leave her also so that she might keep it until the day of my burial," a few later manuscripts have the perfect tense "has kept" (τετήρηκεν without the ἵνα) rather than the subjunctive "might keep" (τηρήσῃ). While τετήρηκεν is certainly not the original reading, most scholars agree that it is the correct interpretation, namely, that Mary had kept the perfume until now in order to anoint Jesus. The purpose clause (initiated by ἵνα) thus explains why the ointment was not sold (responding to Judas' question): it was saved for Jesus' burial. See Brown, *Gospel*, 449; Schnackenburg, *Gospel*, 2:368–9. The NRSV renders the statement this way: "Leave her alone. *She bought it* so that she might keep it for the day of my burial" (italicized words are added by translator). With little confidence, Barrett (*Gospel*, 413–5) also suggests that it could be translated, "Let her remember it on the day of my burial."

[10] See O'Day, "John," 388; M. Sabbe, "Footwashing in John 13 and Its Relation to the Synoptic Gospels," *ETL* 58 (1982): 298.

garments and dries the disciples' feet with a towel (11:2; 12:3; 13:5).[11] As Mary's anointing pre-figures Jesus' death, so too does the footwashing pre-figure Jesus' death, as we shall see. Both narratives are set in the context of a supper (δεῖπνον) at which people recline (ἀνακειμένων, 12:2; 13:2, 12). Neither of the two narratives focuses on the food eaten nor the drink consumed; both focus on the symbolic actions of first Mary and then Jesus. Thus, we might conclude that Mary's pre-death anointing functions as a proleptic or prophetic gesture anticipating Jesus' death[12] and does not merely anticipate Jesus post-death anointing.

Finally, the anointing of Mary confirms Jesus as the Messiah, the "anointed one" (cf. 1:41). The verb to anoint, ἀλείφω, is used twice in the Gospel of John, both times to refer to the action that Mary performs on Jesus (11:2; 12:3), but the noun that refers to "one who has been anointed" (ὁ χριστός, "Christ") and its Hebrew translation Μεσσίας ("Messiah") are found twenty-one times in the Gospel. The identification of Jesus with the Messiah is made unequivocally by the narrator (1:17; 20:31), by Andrew (1:25), by Martha (11:27), and by Jesus himself (17:3).[13] The people in general, however, are less sure of Jesus' identity as the Messiah (7:26, 31, 41; 9:22). The action of Mary thus confirms what the Gospel claims about Jesus: that he is the Messiah, the anointed one.

The description and the function of the figure known as the Messiah is by no means fixed within the Second Temple Period, but certain characteristics can be noted. According to Marinus de Jonge, there are roughly three groups of people who are anointed: kings, priests, and, less frequently, prophets.[14] For example, David was anointed king over the house of Judah (2 Sam 2:4–7) and then over the house of Israel (2 Sam 5:4, 17); Solomon was anointed by the priest Zadok and the prophet Nathan (1 Kgs 1:34, 45). Aaron was anointed as a priest by Moses (Exod 29:7; Lev 8:12). In 1 Kings 19:16, Elisha the prophet is "anointed" when Elijah lays his cloak over his shoulders (1 Kgs 19:19–21; cf. 2 Kgs 2:1–14), indicating that the application of oil is less important than the gift of the Spirit of God (see Isa 61:1). Hence, various individuals, especially kings and priests, are described as "the Lord's anointed" (Lev 4: 3, 5, 16; 1 Sam 12:3, 5; 16:6; 2 Sam 23:1; Isa 45:1). Over time, the Royal Psalms (e.g., Ps 18, 45,

---

[11] Both stories also feature Judas' supposed interest in the poor (12:5, 6, 8; 13:29). Based on the verbal parallels in these two passages, Sabbe ("Footwashing," 298) concludes that the anointing and the footwashing are two components of one symbolic action (cf. Matt 6:17; Ruth 3:3; 2 Kgs 12:20).

[12] Brown, *Gospel*, 454; Schnackenburg, *Gospel*, 2:370; Reinhartz, *Searching*, 583.

[13] Compare the tentative nature of a similar identification made by the Samaritan woman (4:25, 29).

[14] For a full description of the term "anointed," see M. de Jonge, "Messiah," *ABD* 4:777–88; "The Use of the Word 'Anointed' in the Time of Jesus," *NT* 8 (1966):132–48.

89), which were likely written in reference to historical figures, became more generic and articulated a hope in an ideal king. This kingly ideal is reflected in the prophetic literature: he is a descendant of David and God's agent in bringing about a new era in which the exiles will return to the land, Israel and Judah will be reunited, and war will cease.[15]

In early Jewish writings (from about 200 B.C.E. to about 100 C.E.), the figure of the ideal king is more closely associated with priestly figures; sometimes the king and priest are one and the same person. Often the priest is given a higher status. Sirach, for example, emphasizes the failure of most of the Davidic kings to restore peace to Israel and emphasizes instead the virtues of the high priesthood (47:1–22; 49:11–12; 51:12). Priestly leaders who continually depend on the help of the LORD are described in 1 Macc. In particular, Simon the high priest is given the title "commander and ethnarch [literally: ruler of the people] of the Jews and priests," and the "protector of them all" (1 Macc 14:47; cf. 14:35–15:2).[16] The *Book of Jubilees* refers to Levi and his sons as "princes and chiefs" and to Judah as "a prince" (31:13–20). The *Testaments of the Twelve Patriarchs* also represent Levi as superior to Judah; Levi is a priest as well as a warrior, judge, ruler, and teacher (*T. Jud.* 21:1–6a; *T. Reu.* 6:5–7, 8, 10–12; *T. Sim.* 5:4–6; *T. Levi* 4:2–6; chapters 5–6; 8: 2–17). Some of the Qumran texts set the offices of ruler and priest together, as "the anointed one of Aaron" and the "anointed one of Israel"; at other times, the priestly figure leads the people.[17] In contrast, the *Psalms of Solomon* focus on the "anointed" Davidic king who will represent God on earth and restore Israel to the land under wise leadership (*Pss. Sol.* 17, 18). Similarly, apocalyptic literature of the first century C.E. refers to an anointed royal figure who will reign temporarily at the end of time.[18] All of these passages suggest that there is an expectation of some sort of anointed one, whether it is a king or priest (or both), who will lead the people as God's agent.

---

[15] See, for example, Isa 7:14; 9:1–6; 11:1–9; Mic 5:2–4; Jer 23:1–6; 33:14–26; Ezek 17:1–24; 34; 37; Hos 3:5. See D. Juel, *Messianic Exegesis: Christological Interpretation of the Old Testament in Early Christianity* (Philadelphia: Fortress, 1988); J. Ashton, *Understanding the Fourth Gospel* (New York: Oxford, 1991), 238–79. M. de Jonge ("Messiah," 780–781; "Use," 31–32) warns against oversimplifying the notion of "Messiah" and this study does not attempt to do so. These passages are cited to illustrate the purpose of anointing and the type of people who might be anointed. They are used to provoke some questions that might be asked of John's presentation of Jesus as Messiah and, specifically here, to understand the purpose of Mary's actions.

[16] See Bauer, *Lexicon*, 112, 218.

[17] For example, see 1QM, which refers to priests leading the people (II, 1; XV, 4; XVI, 13; XVIII, 5). The Messiah of Aaron and of Israel are mentioned in CD XII, 23; XIV, 19; XIX, 10–11; XX, 1; 1QS IX, 11; 1QSa II, 11–14, 20.

[18] See *2 Bar.* 29:3; 30:1; chapters 36–37; 39:7; 40:1; 70:9; 72:2; *4 Ezra* 7:26–44; 11:1–12:3.

The title "Messiah" is ascribed to Jesus in the Gospel of John, but the representation of the Messiah figure is not clearly dependent on these earlier images.

Jesus is specifically called a king (1:49; 6:15; 12:13–15; 18:33–39; 19:3, 14–19). As a king, Jesus presides over a kingdom "not of this world" (18:36). Barrett suggests that Mary's anointing identifies Jesus as the "anointed king" because he later enters Jerusalem on a donkey, and the people proclaim him to be "the king of Israel" (12:13; cf. Zech 9:9).[19] The problem with this idea is that Mary anoints Jesus' feet rather than his head in the traditional manner of anointing kings (cf. Exod 29:7; Lev 8:12; 21:10; 1 Sam 10:1; 2 Kgs 9:3, 6; Ps 141:5; cf. Luke 7:46).[20] Jesus is also called a prophet (4:19, 44; 6:14; 7:40, 52; 9:17); he both performs signs and predicts events.[21] There are only allusions to Jesus as priest. Like a priest, Jesus consecrates himself for those who believe him (17:19), and he wears a seamless robe, reminiscent of the priestly garb (19:23).[22] It is not clear, therefore, in what specific way the Gospel of John understands Jesus as the Messiah with respect to the Messiah known from other texts. Suffice it to say at this point that the Gospel appropriates this title for Jesus.

Sometimes, the coming of the eschatological Messiah is associated with a banquet. According to Dennis Smith, the classic image is described in Isaiah 25:6–8 and is given full messianic expression in *2 Bar.* 29:1–8. Both passages refer to the consumption of abundant food and a festive meal that signifies immortality and the joys at the end of time or afterlife.[23] The meal is called a "messianic banquet" if the Messiah is present. The supper in Bethany may be designated a messianic banquet for a number of reasons. First, the "Messiah/ Anointed One" is present; the fact that Jesus is anointed at this event secures this identification. There is also an element of celebration in the use of the ointment. The house is filled (ἐπληρώθη) with the abundant fragrance of expensive perfume (12:3).[24] There was so much ointment that Mary was able to

---

[19] Barrett, *Gospel*, 409; Beasley-Murray, *John*, 208.

[20] Barrett, *Gospel*, 412.

[21] For a discussion of the prophetic activity of Jesus in the Gospel of John, see Reinhartz, "Jesus as Prophet," 3–16, and Meeks, *Prophet-King*.

[22] Supported by the description of Jesus as a priest in Hebrews, Brown (*Gospel*, 920– 921) argues that Jesus' seamless tunic woven in one piece is meant to remind the reader of the high priest and thus that Jesus died as a priest. Philo (*Flight* 20.110–112) says that the clothing of the high priest represents the clothing that the λόγος makes of the universe; it thus cannot be rent. Josephus (*Ant.* 3.7.4) describes the priest's garment as one piece.

[23] Smith, "Messianic," 4:788–9.

[24] O'Day ("John," 387) points out that this is the second time that the Bethany family is associated with scents. In 11:39, Martha expresses concern that the odor of Lazarus' dead and rotting body will be offensive. In John 12:3, however, the house is filled with the fragrance

enjoy the excess (12:3).[25] Finally, while other Johannine meal narratives say little about Jesus as Messiah and more about the typical food and drink of messianic banquets,[26] this narrative says more about anointing and nothing about food and drink. The narratives complement one another and round out the picture of the messianic banquet motif.

Mary's anointing makes little sense if the anointing is understood to be solely a hospitable gesture, a pre-death anointing, or the recognition of Jesus as Messiah. Most likely, the anointing of Jesus includes aspects of all three of these possibilities, that is, Mary celebrates the fact that Jesus is the Messiah who is present with them now but who is soon going to be "lifted up" in his death.[27]

John 12:1–8 is included in this study of the ingesting motif because it recounts the events of a supper in Bethany in which Jesus is the honored guest about to go to his imminent death. Unlike other passages that feature ingesting language, Jesus is indisputably a guest and does not slip into the role of host. Here, Jesus is not presented as the provider of the food that gives eternal life. By evoking the ingesting motif, however, and coupling it with actions that anticipate Jesus' death, the Gospel again sets before the reader, albeit in allusive form, the fact that Jesus must die in order that others might "eat him" and live. Jesus' death is to be celebrated rather than mourned, for his death brings life to others. This underlying theme is communicated through traces of the messianic banquet motif.

THE ROLE OF THE DISCIPLES

Those who are usually called disciples in the Gospel of John (Peter, the beloved disciple, Nathanael, Philip, and Andrew) are not explicitly mentioned in this narrative—except for Judas. Instead, the narrative focuses on Lazarus, Mary, and Martha. Lazarus is known from 11:1–44 as the man from Bethany whom Jesus loved.[28] Jesus raises him from the dead after four days in the tomb. This sign brought many people to believe in Jesus, and, as a consequence, the

---

of nard: "The odor of death has been replaced by the odor emanating from Mary's extravagant love." See also, Coakley, "Anointing," 243.

[25] Compare other Johannine narratives that feature abundance (cf. 2:1–11; 6:1–15; 21:8). This is a common Johannine theme made clear by Jesus' statement: "I came that they may have life and have it abundantly" (10:10).

[26] See the meal narratives in John 2:1–11, 4:4–42, 6:1–15, and 21:1–14 that feature the typical "messianic banquet foods" of water, wine, bread, and fish. Smith, "Messianic," 4:789–90.

[27] See Koester, *Symbolism*, 112–5; Culpepper, *Gospel*, 193; Quast, *Reading*, 88.

[28] There is a possibility that Lazarus is the "disciple whom Jesus loved" (see 13:23; 19:26–27; 20:1–10; 21:7, 20–24). See Culpepper, *Anatomy*, 141.

Pharisees and the council planned to put both Jesus and Lazarus to death (11:45–53; 12:9–11). Lazarus is a silent actor in the Gospel; his narrative contribution rests in his passive resurrection by Jesus. The Gospel uses this narrative, however, to foreshadow Jesus' resurrection from the dead after three days and the subsequent feasting with the disciples in John 21.

Lazarus' sister, Martha, who is also loved by Jesus (11:5), participates more actively in the narrative of Lazarus' resurrection. She sends a message to Jesus and meets him on the way to Bethany, expressing confidence that Jesus could have saved her brother from death had he arrived earlier (11:21). She declares her belief that Jesus is "the Messiah, the Son of God, the one coming into the world" (11:27). At the tomb, Martha expresses concern that Lazarus' body will have a strong odor (11:39). She witnesses the resurrection of her brother, and hence, "the glory of God" (11:40). At the supper at Bethany narrative, however, Martha serves in silence (12:2).

In contrast to Lazarus and Martha, Mary has a major role both in the narrative of Lazarus' resurrection and in the narrative of the anointing of Jesus. She, too, is identified as a sister of Lazarus and Martha and as one who is loved by Jesus (11:5). With Martha, she sends a message to Jesus that Lazarus is ill (12:3) and, after Martha, she too meets Jesus on the road to Bethany (11:30–32). There she falls at his feet and weeps, moving Jesus and the crowd to tears (12:32–36). Mary also witnesses the resurrection of her brother (11:45). At the supper in Bethany, Mary anoints the feet of Jesus. In fact, it is for this act that Mary is known, for John 11:1–2 says: "Now a certain man was ill, Lazarus of Bethany, the village of Mary and her sister Martha. Mary was the one who anointed the Lord with perfume and wiped his feet with her hair." As a reference to events that have not yet occurred, this statement functions as an internal prolepsis (i.e., the event will occur before the narrative's conclusion).[29] Thus, it not only foretells the event and underlines its significance but it also highlights the importance of Mary's role in the event.

Lazarus, Mary, and Martha appear at the outset of the most intense point of narrative conflict; that is, once these three are introduced, the conflict within the Gospel reaches its climax quickly as a direct result of the raising of Lazarus (11:45–53; 12:9–11). As pivotal figures, their actions anticipate the remaining events of Jesus' life: like Martha, Jesus serves others; like Mary, he washes feet; and, like Lazarus, he is raised from the dead.

Judas is again established as a counterpoint to the other disciples and, more specifically in this case, to Lazarus, Martha, and Mary. Judas is identified as

---

[29] Culpepper (*Anatomy*, 60) calls 11:2 a misplaced analepsis because it technically "looks back" at an event involving Mary, but the event has not yet occurred in the narrative chronology.

Judas Iscariot, instead of the more common title, Judas son of Simon Iscariot (cf. 6:71; 13:2, 26). He is also identified as "one of the disciples" (12:4), and his presence suggests that the other disciples were also present, though the text does not explicitly say so. As usual, the name of Judas is followed by the designation, "the one who was about to betray him" (12:4; cf. 6:71; 13:2; 18:2). Here, however, Judas is described as the one who carries the money box, likely handling the financial matters of the group (see also 13:29). Yet Judas is a thief (κλέπτης) and takes whatever money is added to the box (12:6). This evokes the contrast made in John 10 between the shepherd, who looks after the sheep, and the thief (κλέπτης), who comes to steal, kill, and destroy (10:10). The narrator also informs us that Judas is not concerned for the poor (12:6) although he expresses this concern (12:5); thus, Judas is also a liar (see 8:44). As usual, the Gospel highlights the strengths and weaknesses of the characters in the story through contrast; in this case, Judas' desire for money is offset by Mary's extravagance.

Belief is not a major theme in the narrative of the anointing in Bethany, but the actions of Mary, whether she understands or not, attest to her acceptance of the fate of Jesus. Her anointing anticipates the death and burial of Jesus, but this is not the end of the story. As the anointed one, the Messiah, Jesus rises from the dead. His death and resurrection mark the end of mourning and the beginning of celebration (occasions for anointing certainly), and are symbolically anticipated in the pleasing scent of the perfume filling the house (12:3; cf. 3:29; 10:10; 15:11; 16:24). Set in the context of a meal where no eating is mentioned, this supper of anointing focuses on Jesus' death.

Chapter 6

The Last Supper (13:1–30; 15:1–17)

This chapter will examine the Last Supper and one section of its accompanying discourse. The first section will look carefully at the explicit "meal narrative" found in John 13:1–30. The references to eating and meal postures are more developed in this narrative than in the Supper at Bethany, but like the Bethany meal, the Last Supper focuses more on the symbolic actions than the actual eating and drinking that takes place. These actions pick up on themes that have been previously introduced through the ingesting motif and extend them now in new directions. The second section of this chapter deals with a less significant passage within the ingesting motif. This is the vine and branches metaphor used by Jesus to describe the interconnection of the Father, Jesus, and the disciples. Although it is more of an agricultural metaphor than an ingesting one, it is included in this survey of the ingesting motif because it notes that the disciples bear fruit. The assumption is that this "fruit" will be consumed.

THE LAST SUPPER (JOHN 13:1–30)

Before the festival of Passover, Jesus washes the disciples' feet during supper. When Peter misunderstands why he does this, Jesus explains that he is showing them by example what they are to do for each other. He hints about one who is not clean and finally discloses to the disciples that someone will betray him (although the reader has known the identity of the betrayer since 6:71). Peter motions to the beloved disciple to ask Jesus who the betrayer is. Jesus says that he will dip a piece of bread and give it to the one who will betray him. He gives it to Judas and Judas leaves. The disciples still do not understand. Jesus then teaches, blesses, and prays for them in an extended discourse (13:31–17:26).

The Last Supper is the third narrative that uses ingesting language in the context of the Passover: in the first, Jesus cleanses the temple (2:13–25) and, in the second, he feeds the multitude (6:1–15). In contrast to the Synoptic Gospels, which locate the Last Supper on the actual night of Passover, the Gospel of John situates the Last Supper on the eve of Passover. Both accounts describe the meal that takes place on the night that Jesus is betrayed by Judas and arrested. The dating of the Last Supper in the Synoptic Gospels has led several scholars to interpret John 13 as if it were also a Passover meal and, thus, to draw on paschal traditions to explain the various actions of Jesus and the disciples.[1] The Gospel of John is explicit, however, that the Last Supper is not a Passover meal. It is "before (πρό) the festival of the Passover" (13:1)[2] and confirmed by later narrative events. For instance, the Jews refuse to enter Pilate's *praetorium* for Jesus' trial in order to avoid ritual impurity and still eat the Passover (18:28). Jesus is condemned "on the Day of Preparation for the Passover" at the time of the Passover sacrifice (19:14).[3] The Last Supper in John is not a Passover meal, but the Passover looms on the narrative horizon.

John 13:1–30 is clearly situated within the context of a meal.[4] It is not necessarily a special meal (note that there is no definite article before the word δεῖπνον in 13:2). It was likely the evening meal (13:30); an evening meal was common at that time, and constituted the major meal of the day. Customarily, people would lie on their left side, elevated on their left elbow, and use their right arm to bring food to their mouths.[5] The feet of the guests were easy to get

---

[1] See especially Jeremias (*Eucharistic*) and the opposing arguments in S. Zeitlin, "The Last Supper Was an Ordinary Meal in the Fourth Gospel," *JQR* 42 (1952): 251–60, and C. Torrey, "In the Fourth Gospel the Last Supper Was a Paschal Meal," *JQR* 42 (1952): 237–50. Jeremias (*Eucharistic*, 42–53) claims that the Last Supper was on the 15th of Nissan, that is, on Passover, because only on Passover did Jews drink red wine, limit their number to twelve, break bread after the meal was started and sing hymns. He includes evidence of Passover feasting from John 13: only on Passover do Jews recline at meals (13:12), eat at night (13:30), and eat in a state of Levitical purity (i.e., footwashing, 13:5–11). Furthermore, Jesus speaks words of interpretation over the food (13:31–17:26), and the disciples think that Judas has gone to give something to the poor, a Passover tradition (13:29). Jeremias concludes that the Christian Eucharist began as a Christian Passover celebration. Disagreeing with Jeremias, Brown (*Gospel*, 556) is not convinced that so much activity (Jesus and the disciples travel to Gethsemane; temple guards bear arms; people bury Jesus) would occur on the night of Passover. He dates the Johannine Last Supper to the day before Passover. See the survey and bibliography on this question in Brown, *Gospel*, 555–6.

[2] Jeremias (*Eucharistic*, 80), Bultmann (*Gospel*, 463), and Torrey ("Paschal," 240–242) argue that Jesus *knew before* the Passover that his hour had come and so was now prepared to eat the Passover meal.

[3] *Jub.* 49:10, 19 ("on the third part of the day"); Philo, *Spec. Laws* 2.145 ("beginning at noon"). See J. Bonsirven, "Hora Talmudica," *Biblica* 33 (1952): 511–5.

[4] According to Smith, references to meal customs and rules of etiquette in the New Testament presuppose the influence of the surrounding Greco-Roman culture. See "Meal Customs: Greco-Roman Meal Customs," *ABD* 4:650–655; "Jesus at Table," 466–86; "Social Obligation"; "Meals," 319–39; "Table Fellowship," 613–38; "Reconsidered," 64–73; "Messianic Banquet," *ABD* 4:788–91.

[5] The practice of reclining at meals seems to have arisen in the East and was known to the Jewish people as early as the 8th century (Amos 6:4–7). See also Jdt 12:15; Tob 2:1; Tob S 7:9; Sir 25:18; 32:2; Mark 6:40; 8:6; Matt 15:35; Luke 14:10; 17:7. By the 6th century,

to from the outside of the circle, and servants would wash the guests' feet before the meal began.[6] This explains how Mary of Bethany was able to reach Jesus' feet in order to anoint them (John 12:3) and how Jesus was able to wash the disciples' feet during their Last Supper. Typically, three couches (*triclinium*) surrounded either a rectangular or circular/oval table. The fourth side was open to allow access by servants. There would normally be three guests on each couch. They were assigned a place at the table by the host. In Palestine in the first century, the place of honor was most consistently the middle place of the middle couch. The next best location was usually to the left of this guest, and the third place of honor was to his right.[7] In the same way, the disciples and Jesus are said to be lying down, or reclining (13:12, 23, 28).[8]

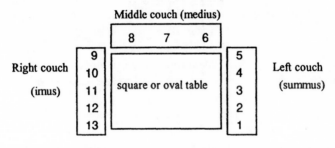

Figure 1[9]

It is an interesting exercise to speculate on the positions of those at table in John 13. If Jesus, as the guest of honor, was reclining in the middle position of

---

Greeks appeared to have adopted the custom from the Assyrians; the Romans adopted the custom soon afterward. See, for example, Plato, *Symposium*, 174e; Pliny, *Ep.* 4.22.4. J.-M. Dentzer, "Aux origines de l'iconographie du banquet couché," *Revue archéologique* (1971): 215–58; "Le motif du banquet couché dans le Proche-Orient et le monde grec du 7e au 4e siecle avant J.-C.," in *Bibliothèque des écoles françaises d'Athènes et de Rome* 246e (Rome, 1982). Only the Cretans continued to eat their meals seated at a table. F. Prat, "Les places d'honneur chez les Juifs contemporains du Christ," *RSR* 15 (1925): 515. See Smith, "Meal Customs," 4: 650–655.

[6] Plato, *Symposium*, 175a.

[7] See Prat ("Places," 518) for primary source evidence. The place of honor assigned by a host was sometimes the cause of social embarrassment. This is seen in the struggle for precedence by the scribes and Pharisees in Matthew 23:6, by the mother of James and John on their behest in Matthew 20:20–28, and by the disciples themselves at the Last Supper in Luke 22:24.

[8] Cf. Jeremias (*Eucharistic*, 49) who says, "it is *absolutely impossible* that Jesus and his disciples should have *reclined* at table for their ordinary meals" (his italics). See John 12:1–2 where Jesus and Lazarus were reclining (ἀνακειμένων) six days before the Passover.

[9] Adapted from Prat, "Places," 513.

the middle couch (see figure 1 above, 7), then the beloved disciple would be to his right (8), the third place of honor, because he "reclined on the breast of Jesus" (13:23). He would be able to lean back and whisper discreetly to Jesus.[10] Judas must have been to the left of Jesus (6), that is, the second place of honor, for Jesus was able to pass him bread (13:27). Were Judas anywhere else, Jesus would have had to reach to the right over the body of the beloved disciple, or to the left, past the fully extended body of the person on the adjacent couch (5). This seems unlikely. Peter was most probably seated somewhere to the right of Jesus and the beloved disciple (possibly 9) for he was able to motion to the disciple to ask Jesus a question but was not close enough to ask Jesus himself (13:24).[11]

From this recumbent position, Jesus gets up to wash the disciples' feet (13:4)[12] and then returns afterwards (13:12). It is thus "during supper" or "while supper is happening" ($\kappa\alpha\grave{\iota}$ $\delta\epsilon\acute{\iota}\pi\nu\text{ou}$ $\gamma\iota\nu\text{o}\mu\acute{\epsilon}\nu\text{ou}$)[13] that Jesus washes the feet of the disciples and talks to them. This is confirmed in 13:26–30 for they are still eating: Jesus passes bread to Judas. Recurring references to eating postures and food situate the footwashing and the interpretive discourse within a meal narrative.

The approaching Passover dominates this passage, not because the meal itself is the Passover supper, but because the narrative has been moving towards this festival with growing intensity. In the Cleansing of the Temple and the Feeding of the Multitude narratives, also set at the time of Passover (2:13; 6:4), Jesus' death is anticipated. The approach to the final Passover in the Gospel begins in chapter 11.

> Now the Passover of the Jews was near, and many went up from the country to Jerusalem before the Passover to purify themselves. They were looking for Jesus and were asking one another as they stood in the temple, "What do you think? Surely he will not come to the festival, will he?" Now the chief priests and the Pharisees had given orders that anyone who knew where Jesus was should let them know, so that they might arrest him. (11:55–56)

---

[10] Brown, *Gospel*, 574; Barrett, *Gospel*, 446–7. See Plutarch, *Quaest. Conv.* 1.2; 619B; 615D; Luke 14:7–11.

[11] Prat's suggestion ("Places," 519) that Peter was in position 6 because he was the head disciple and thus in the seat of honor makes no sense given this arrangement. Peter would have had to reach over (or around) Jesus to get the beloved disciple's attention. Likewise, Judas is placed in position 9, too far for Jesus to reach.

[12] Footwashing before meals is frequently mentioned in the biblical text. See Gen 18:4; 19:2; 24:32; 43:24; Luke 7:38, 44, 48, etc. According to Josephus (*J.W.* 2.129), the Essenes took complete baths before meals.

[13] The text is doubtful here: p[66] has $\gamma\epsilon\nu\text{o}\mu\acute{\epsilon}\nu\text{ou}$, which is little help; $\aleph$ has $\gamma\epsilon\nu\text{o}\mu\acute{\epsilon}\nu\text{ou}$ corrected to $\gamma\iota\nu\text{o}\mu\acute{\epsilon}\nu\text{ou}$; other early authorities support $\gamma\iota\nu\text{o}\mu\acute{\epsilon}\nu\text{ou}$. The present participle is here translated in the concurrent sense.

The supper in Bethany, which occurs six days before Passover, brings us closer still (12:1). On the next day (presumably the fifth day before Passover), Jesus' entry into Jerusalem is both heralded by the crowd and feared by the Pharisees (12:12–19). In the context of this approaching festival, some Greeks come looking for Jesus (12:20). The coming festival is linked to the hour of Jesus' death (12:33), referred to as the hour of his glorification (12:23). Finally, in John 13:1, the festival of the Passover is imminent and Jesus "knew that his hour had come to depart from this world and go to the Father." The Last Supper thus serves as a step closer to the death of Jesus.

Special significance is given to the last words spoken by someone facing death. We see this in the biblical accounts of the parting words of Jacob (Gen 48–49), Moses (Deut 33), Joshua (Josh 23–24), and possibly Paul (Acts 20:17–38). James Charlesworth describes this literary genre, which he identifies as the testament genre, as follows:

> The ideal figure faces death and causes his relatives and intimate friends to circle around his bed. He occasionally informs them of his fatal flaw and exhorts them to avoid certain temptations; he typically instructs them regarding the way of righteousness and utters blessings and curses. Often he illustrates his words—as the seer in apocalypses—with descriptions of the future as it has been revealed to him in a dream or vision.[14]

Some of these elements are present in the Farewell Discourse of Jesus in John 13–17. For example, Jesus gathers his beloved friends before his death (13:1). He warns them of the world's hatred "to keep them from stumbling" (16:1). He foretells the betrayal of Judas (13:21–30), the denial of Peter (13:36–38), and the scattering of the disciples (16:32). He instructs the disciples regarding the way of righteousness by demonstrating the active service of footwashing and says they will be blessed if they also do it. He promises them that they will receive an inheritance (13:8 [see below]; 14:1–3; 17:24) and the Spirit (14:15–31; 16:1–15). He concludes the discourse with a prayer for protection (17:11, 15). As the patriarchs' last words are informed by their heavenly visions or dreams, the whole discourse of John 13–17 is informed by Jesus' knowledge of the Father and thus of the future. The words and the actions of the Last Supper therefore represent the introduction to the final testimony of Jesus.

The Gospel also considers that the words and actions of Jesus at the Last Supper are motivated by love. John 13:1 says that Jesus "having loved his own who were in the world, he loved them to the end" (ἀγαπήσας τοὺς ἰδίους τοὺς

---

[14] J. H. Charlesworth, "Testaments Often with Apocalyptic Sections: Introduction," in *Old Testament Pseudepigrapha* Vol. 1 (ed. J. H. Charlesworth; New York: Doubleday, 1983), 773. See also J. J. Collins, "Testaments," in *Jewish Writings of the Second Temple Period* (ed. M. Stone; Philadelphia: Fortress, 1984), 325–55; G. Nickelsburg, *Jewish Literature between the Bible and the Mishnah* (Philadelphia: Fortress, 1981).

ἐν τῷ κόσμῳ εἰς τέλος ἠγάπησεν αὐτούς). The objects of Jesus' love are "his own" (τοὺς ἰδίους). As the sheep belong to a shepherd (10:14–15), the disciples belong to Jesus (15:19; cf. 17:6–10). Jesus loves his own "to the end" (εἰς τέλος). Because the word τέλος is unarticulated and preceded by the preposition εἰς, it may have an adverbial sense indicating degree, as in "he loved them completely/absolutely/fully." Alternatively, it may be an indication of time, such that "he loved them until the end."[15] Whether this means to the end of his life, as Brown supposes,[16] or to the end of all time is not clear. Both meanings may be supported by the context: Jesus loves his own to the point of death (10:14; see the related verb τελέω on the lips of Jesus while he dies, 19:30) and he loves them to the end of time (cf. 3:36; 5:24; 6:40, 47, 68; etc.). Schnackenburg points out that the Gospel uses a finite verb ἠγάπησεν ("he loved") to indicate that Jesus loves his own completely in that one act of death.[17] We may recall from John 4:34 that Jesus says his food is to do the will of God and to *complete* (τελείοω) his work. In the context of yet another meal, words drawn from the semantic field of τέλος point to the death of Jesus.[18]

The Gospel of John presents Jesus as one who knows all things (16:30; 21:17).[19] As the "word" (λόγος), Jesus is present in creation (1:3). Having come from the Father, he alone knows the Father (8:19, 55). He knows where he has come from and where he is going (7:27–28; 8:14; 9:29–30; 13:3; 14:4; cf. 18:4). He knows in advance what he will do (6:6), what the disciples think (6:61), and which of them believes in him (6:64; cf. 13:18). Similarly, John 13 is shaped by the knowledge of Jesus: he knows that his hour has come (13:1) and that all things have been given into his hands (13:3). He knows that he is going to the Father (13:3). He knows whom he has chosen (13:18) and who will betray him (13:2, 11). It is with full knowledge that Jesus hands his life over to his enemies.

Having set the stage with the foreshadowing of Jesus' imminent death, the Gospel introduces a symbolic action that also foreshadows his death: Jesus washes the disciples' feet.

> He got up from the table, took off his outer robe, and tied a towel around himself. Then he poured water into a basin and began to wash the disciples' feet and to wipe them with the towel that was tied around him (13:4–5). . . . After he had washed their feet, had put on his robe, and had returned to the table, he said to them, "Do you know what I have done to you?" (13:12)

---

[15]   Bauer, *Lexicon*, 228–9.

[16]   *Gospel*, 550.

[17]   *Gospel*, 3:16.

[18]   See C. Spicq, "La charité est amour manifeste," *RB* 65 (1958): 360–362.

[19]   See Gaffney ("Believing," 215–41) for a full discussion of the words "to know" and "to believe."

ἐγείρεται ἐκ τοῦ δείπνου καὶ τίθησιν τὰ ἱμάτια καὶ λαβὼν λέντιον διέζωσεν
ἑαυτόν· εἶτα βάλλει ὕδωρ εἰς τὸν νιπτῆρα καὶ ἤρξατο νίπτειν τοὺς πόδας τῶν
μαθητῶν καὶ ἐκμάσσειν τῷ λεντίῳ ᾧ ἦν διεζωσμένος (13:4–5)."Οτε οὖν ἔνιψεν τοὺς
πόδας αὐτῶν [καὶ] ἔλαβεν τὰ ἱμάτια αὐτοῦ καὶ ἀνέπεσεν πάλιν, εἶπεν αὐτοῖς,
Γινώσκετε τί πεποίηκα ὑμῖν; (13:12)

The language used to describe this action evokes the image of Jesus' death and
resurrection. While the word τίθυμι has the meaning of "putting or setting
down" an object, in this case, "garments" (13:4; see also "wine" in 2:10, and
"sign" in 19:19), in the Gospel of John it is used eight times to refer to someone
laying down his life. The good shepherd (i.e., Jesus) lays down (τίθησιν) his
life for his sheep (10:11, 15, 17, 18 bis). Peter declares to Jesus, "I will lay
down (θήσω) my life for you" (13:37), and Jesus counters with, "Will you lay
down (θήσεις) your life for me?" (13:38). Furthermore, Jesus tells his disciples,
"This is my commandment, that you love one another as I have loved you. No
one has greater love than this, to lay down (θῇ) one's life for one's friends"
(15:12–13).[20] When Jesus lays down his garments, therefore, it alludes to the
laying down of his life.

The laying down of garments as a symbol for Jesus' laying down his life is
reinforced in 13:12 where the Gospel says that Jesus again "took up (ἔλαβεν)
his garments." The same verb, λαμβάνω, is also used in 10:17–18: "For this
reason the Father loves me, because I lay down (τίθημι) my life in order to take
it up (λάβω) again" (10:17). Jesus lays down his garments (and his life) and
takes up his garments (and his life) again.[21]

Similarly, the text of 13:4 talks of Jesus "getting up" or "rising" (ἐγείρω).
Elsewhere in the Gospel of John, this word is used in the active voice three
times to refer to someone "getting up" (5:8[22]; 11:29; 14:31), but it is used in the
passive voice eleven times to refer to someone "being raised" from the dead.
Jesus raises Lazarus from the dead (ὃν ἤγειρεν ἐκ νεκρῶν) after four days
(12:1, 9, 17) and says that he will raise (ἐγερῶ) the temple in three days after it
is destroyed (2:19). He refers here, according to the narrator in 2:22, to his own
body being raised from the dead (ἠγέρθη ἐκ νεκρῶν). This is confirmed in
21:14 where Jesus appears to the disciples for the third time after he is "raised
from the dead" (ἐγερθεὶς ἐκ νεκρῶν). The passive here (ἐγερθεὶς) refers to the

---

[20] It is used four times to refer to the "laying out" of Jesus' body (19:42; 20:2, 13, 15; cf.
11:34, 19:41). In one case it is used in the sense of "appoint." Jesus says, "I appointed
(ἔθηκα) you to go out and bear fruit, fruit that will last" (15:16).

[21] Brown (Gospel, 551) says "a deliberate parallel is not out of the question" and "all of
this serves to relate the footwashing to the death of the Lord." For a similar position, see
Barrett, Gospel, 439; J. Marsh, Saint John (Harmondsworth: Penguin, 1968), 483; B.
Lindars, The Gospel of John (London: Butler & Tanner, 1972), 450. Cf. Dodd
(Interpretation, 401–402) who understands the footwashing as a "sign" of the incarnation.

[22] Jesus tells the lame man to stand, so in a sense Jesus raises him from illness.

action of the Father who "raises the dead and gives them life" (5:21). Therefore, when Jesus "arises" to wash the disciples' feet and lays down his garments in order to take them up again, the Gospel points to his imminent death and resurrection.

In a similar way, the action of tying a linen towel around himself also prefigures Jesus' death. The word λέντιον is a loan word from the Latin *linteum*, meaning "linen cloth." It is not found elsewhere in the New Testament, but is found frequently in Greek and Latin texts to refer to table linens, sails, curtains, and linen cloth.[23] Though the same word is not used, Jesus' body is wrapped in "linen cloth" and then placed in a tomb. The word used for this type of cloth is ὀθόνιον (John 20:6–7; see also 19:40; Luke 24:12).[24] The word ὀθόνιον is translated as *linteamina* in the Vulgate, reflecting its association with linen products. Thus, it is possible that the action of wrapping himself in linen prefigures the wrapping of his body in linen after death.

Furthermore, according to the LXX, priests wore linen garments called λίνους under their robes next to their skin. For example, Aaron puts on linen clothing as part of the preparation for making a sacrifice (Lev 16:3–5; see also Exod 28:42). According to Ezekiel, these linen garments could pass on holiness to others, so they had to be kept separate from common clothes (Ezek 44:15–19). Therefore, it is possible that Jesus' action of girding himself with a towel both foreshadows his death, on the one hand, and recalls the priestly action of purification, on the other hand.[25] The action of footwashing must therefore be understood in the context of Jesus' death and resurrection.

Of course the action of footwashing also has "earthly meaning" quite apart from its symbolic action. Feet shod in sandals easily become encrusted with dust. It was the custom in Palestine at this time for a servant in the household to wash the feet of guests as a gesture of hospitality. This was usually done before the meal. Sometimes, feet were also anointed with oil.[26] The peculiar aspect of

---

[23] Bauer, *Lexicon*, 471.

[24] Bauer, *Lexicon*, 555. Judg 14:13B; Hos 2:7, 11; *Let. Arist.* 220; Homer, *Od.* 7.107. The word used in Matthew and Mark for the cloth that wrapped Jesus' body is σινδών (Matt 27:59; Mark 15:46).

[25] Lightfoot (*John*, 261–2) makes the unlikely suggestion that baptism is meant here but that it is intentionally obscured to protect the ritual from misappropriation or misunderstanding (but see John 1:26–27; 4:2). According to M.-É. Boismard ("Le lavement des pieds [Jean 13:1–17]," *RB* 71 [1964]: 17), 13:8–10 refers without doubt to baptism because of its parallels with 3:3–5. Robinson ("Significance," 145) does not rule out the overtone of baptism but does not agree that this passage is principally about this rite. I follow his lead in this exegesis.

[26] For footwashing as a sign of hospitality, see Gen 18:4–5; 19:1–3; 24:32; 43:24–25; Judg 19:21; 1 Sam 25:41; cf. 2 Sam 11:8. The LXX translates the word רחץ as νίπτω, the same verb used in John 13:5, 7, 8, and 10. In each case except 1 Sam 25:41, the basin of

the footwashing in John 13 is that it appears to occur during the meal, rather than before it. In fact, footwashing occurs when one would expect there to be eating, yet there is no mention of anyone eating, except for Judas (see below).

To summarize briefly, the combination of a meal setting and accompanying non-meal activities suggest that this narrative should be read symbolically. We recall that Freedman identifies a literary motif by a word choice that is easily avoided or that is unlikely.[27] In this case, word choices that reflect Jesus' death find their way into a meal setting, a setting that is made more significant by its climactic point in the narrative. In this way, the motif recalls effectively the relationship between eating and Jesus' death.

The narrative itself provides two reasons for the footwashing. The first reason, set out in 13:6–12, is that Jesus cleans the disciples so that they might have a "part" with him (we will return to this notion presently). The second reason that Jesus washes their feet is to teach them by example (13:13–17). These two reasons, juxtaposed as they are, have been explained as emanating from different sources.[28] Rather than ask where these explanations come from, however, we will ask what they mean first alone and then placed side by side.

The first reason for Jesus' act of footwashing arises in a dialogue between Jesus and Peter. This dialogue follows other Johannine patterns wherein the person speaking to Jesus misunderstands and Jesus takes the opportunity to explain further. In John 13:6, Peter says to Jesus, "Lord, do *you* wash *my* feet?" (κύριε, σύ μου νίπτεις τοὺς πόδας;). The pronoun placement and use of the title "Lord" indicates Peter's misunderstanding: usually the servant, not the master (κύριος), washes the feet of guests. Jesus responds that Peter does not

---

water is provided and the guests presumably wash their own feet. In 1 Sam 25:41, Abigail calls herself a servant (אָמָה, δούλη) "to wash the feet of the servants of my lord (i.e., David)." Luke 7:44 shows that footwashing was still considered an act of hospitality in the first century C.E. See also *T. Ab.* 3:7–12; *Jos. Asen.* 7:1; 13:12; 20:1–5; 1 Tim 5:10. As an action anticipating the divine presence, see Exod 30:19–21; Philo, *Moses* 2.139; *Spec. Laws* 1.207. Referring to Luke 7:38, 44–46 which mentions both washing and anointing feet, Sabbe ("Footwashing," 300) argues that the footwashing in John 13 must be paired with the anointing in John 12.

[27] Freedman, "Motif," 126–7. S. Schneiders ("The Foot Washing [John 13:1–20]: An Experiment in Hermeneutics," *CBQ* 43 [1981]: 82) argues that the "presence of the extraordinary in the ordinary" (namely, that Jesus and not a servant washes their feet) is a clue to the presence of the symbolic.

[28] Boismard ("Lavement") was the first to suggest that the two explanations for the footwashing, that is paraenetic and sacramental, represent two different sources, one archaic and the other an addition by a redactor. The addition theory has subsequently been adopted and developed by a growing number of exegetes. For a survey of these positions, see Sabbe, "Footwashing," 279–82; F. Segovia, "John 13:1–20, the Footwashing in the Johannine Tradition," *Zeitschrift für die neutestamentliche Wissenschaft und die Kunde der älteren Kirche* 73 (1982): 31–37.

know (οὐκ οἶδας) now but will know (γνώσῃ) after these things (ταῦτα, 13:7). The implication is that the action of footwashing is symbolic.[29]

The meaning of "these things" (ταῦτα) is unclear. There appear to be two options. First, "these things" refer to the footwashing itself. Once Peter understands that footwashing is an act of humility that the disciples are to imitate, then he will understand fully (see 13:12, 17). Second, "these things" refer to the death of Jesus. As we have seen, Jesus arises, lays down his garments, and takes them up again as a foreshadowing of his death and resurrection. In the Cleansing of the Temple narrative, we learn that the disciples come to understanding after Jesus is raised from the dead (2:22). Likewise, after Jesus' entry into Jerusalem on a young donkey, the disciples "did not understand these things at first; but when Jesus was glorified, then they remembered that these things had been written of him and had been done to him" (12:16). They will understand only after they receive the Holy Spirit (7:37–39; 12:16; 14:26).[30] Both of these options are possible: "these things" can refer to the footwashing and/or Jesus' death.

Peter becomes more insistent and swears, as if with an oath, that Jesus will never wash his feet.[31] Jesus tells him that unless he washes Peter's feet, Peter will have no part with him (ἐὰν μὴ νίψω σε, οὐκ ἔχεις μέρος μετ' ἐμοῦ). The force of ἐὰν μή has been seen before in 6:53: "Truly truly, I say to you, unless (ἐὰν μή) you eat the flesh of the Son of Man and drink his blood, you do not have life in you." Just as eating the flesh of Jesus and drinking his blood—understood as believing—are required for eternal life, so also is footwashing by Jesus required.

The phrase, οὐκ ἔχεις μέρος μετ' ἐμοῦ, presents a number of exegetical problems that, given its importance to the Gospel's soteriology, need to be addressed in some detail. The first problem concerns the tense of the verb. While in form the verb ἔχεις is present active indicative (second person), it also has a future sense (see also 12:8, 48; 16:33), made stronger by the condition not yet realized in the protasis, "unless I wash you." The translation may be rendered thus: "you do not have/are not having" and/or "you will not have." The ambiguity of the verb tense permits both readings.

The second exegetical problem regards the meaning of the phrase "a part with me" (μέρος μετ' ἐμοῦ). The word μέρος is used in the New Testament and LXX in the sense of a "part," "portion of the whole," "district" or "region," "side," "piece," "matter," or "share." Its meaning is often conflated with that of

---

[29] Segovia, "Footwashing," 43.

[30] Barrett, *Gospel*, 440; Schnackenburg, *Gospel*, 2:19; Segovia, "Footwashing," 43.

[31] Jeremias, *Eucharistic*, 209–10; Barrett, *Gospel*, 440. Schneiders ("Foot Washing," 87) argues that Peter objects because he does not want Jesus to subvert relationships of power.

? Semantically

another word, μερίς, which resembles μέρος morphologically and is also used in the sense of a "part of the whole," "share," or "portion." In some early classical Greek texts, these two words may be said to be synonymous.[32] Statistically, however, μερίς is used much more frequently in the sense of "inheritance" than is μέρος.[33] For example, the LXX uses μερίς fifty-six times (or forty-six percent of all cases) to translate the Hebrew חלק, a word that has the fundamental sense of "divide" or "share," and, most particularly, an "inheritance of patrimonial land." In later texts, this notion was understood as an eschatological inheritance.[34] In contrast, μέρος is used to translate חלק in only two cases (that is, less than two percent of all cases; Prov 17:2; Eccl 5:19 [18]). Μερίς, then, is more commonly associated with "inheritance" than is μέρος. Μέρος, on the other hand, is most frequently used in the sense of "portion" or "part of the whole" and is used this way in forty-six percent of the cases in the LXX and twenty-six percent of the cases in the New Testament. (Most of the other cases favor the sense of "side" or "district.") It seems logical to favor the most customary use of the word in John 13:8, rendering a translation something like, "You will have no portion/part with me."

Nevertheless, many scholars favor a translation of "inheritance" in spite of the statistics, preferring to read into μέρος the complex meanings of חלק. Brown, for example, argues that οὐκ ἔχεις μέρος μετ' ἐμοῦ should be translated, "You will have no heritage with me." In other words, John 13:8 means that those who are unwashed will not find their eternal reward with Jesus.[35] Bultmann takes this phrase to mean that whoever accepts the footwashing of Jesus "has fellowship with him, remains united with him, that is, as he is on his way to the δόξα," meaning that the washed would share Jesus' destiny. Like Brown, he conflates the use of μέρος and μερίς, citing from the

---

[32] See Bauer, *Lexicon*, 505.

[33] In the LXX, μέρος is used fifty-nine times (fifty-three percent) to refer to an "edge, side, or corner," fifty-one times (forty-six percent), as a "portion of the whole," and two times (one percent) as an "inheritance." In the New Testament, it is used as "side" once (two percent), "district" eight times (twenty-one percent), a "portion of the whole" twenty-six times (sixty-eight percent), and "inheritance" three times (seven percent; Rev 20:6; 21:8; 22:19). Based on Matt 24:51 and Luke 12:46, E. A. Abbott (*Johannine Vocabulary* [London: Adam & Black, 1905], 341) translates μέρος as "destiny" or "lot." Μερίς is used in the LXX as "portion" fifty times (thirty-seven percent), "side" six times (four percent), "district" three times (two percent), and "inheritance" seventy-eight times (fifty-seven percent). It is used five times in the New Testament: in the sense of "district" once, "portion" twice, and "inheritance" twice.

[34] For the meaning of חלק, see F. Dreyfus, "Le thème de l'héritage dans l'Ancien Testament," *RSPT* 42 (1958): 3–49. Μερίς has the same sense in another twenty-three cases in the LXX.

[35] *Gospel*, 565–6. He also depends on the use of μέρος in Rev 20:6; 21:8; 22:19.

LXX only instances of μερίς.[36] Schnackenburg also defends this position, but does so by also citing references in the Gospel of John to demonstrate that Jesus will share his destiny with believers (12:26; 14:3, 19; 17:24).[37] In a similar vein, Barrett, who understands the footwashing to prefigure Jesus' crucifixion, suggests that those who are unwashed will have "no share in the benefits of Jesus' passion and no place among his people" because they have not been baptized into Jesus' death (cf. Acts 8:21).[38] All of these arguments depend on equating μέρος to μερίς, a claim that has gained acceptance without solid argument. Based on the statistical use of μέρος in the LXX and New Testament, the most likely reading should be as some kind of portion or piece.[39]

What kind of portion or piece does this refer to? The word μέρος is used to refer to parts of various elements throughout the New Testament. For example, it is used to refer to the parts of a body (Matt 24:51; Luke 11:36; 12:46), an argument (Rom 15:15), a garment (John 19:23), or a group of people (Acts 23:6, 9). Though its use is rare, it is used for food in Luke 24:42, where it refers to a piece of fish. The word μέρος can therefore refer to a portion of food.

We move on to the next part of the phrase: μετ' ἐμοῦ. Μετά followed by a personal pronoun in the genitive usually indicates accompaniment, especially when it follows an active verb.[40] The phrase, μετ' ἐμοῦ, is often found in the

---

[36] Bultmann, *Gospel*, 468. He cites Deut 10:9; 14:27, 29; 2 Sam 20:1; Isa 57:6; Ps 49:18. He also depends on the ambiguous translation of Matt 24:51: "He will cut him in two and he will place τὸ μέρος αὐτοῦ (the part or destiny?) of him with the hypocrites; there is the weeping and gnashing of teeth" [my literal translation]. Given that only Revelation in the NT uses μέρος to refer explicitly to destiny and it used elsewhere 38 times to refer to "portion," the statistics favor reading μέρος as "part." Also citing only those verses using μερίς in the LXX and on the basis of parallel grammatical structure in 3:3, Boismard ("Lavement," 8, 16) argues that "to have a part with Jesus" means "*participer au royaume eschatologique.*" F. Manns ("Le lavement de pieds," *RSR* 55 [1981]: 167–169) suggests that, based on Passover themes in John 13 (girding loins, in particular), μέρος refers to a portion of the (promised) land that is only achieved through purification. While the Jews faced the loss of their land in 70 C.E., the Christians were promised a new kind of inheritance by following the example of Jesus' death. Without argument, Malina and Rohrbaugh (*Social*, 221) see the meaning as group solidarity. Based on precedence in Luke, Sabbe ("Footwashing," 297) argues that "you have no part with me" is an "invitation to the disciples to participate in the suffering and the death of Jesus, who is acting as one who serves (Luke 22:27) and gives his life for others." While this may be true in essence, as we shall see below, Sabbe's use of Luke to reach this conclusion is problematic.

[37] *Gospel*, 3:19.

[38] Barrett, *Gospel*, 440–442.

[39] In the LXX and the New Testament, μέρος is combined with the following preposition μετά only in John 3:8. Bauer (*Lexicon*, 506) gives no other instance of this combination.

[40] When μετ' ἐμοῦ is used with εἰμι, it has the sense of "in my presence." For example, "My children are with me" (Luke 11:7); "You will be with me in paradise" (Luke 23:43); "The Father is with me" (John 16:32); "Only Luke is with me" (2 Tim 4:11). See also Luke

context of eating:[41]

> He answered, "The one who has dipped his hand into the bowl with me (μετ' ἐμοῦ) will betray me." (Matt 26:23)

> And when they had taken their places and were eating, Jesus said, "Truly I tell you, one of you will betray me, one who is eating with me (μετ' ἐμοῦ)." (Mark 14:18)

> And he did the same with the cup after supper, saying, "This cup that is poured out for you is the new covenant in my blood. But see, the one who betrays me is with me (μετ' ἐμοῦ), and his hand is on the table." (Luke 22:21)

> "Listen! I am standing at the door, knocking; if anyone hears my voice and opens the door, I will come in to him and dine with him, and he with me (μετ' ἐμοῦ)." (Rev 3:20)

An important textual variant in John 13:18 also has this combination:

> The one who eats *my* bread will lift his heel against me.

> Ὁ τρώγων *μου* τὸν ἄρτον ἐπῆρεν ἐπ' ἐμὲ τὴν πτέρναν αὐτοῦ. [42]

> The one who eats bread *with me* will lift his heel against me.

> Ὁ τρώγων *μετ' ἐμοῦ* τὸν ἄρτον ἐπῆρεν ἐπ' ἐμὲ τὴν πτέρναν αὐτοῦ. [43]

This phrase is a citation of Ps 40:10 (41:9 MT) and serves as a prophecy for the disclosure of Judas (which will be treated in more detail below). While the first reading conforms to the LXX (and the Hebrew syntax), the second reading is more probable because it does not conform to the LXX. Obviously, the text was corrected in order to agree with the citation.[44] So we have another example of μετ' ἐμοῦ in the context of eating. Given that μετ' ἐμοῦ finds its home frequently in a meal context elsewhere in the New Testament and that it is found again here in a meal context, might we conclude that John 13:8 is referring to food? Thus οὐκ ἔχεις μέρος μετ' ἐμοῦ would be translated as "You do/will not have a portion/piece with me," that is, a portion most probably of

---

15:31, 22:28; John 8:29; 15:27; 17:24; Acts 20:34; Titus 3:15; Rev 22:2. To "be with" someone is a common expression in the Gospel of John and is used 19 times.

[41] See also "stay awake with me" (Matt 26:38, 40), "share an inheritance with me," (Luke 12:13); "walk with me" (Rev 3:4); "speak with me" ("with me" is used instead of the usual dative personal pronoun following verbs of speech; Rev 1:12; 4:1; 10:8; 17:1; 21:9; 21:15; cf. John 4:27; 9:37; 11:56; 14:30) and "sit with me" (Rev 3:21).

[42] B C L 892 1071 vg^mss cop^sa eth Origen^1/2 Cyril^com Ambrose^1/3

[43] p^66 ℵ A D W Δ Θ Ψ 0141 *f*^1 *f*^13 28 33 157 180 205 579 597 700 1006 1010^supp 1241 1243 1292 1342 1424 1505 *Byz* [E F G H] *Lect* it^a, aur, b, c, (e), f, ff2, l, rl vg syr^s, p, h, pal cop^bo-pt arm geo slav Hippolytus Origen^1/2 Eusebius Epiphanius Chrysostom Cyril^lem Theodoret Tertullian Ambrose^2/3 Augustine. A few later mss have both μετ' ἐμοῦ and μου. This is obviously an attempt to harmonize the variants.

[44] See also Barrett, *Gospel*, 444; Brown, *Gospel*, 554.

bread (see 13:18) or perhaps fish (see Luke 24:42) or a piece of the paschal lamb.[45] More periphrastically, this would read, "You are not eating with me" or "You will not be eating with me."[46] This revised reading of οὐκ ἔχεις μέρος μετ' ἐμοῦ calls into question the usual interpretation of John 13:8. That is, Jesus is not necessarily talking about dividing an inheritance; he may be talking about sharing food.

What does it mean, then, to eat with Jesus in the context of John 13? (1) What would it mean to eat with Jesus at this supper (i.e., in the present)? (2) What would it mean to eat with Jesus in the future? Although the use of ingesting language is abundant in the Gospel, the act of eating with Jesus in the narrative present is not prevalent at all, especially in comparison with the Synoptics.[47] In narratives that feature eating and drinking, there is no clear statement about Jesus eating or drinking (see especially 4:34). The only time that the Gospel states that Jesus eats or drinks is when he is on the cross (19:30); there, he drinks alone. Therefore, to eat with Jesus in the narrative present would mean to share the only food of which Jesus partakes—the cup of his death: he says, "Am I not to drink the cup that the Father has given me?" (19:11; cf. 15:20).[48] In other words, to eat and drink with Jesus suggests that the disciples must be prepared to die for the sake of Jesus, a theme that pervades the Gospel (see, for example, 13:37; 15:13; 21:18–19).

To eat and drink with Jesus in the future sense is understood eschatologically. In John 6, we found that ingesting language can be used figuratively to refer to believing in Jesus. Just as eating physical food provides temporary life for those who eat, "eating Jesus," that is, believing in the necessity of Jesus' death, provides eternal life. Eating Jesus is the means of salvation, and eternal life is the result. In John 13, the imagery is extended: when one believes in the efficacy of Jesus' death, one eats with Jesus "after these things" (μετὰ ταῦτα, 13:7), that is, after his death. Thus, to eat Jesus could well mean to believe in the efficacy of Jesus' death, also enabling the believer to eat with Jesus after death. In any case, since Jesus is "going to the

---

[45] If the portion is a piece of the paschal lamb, then the disciples would eat a piece of Jesus who replaces the paschal lamb in this Gospel. Then the phrase μετ' ἐμοῦ could be translated "of me." Bauer (*Lexicon*, 508–10) does not support such a reading.

[46] Morris (*Gospel*, 617) states that "unless Peter submits to the feet-washing he may not eat with Jesus" but later concludes that "apart from this a man will have part in Christ."

[47] He does, however, distribute food to others; we see this is the Feeding of the Multitude (6:1–15), the presentation of a morsel to Judas (13:30), and the Resurrection Breakfast (21:1–14).

[48] Robinson ("Significance," 145) argues for the same interpretation of this passage, not because of linguistic reasons, but because of the similarity between this passage and Mark 10:32–45 (the prediction of Jesus' death followed by the request by James and John for favorable positions).

Father" (13:1), doing anything "with Jesus" in the future must refer to being with Jesus and the Father (14:2–3; 17:24) in "the world above" (8:23; 12:25–26).[49] From this perspective, the footwashing may be understood as an anticipation of eschatological hospitality.[50]

It is likely, therefore, that the phrase οὐκ ἔχεις μέρος μετ' ἐμοῦ reflects the ingesting motif which, as we have seen, often connects eating and drinking with the death of Jesus. In addition, it directly ties the need for footwashing to the need to eat with Jesus as a prerequisite of salvation. This is further supported by the meal context for the footwashing event.

Peter's response to Jesus, "Lord, not my feet only but also my hands and my head" (13:9), takes the discourse in a different direction. It is no longer a matter of the proper roles of servant and master and the fact of washing; it is now a question of the degree of washing. This misunderstanding is also corrected: only the feet are still to be washed.[51] In John 15:3, Jesus tells the disciples, "You have already been cleansed by the word that I have spoken to you." The death and resurrection of Jesus, which are prefigured in the footwashing and understood to clean people from their sin (1:29; 5:14; 16:9), complete finally what has been started through the words and deeds of Jesus. The expected response of the disciples is belief—"I told you that you would die in your sins, for you will die in your sins unless you believe that I am he" (8:24)—and, as we will see shortly, imitation of the words and deeds of Jesus. Segovia describes it this way:

> The "bathing" that has taken place would refer to the fact that the disciples have already expressed correct belief in Jesus (e.g., 1:35–51; 2:1–11; 6:66–71), while the further "washing" that remains would indicate that such a belief is not yet perfect, i.e., it does not yet include the still outstanding and impending glorification of Jesus. In other words, belief in the Son of God must include an acceptance of his death as the goal and culmination of his mission.[52]

Accepting the footwashing is therefore akin to accepting the efficacy of Jesus' death, making sense of the comment on Jesus' lips, "You do not know now what I am doing, but later you will understand" (13:7; cf. 2:22; 12:16).

To review briefly, the first interpretation of the footwashing is inherent in the act itself. The footwashing is a symbol of the cleansing benefit of the final act of the death and resurrection of Jesus. To accept the death of Jesus and its

---

[49] Boismard, *Lavement*, 9–10; Segovia, "Footwashing," 43. The post-resurrection meal with Jesus is pre-figured in John 21.

[50] A. Hultgren, "The Johannine Footwashing (13:1–11) as Symbol of Eschatological Hospitality," *NTS* 28 (1982): 539–46.

[51] The words εἰ μὴ τοὺς πόδας appear in p[66] B C* W but are omitted in ℵ it[aur, c] vg[ww] Origen Tertullian.

[52] Segovia, "Footwashing," 44–45.

efficacy enables the disciples to participate in the rewards of eternal life, that is, "to share a portion" with Jesus. In this way, the first explanation sets out the role of Jesus in the plan of salvation.

THE ROLE OF THE DISCIPLES

The second explanation for the footwashing is found in 13:12–17 and focuses on the role of the disciples. In contrast to the first explanation in 13:6–11 that focuses on the one-time death of Jesus and its cleansing effect, the second explanation explains the footwashing as an example (ὑπόδειγμα)[53] and addresses more directly Peter's question, "Lord, are *you* going to wash *my* feet?" Although Jesus is their teacher and lord, he washes the disciples' feet. Since the disciples are not greater than their master is, they are to continue to wash the feet of others.[54] Given the first explanation, then, does this mean that the disciples should also go to their death for the benefit of others? This is likely, for elsewhere, the disciples, motivated by love, are asked to lay down their lives for their friends (11:16; 13:36; 15:12–17; 21:15–19).[55]

As we have seen previously, especially in John 6, the description of the varying responses of the disciples to the words and actions of Jesus serve as both instruction and warning. In this case, three disciples are named and each responds to Jesus differently. Peter is the disciple who questions Jesus' actions and who tries to prohibit him (13:6–9; cf. Matt 16:22; Mark 8:32). His triple misunderstanding sets the context for more detailed explanations. He misunderstands, first, the appropriateness of Jesus' washing the disciples' feet. When Jesus tells him that he will understand later, Peter swears that Jesus will never wash his feet. Then when Jesus makes his footwashing a condition for "having a part" with him, Peter again misunderstands and wants his head and hands to be washed as well, moving from prohibition to over-zealousness. Both extremes are corrected by the text: the one act of Jesus is all that is needed, but

---

[53] Imitating the actions of Jesus is not a unique concept in the New Testament. See 1 Cor 11:1; Rom 15:7; Eph 5:2; Heb 12:2; 1 Pet 2:18–25; 3:17. Schnackenburg (*Gospel*, 2:402) notes that imitating Jesus is subordinated to following Jesus (see John 12:26; 13:36).

[54] The present infinitive νίπτειν suggests continuous action. See W. Mounce, *Basics of Biblical Greek:Grammar* (Grand Rapids: Zondervan, 1993), 295.

[55] Manns, "Lavement," 164. See the development of this idea in the discussion on John 21. Segovia ("Footwashing") denies any aspect of martyrdom and sees here only a call to love one another as Jesus loved them, up to but not including death, one supposes. Robinson ("Significance," 145) sees Jesus' washing of the disciples' feet "as a bid for solidarity with him as he goes to his death." This means, for Robinson, that the disciples must accept the role of servant in order to have a share in Christ. H. Weiss ("Foot Washing in the Johannine Community," *NT* 21 [1979]: 300) argues that footwashing was a sacrament performed by the Johannine community to prepare people for their imminent martyrdom.

that one act is absolutely necessary. Peter thus exemplifies a disciple (1) who knows only in part but who will know after the death and resurrection of Jesus (13:7), (2) who accepts the washing of Jesus (that is, his cleansing death), and (3) who will follow Jesus' example and wash the feet of others.

The "good disciple" is exemplified in the character of the beloved disciple, introduced in 13:23 for the first time. The relationship of the beloved disciple to Jesus is described in ways that reflect the nature of the relationship between Jesus and the Father. He reclines "on the chest" of Jesus (13:23; 21:20) just as Jesus is "on the chest" of the Father (1:18). He is loved by Jesus (13:1, 23) as Jesus is loved by the Father (3:35; 5:20; 10:17; 15:9, 10; 17:23–26). He has the ear of Jesus (13:24; cf. 14:13), as Jesus has the ear of the Father (11:41–42). He testifies to the truth (21:24; also possibly 19:35) as Jesus testifies to the truth (5:36; 8:14; 18:37). He knows Jesus (21:7) as Jesus knows the Father (8:55; 17:25). Furthermore, the beloved disciple is with Jesus throughout the passion narrative: at the crucifixion, he takes Jesus' mother into his home as his own (19:26–27); outrunning Peter to the tomb, he is the first to believe (20:2–10); and he eats the breakfast prepared by Jesus (21:12–15). His death (or non-death) leads to talk in the community (21:23). Indeed, he exemplifies the role of the insider. Closer to Jesus than Peter, he is able to ask questions (13:23; 21:20) and, as the implied author and authoritative witness of the Gospel (21:24), he receives answers which no one else understands (13:29). As a "member of the family," he is given the responsibility of Jesus' mother as a "son" (19:25–27). Unlike Peter, the beloved disciple does not need correction (13:6–9), convincing (20:8–9), or restitution (21:15–17). He does not deny Jesus at the point of death—as Peter does (18:15–18, 25–27)—but remains with Jesus throughout the crucifixion (19:25–27). The beloved disciple, though unnamed, enacts the ideal response expected from a disciple and the reader.[56]

Judas, on the other hand, is the negative counterpart to the ideal disciple. In fact, John 13 is threaded with comments and allusions to Judas that heighten the contrast between those who are with Jesus and those who are against him. In a series of five participles, the convoluted introduction to John 13:1–3 ties Jesus' fate, the disciples' role, and the Last Supper into one complex. It might be diagrammed thus:[57]

---

[56] Brown, *Gospel*, xciii–viii; Barrett, *Gospel*, 116–9; R. Bauckham, "The Beloved Disciple as Ideal Author," *JSNT* 49 (1993): 21–44; D. Beck, "The Narrative Function of Anonymity in Fourth Gospel Characterization," *Semeia* 53 (1991): 143–58; B. Byrne, "The Faith of the Beloved Disciple and the Community in John 20," *JSNT* 23 (1985): 83–97; O. Cullmann, *The Johannine Circle* (London: SCM, 1979), especially 2–5, 74–76; M. Pamment, "The Fourth Gospel's Beloved Disciple," *ET* 94 (1983): 363–7.

[57] Obviously awkward, my translation attempts to highlight the Greek structure.

a. Jesus knowing (εἰδώς) that his hour had come . . .
   b. loving (ἀγαπήσας) his own who were in the world to the end
      c. supper happening (γινομένου)
   b¹. the devil already having entered (βεβληκότος) the heart of Judas
a¹. knowing (εἰδώς) that the Father had given all things into his hands

This chiasmus illustrates the centrality of the meal narrative (c). It demonstrates how Jesus' knowledge (a-a¹) is seen to frame all that is to happen in the forthcoming narrative, even his own betrayal. It also makes the distinction clear between those who are for Jesus and those who are against him, that is, the contrast between those "whom Jesus loved to the end" and the one who betrayed him (b-b¹). This contrast continues to punctuate the remaining narrative. After Jesus washes the disciples' feet, he tells them, "You are clean, though not all of you" (13:10). Jesus' prescience is again emphasized in this context: "For he knew who was to betray him; for this reason he said, 'Not all of you are clean'" (13:11). At another point, Jesus tells the disciples that if they wash one another's feet, they will be blessed, *but not all of them*, i.e., Judas is excluded from participation in the mutual washing as well as from the resultant blessing (13:15–18). In fact, though he is one of the chosen Twelve (6:70, 71; 12:4), he will "lift his heel" against Jesus in betrayal (13:18). Judas thus serves as a negative foil to the ideal beloved disciple and to the questioning but zealous Peter, a counterpoint that highlights the appropriate response to Jesus (cf. 13:20).

Judas' role as the betrayer, insofar as he is the earthly agent responsible for Jesus' arrest (18:1–9), also extends to the realm of the spiritual. Judas is recognized as a devil in the words of Jesus in 6:70. According to 13:2, "the devil had already put it into the heart of Judas son of Simon Iscariot to betray (παραδοῖ) him." Thus, while the Father gave (ἔδωκεν from δίδωμι) all things into the hands of Jesus, Judas "gives Jesus over" (παραδοῖ from παρα-δίδωμι) to death. This is made possible, it seems, through the act of Jesus himself: he hands Judas a morsel of bread "and with it, Satan entered into him" (13:27). A closer look at this sequence is needed, given its use of ingesting language.

In John 13:18, the text states,

"I am not speaking to all of you; I know whom I have chosen. But it is to fulfill the scripture, 'The one who ate my bread had lifted his heel against me.'"

οὐ περὶ πάντων ὑμῶν λέγω ἐγὼ οἶδα τίνας ἐξελεξάμην ἀλλ' ἵνα ἡ γραφὴ πληρωθῇ,
'Ὁ τρώγων μου τὸν ἄρτον ἐπῆρεν ἐπ' ἐμὲ τὴν πτέρναν αὐτοῦ.

The scripture citation comes from Ps 40:10 (LXX), a psalm that compares the faithfulness of God and that of friends. At the time of his death, the enemies of the Psalmist "gather mischief" and hope for his demise.

Even the man of my peace in whom I trusted (ὁ ἄνθρωπος τῆς εἰρήνης μου ἐφ᾽ ὃν ἤλπισα), who ate of my bread, has lifted his heel against me. But you, O LORD, be gracious to me and raise me up, and I may repay them. By this, I know that you are pleased with me; because my enemy has not triumphed over me. Yet you have upheld me because of my integrity, and set me in your presence forever (Ps 40:10–13 LXX).

The key phrase in John 13:18 (with textual variants, see above), in Ps 40:10 (LXX), and in the BHS is given as follows:

John 13:18a   Ὁ τρώγων μου τὸν ἄρτον ἐπῆρεν ἐπ᾽ ἐμὲ τὴν πτέρναν αὐτοῦ.

John 13:18b   Ὁ τρώγων μετ᾽ ἐμοῦ τὸν ἄρτον ἐπῆρεν ἐπ᾽ ἐμε τὴν πτέρναν αὐτοῦ.

Ps 40:11   Ὁ ἐσθίων ἄρτους μου ἐμεγάλυνεν ἐπ᾽ ἐμὲ πτερνισμόν.

Ps 41:9   אוֹכֵל לַחְמִי הִגְדִּיל עָלַי עָקֵב׃

Several differences may be noted in the text. While the Hebrew and LXX use the more common word for "eating," John 13 uses the present active participle of τρώγω. We have seen a similar change in verb choice in John 6, where Jesus says, "Whoever eats (τρώγων) my flesh and drinks my blood has eternal life" (6:54). There, it appears to act as an intensification of the word "to eat" as it does also here. Second, the pronoun modifier μου ("of me") follows the noun in the LXX (and the Hebrew for that matter) but precedes it in John's variant a. As genitival modifiers usually follow their governing word, the place of μου before τὸν ἄρτον indicates some sort of emphasis in John; it is thus, "*my* bread."[58] Third, "bread" is plural in the LXX, but singular in the Hebrew and in John. The use of "bread" as both a plural and singular noun in John 6 suggests that this distinction is not important. Fourth, the Hebrew and LXX both use verbs that imply "making great," while John's word, ἐπῆρεν, has more of the sense of "lifting up." It is unclear whether this change is significant.[59] Fifth, as noted above, a strong variant reading has μετ᾽ ἐμοῦ rather than μου and given the context of John 13 as a meal narrative and a previous reference to having "a portion" with Jesus in 13:8, this is a more likely reading. Finally, "heel" is specified as "his heel" in John. Comparisons of these four texts highlight various components of the Gospel. In particular, the use of τρώγω recalls the declaration that one must eat Jesus' flesh in order to have eternal life. The variant reading of μου τὸν ἄρτον emphasizes the source of the bread as Jesus. The choice of this Psalm as a prophetic saying in the mouth of Jesus thus seems most apt. Like the Psalmist, Jesus is betrayed by a trusted friend, one of the

---

[58] See S. Porter, *Idioms of the Greek New Testament* (2d ed.; Sheffield: Sheffield Academic Press, 1999), 291–2; Daly-Denton, *David*, 198.

[59] See M. Menken, "The Translation of Psalm 41:10 in John 13:18," *JSNT* 40 (1990): 61–79.

Twelve who has shared his bread.[60]

The citation is meant as a prophetic saying in the mouth of Jesus: it is "to fulfill the scripture" (13:18). Jesus tells the disciples "before it happens," so that "when it happens," they might believe (13:19). The Gospel makes the prophecy more explicit: Jesus declares in a solemn statement, "Very truly I say to you, one of you will betray me" (13:21). To the beloved disciple (alone perhaps), Jesus reveals that the one who will betray him is the one to whom he gives a morsel (ψωμίον) after dipping it in a dish (13:26).[61] The next sentence describes this very action: Jesus gives the morsel to Judas.[62] Granted that the earlier prediction (the citation of the Psalm) refers to bread, the word ψωμίον in this prediction likely refers to bread also. After Judas receives this morsel, Satan enters him (13:27). Jesus tells Judas to do what he must do quickly (13:28). Judas goes out and it is night (13:30). The Gospel reveals later that Judas does indeed betray Jesus to the authorities (18:1–9). He is the one "destined to be lost" (17:12). In this way, the Gospel presents Jesus as one who knows all that is about to happen to him and who does, in fact, set it in motion. In contrast, Judas is a silent puppet.

The prediction and initiation of Judas' betrayal of Jesus are underscored by an ironic correspondence with John 6. In John 6, Jesus refers to himself as the "bread that comes down from heaven" (6:32, 35, 51). Whoever eats (τρώγων) this "bread," that is, Jesus' flesh, will not die (6:50–51, 53–56). Jesus urges people to seek this kind of bread, bread that satisfies hunger forever (6:35), rather than the bread that perishes (6:26). Here in John 13, however, Jesus gives (δίδωσιν) bread to someone to eat (τρώγειν), and with the bread, he also hands over his life (cf. 13:3).[63] This action sets into motion the events leading to Jesus' crucifixion which will, in turn, give life to all who believe. Yet in this case, rather than life entering Judas, Satan enters Judas (13:27). This irony underscores the importance of receiving Jesus (13:20): ingesting the physical food that Jesus offers is not enough. The "true bread" (6:55), that is belief in

---

[60] See J. Ramsey Michaels, "Betrayal and the Betrayer: The Uses of Scripture in John 13:18–19," in The Gospels and the Scriptures of Israel (JSNTSS 104; ed. C. A. Evans and W. Stegner; Sheffield: Sheffield Academic Press, 1994), 459–74. Michaels argues that this citation refers to the phenomenon of betrayal in general within the Christian community, and not specifically the betrayal of Judas.

[61] Into what was the morsel dipped? The use of βαπτίζω suggests water (see Lev 11:32; Num 19:18; Josh 3:15; Luke 16:24). Or was it oil (Lev 14:16; Deut 33:24)? Literal correspondence with Ruth 2:14 suggests that it was most likely sour wine.

[62] Some later mss have βάψας οὖν τὸ ψωμίον λαμβάνει καὶ δίδωσιν. The use of λαμβάνω echoes Eucharistic language (as in John 6:11 and 21:13), but a reference to the Eucharist is denied by most scholars. See Schnackenburg, Gospel, 3:30; Brown, Gospel, 575.

[63] Michaels ("Betrayal," 467) concludes that the verbal parallels are merely a matter of style and that they have no theological significance.

and faithfulness to Jesus, must be ingested, for it has a greater value.

As a consequence of his betrayal, Judas is "lost" (17:12). He goes into the night (13:30; cf. 18:3), rather than into the light (3:19–21; 9:5; 11:9–10; 12:35–36, 46). As one who moves in the night, he stumbles (11:10; cf. 18:6) and does not know where he is going (12:35); his deeds are evil (3:19–21). Although Judas is one of the Twelve, he is not one of the chosen (13:8): he is the one "destined to be lost" (17:12). He will receive death, not life (cf. 1:4).

Beginning in John 13, the Gospel focuses more acutely on the expected response of the disciples to Jesus than previously: the disciples are to follow the example of Jesus.[64] Jesus washes their feet as a sign both of the effectiveness of his death and of his humble service. Three disciples and their responses to Jesus are set forth. Peter does not hesitate to question Jesus. He acts impulsively and over-zealously but is open to correction. The beloved disciple, on the other hand, is the intimate of Jesus, the one who is there at Jesus' crucifixion, sees the empty tomb, and believes. Judas, certainly one of the twelve disciples, plays the role of the trusted-friend-turned-Satanic-agent who betrays Jesus. The directive teaching of Jesus through word and illustration and the examples of various responses serve to map out the expected response required of disciples who follow Jesus.

CONCLUSION

The Last Supper recounted in John 13 is the most well-developed meal narrative in the Gospel. In contrast to the Synoptic tradition, some details of the meal go unmentioned: we do not learn of an "upper room" in Jerusalem or the institution of the Eucharist, and there is no description of the food and drink. We do learn of the table posture (reclining) and, to some extent, the seating arrangements. The words and actions by the various participants are the focus of the narrative. Instead of eating, Jesus washes the disciples' feet. Instead of giving bread to all the disciples, Jesus gives bread only to Judas. Instead of eating a meal, the disciples are offered "a part with" Jesus. All this is set in the context of a final testament, the last, loving words of a man about to die.

The footwashing actions of Jesus can be interpreted as a symbolic enactment through which he lays down his life (garment) and then picks it up again. By performing this action in the midst of a meal, it is as though Jesus serves himself as "true food" to them through his death. The disciples can accept this or not. Those who believe that Jesus must die and that his death results in eternal life are able to eat "with Jesus." (Judas gets this part wrong.) Furthermore, to eat "with Jesus" is to follow his example, that is, to be prepared

---

[64] Dodd, *Interpretation*, 398–9.

to pass through death in order to enjoy the eschatological feast. This feast is anticipated in the footwashing and, elsewhere, in the miraculous meal events in John 2, 6, and 21. These soteriological statements are expressed through the ingesting motif.

THE VINE AND THE BRANCHES (JOHN 15:1–17)

In the midst of the extensive discourse that follows the footwashing, Jesus identifies himself as the vine, the disciples as the branches, and the Father as the vine-dresser. While strictly speaking this is an agricultural image, it is included in a discussion of the ingesting motif because it refers to the fruit that the disciples produce.

The narrative setting of this discourse is ambiguous. While it appears to be a part of the larger Farewell Discourse which begins in John 13:1, the last line of John 14 has Jesus say, "Rise let us be on our way" (14:31). The text records no response to these words, and the discourse continues with themes carried over from chapter 14. In particular, Jesus says, "I do as the Father has commanded me, so that the world may know that I love the Father" (14:31; cf. 15:9, 17). The visual imagery evoked with this agricultural metaphor of the vine might suggest, however, that Jesus and the disciples are outdoors rather than gathered around a table. Jesus does not pluck the fruit and eat it while walking as he does in similar Synoptic stories (Matt 12:1; Mark 2:23; Luke 6:1). Thus, rather than depending on its setting within a meal narrative, the ingesting motif focuses on the production of fruit.

In a series of metaphors, Jesus identifies himself as the vine, the Father as a vine-dresser, and the disciples as the branches. As the vine-dresser, the Father cares for the vine (Jesus): he takes off (αἴρει) branches that do not bear fruit and prunes or cleans (καθαίρει) the branches that do produce fruit so that they will produce more.[65] The Father is glorified when the branches produce fruit (15:8).[66] As the true vine,[67] Jesus loves the disciples and remains in them (15:5, 9); he also makes them clean (καθαροί)[68] by his word (15:3; cf. 13:10). As the branches, the disciples remain in Jesus (15:4) and thus bear fruit that will remain (15:16).

The notion of remaining or abiding (μένω) is significant in the Gospel of John. The word is introduced in John 1:38–39 when the disciples ask where

---

[65] Note the play of these two words. See Brown, *Gospel*, 660; Morris, *Gospel*, 669–70; Barrett, *Gospel*, 471; Dodd, *Interpretation*, 137.

[66] Jesus glorifies the Father by completing his work (17:4), just as Peter glorifies God by dying (21:19).

[67] Compare John 6:32, where Jesus is the true bread.

[68] The play of words is continued from 15:2.

Jesus is staying; they remain there with him. Elsewhere we are told that Jesus and the disciples remain in various locations (2:12; 4:40; 7:9; 10:40; 11:6, 54). The word "remain" has the sense of permanence in John 6:27 where Jesus compares food that perishes and food that remains for eternal life. This permanence is directly connected to a relationship with Jesus: those who eat the flesh of Jesus and drink his blood remain in Jesus and Jesus remains in them (6:56). Only true disciples remain in Jesus (8:31; cf. 15:8). In a similar way, the Father remains in Jesus (14:10) and Jesus remains in the Father (15:10). John 15:1–8 explores the benefits of remaining in Jesus. First, only those who remain in Jesus bear fruit (15:1, 4, 5, 7, 16). Second, they are "cleaned" by the Father and by the word that Jesus speaks (what he has heard from the Father, 15:15) so that they can produce even more fruit (15:2–3).[69] Third, they will receive whatever they ask from the Father (15:7, 16). Fourth, when disciples remain in Jesus, they obey the commandment (word) of Jesus and love one another (15:9, 10, 12, 17); in the same way, Jesus obeys and loves his Father (15:10). As a result, their joy will be complete (15:11). This love for others extends to the point of death; Jesus is the primary example of this kind of love (15:13; cf. 13:1–4). Finally, whoever remains in Jesus and loves others is called a friend and not a servant (15:14–15).[70] In contrast, those who do not remain in Jesus are like branches that wither and are thrown away; they are gathered, thrown into the fire, and burned (15:6).[71]

Those who remain in Jesus experience complete joy (15:11). Like the joy of the friend who hears the bridegroom coming (3:29) and the joy over the (eschatological) harvest (4:36), the disciples will rejoice in Jesus' love. In 16:16–24, Jesus predicts his death and tells his disciples that they will weep and mourn at first. Their pain, however, will be replaced with rejoicing when they see Jesus again. In this way, after Jesus' death and resurrection, joy is experienced as a salvific gift.[72]

Background for the image of the vine may be found in the Hebrew prophets. For example, Isaiah describes God building a special vineyard, hoping for grapes. When only wild grapes are produced, he destroys the vineyard. This vineyard is identified with Israel, a nation that produces bloodshed instead of justice (5:1–7; cf. 27:2–6; Jer 5:10; 12:10–11). Ezekiel describes the wood of the vine that is burned in the fire; it is useful for nothing. Again, the vine is identified as Israel (15:4–6, cf. 19:12). Israel's faithfulness is compared to a fruitful vine whose branches have also been pruned (Hos 10:1; 14:8 [7]; Jer 6:9;

---

[69] See R. Borig, *Der wahre Weinstock* (Munich: Kösel, 1967), 42.

[70] Jesus promises that the Father will give the disciples another advocate to abide with them forever (14:17).

[71] John 13:10–11, 21–30 says that Judas is not included among those who are clean.

[72] Brown, *Gospel*, 681.

Ezek 15:1–6; 17:5–10; 19:10–14; Ps 80: 9 [8]; *4 Ezra* 5:23). In all of these cases, the vine or the vineyard is equated with Israel and not with an individual. Ezekiel 17:5–10, however, does speak of a vine as an individual person. Other Johannine uses of Ezekiel suggest that this passage might serve as background.[73] By referring to Jesus, the metaphor of the "true vine" in John 15 suggests that Jesus replaces Israel as the beloved focus of God and as the locus of salvation (cf. 4:22).

CONCLUSION

John 15:1–17 defines the role of Jesus as a provider of food through the agency of the disciples. He sustains and provides life to the branches.[74] Without him, they can do nothing. Because of him, they can bear much fruit. The disciples' role is thus to remain in Jesus. They will produce more fruit because the Father prunes them.[75] This agricultural metaphor is relevant to the ingesting theme because it focuses on the role of the disciples in providing fruit for others, though the exact nature of the "fruit" is not given here.

---

[73] See Borig, *Weinstock*, 101. Cf. Dodd, *Interpretation*, 411.

[74] Bultmann (*Gospel*, 530) refers to Jesus as the "tree of life."

[75] P. Minear (*John: The Martyr's Gospel* [New York: Pilgrim, 1984], 84) suggests that the fruit of the branches are converts to Christianity. This seems unlikely in the light of the greater ingesting motif.

Chapter 7

First and Last Drink (19:28–30; 18:11)

In his definition of a literary motif, Freedman states that a motif will make a greater impact when it is used at the crisis point in the plot, especially when it seems to be out of place or is unnecessary.[1] This is certainly true of the ingesting motif in the Gospel of John. At the pinnacle of the plot, the moment in which Jesus dies, the ingesting motif is again evoked. This chapter looks at this moment of death and the last drink of Jesus.

The crucifixion of Jesus is the narrative climax in the Gospel of John. As early as John 1:11, the rejection of Jesus is anticipated. Recurring references speak of the plot to arrest and kill Jesus because of what he does (5:16–18; 9:1–41; 11:45–57; 12:9–11) and says (7:25–32; 8:12–59; 19:7) and because of the response of the people (12:9–11, 19). Punctuated throughout the narrative are references to Judas who hands Jesus over to his death (6:64, 71; 12:4; 13:2, 11, 18, 21, 26; 18:2–3). As the crucifixion approaches, the narrative pace slows; John 1–13 likely covers several years,[2] but John 13:1–19:16 covers only about one day. The narrative tension reaches its peak when the Jews clamor for Jesus to be crucified, shouting, "Away with him! Away with him! Crucify him!" (19:15). The crucifixion thus comes as the narrative climax.

In addition to these specific references to Jesus' death, the Gospel alludes to his death by recounting symbolic actions. For instance, Mary anoints Jesus' body for burial before he goes to his death (12:1–8), and Jesus lays down his garments to wash the disciples' feet as he will lay down his life for his friends (13:1–30). In addition, the Gospel uses metaphorical language to speak of Jesus' death. It waits for Jesus' "hour," anticipating his death when he is lifted up and/or glorified (2:4, 19–20; 7:30, 39; 8:56; 12:7, 16, 23, 27; 13:1, 31; 17:1, 4). The death of Jesus is thus central to the literary structure and concerns of the Gospel of John.

The death of Jesus also marks the completion of Jesus' work, that is, the work that his Father has sent him to do (4:34; 5:36; 9:4; 10:25–38; 14:10–12). The Gospel anticipates this completion throughout the last days of Jesus' life. When the hour has come for him to pass from this world to the Father, Jesus

---

[1] Freedman, "Motif," 126–7.
[2] Several different Passovers are mentioned.

loves his own to the end—or completely (εἰς τέλος)—and demonstrates his love by symbolically enacting his death and resurrection (13:1–30). In a final prayer anticipating his departure in 17:4, Jesus says that he glorifies the Father by finishing (τελειώσας) the work he has been given to do. Then, on the cross (19:28–30), when Jesus knows that all things have been finished (τετέλεσται), he says, in order to fulfill (τελειωθῇ) the scripture (Ps 69:21; 22:15), "I thirst." After he drinks, he says, "It is finished" (τετέλεσται) and dies. (Note that verbs with the τελ- root are used three times in these three short verses.) Thus, Jesus completes both the plan of scripture and the work of his Father on the cross when he dies.[3]

The Gospel stresses that Jesus goes to his death intentionally; he knows everything and is not a hapless victim caught up in some twist of fate (e.g., 6:64, 70–71; 10:17–18; 13:11, 18–19, 21–30; 16:30; 18:2–10, 34–37; 19:9, 11, 26–27). At the Last Supper, for example, Jesus knows (εἰδώς) that his hour has come to depart from this world and go to the Father (13:1). Before his arrest, he knows (εἰδώς) all that is to happen to him (18:4). Now here on the cross, Jesus knows (εἰδώς) that all is completed, so in order to fulfill the scripture, he says, "I thirst."[4] In short, Jesus' expression of thirst reflects his knowledge of the situation and his willingness to complete all things according to the plan of the Father.

Although Jesus' thirst may be understood as a physical need and, indeed, the soldiers respond to him as if it is a sincere request for a drink and give him vinegar, it may also be understood as a spiritual need. The request for a drink refers back to the cup mentioned in 18:11 when Jesus says, "Am I not to drink the cup that the Father has given me?" The image of the cup of God has its precedent in the Psalms and the prophets. On the one hand, the "LORD's portion and cup" is a pleasant thing that gives life (Ps 16:6; cf. 23:5; 116:3). On the other hand, the cup of the LORD is a metaphor for the wrath of God poured out on those who are disobedient (Ps 11:6; Jer 16:7; 25: 15–28; 49:12; Lam 4:21; Ezek 23:31–34; Hab 2:16; cf. Pss. Sol. 8:14). In Isaiah 51:17–23, God says that he has taken "the cup of staggering" from Israel's hand and given it to Israel's tormentors instead. Isaiah sees the cup of God as both an instrument of punishment and an instrument of destruction, but underlying both is the necessity of suffering and the promise of restoration. This is the sense of John 18:11: to drink the cup means to face suffering and death. Jesus is willing to

---

[3] Brown, *Gospel*, 908.

[4] Although the ἵνα clause may refer grammatically to that which precedes it or to that which follows, most commentators take the clause with the following, "Jesus said, 'I thirst.'" Compare the similar use in 1:31; 14:31; 19:31. G Delling ("τέλος κτλ.," *TDNT* 8.82 n.16) argues that the purpose clause precedes the main clause in order to stress its importance. See L. T. Witkamp, "Jesus' Thirst in John 19:28–30: Literal or Figurative?" *JBL* 115 (1996): 494.

face death because he knows that he will be restored. Thus, Jesus' request for a drink reflects his spiritual thirst, a thirst that can be satisfied by laying down his life and returning to the Father.[5]

The choice of vinegar is strange here and may be dependent on Ps 69:21, a psalm that is culled for images and citations throughout the Gospel (see Ps 69:9 and John 2:17; Ps 69:4 and John 15:25). Hodges argues that the vinegar, like a poison, causes Jesus' death, because Jesus as a man "from above" has ingested substances from the earth.[6] This argument is unconvincing, however, because the Gospel claims crucifixion as the cause of death, the marks of which are used as proof of his death to the disciples and to Thomas after his resurrection (20:20, 25, 27).[7] In contrast to Hodges, Witkamp claims that the "vinegar" is really water to which vinegar has been added to keep it fresh in a hot climate. He concludes that Jesus' expression of thirst is a figurative way of saying that Jesus longed to complete the will of God (based on similar use in Ps 42:2–3 and 63:2 in combination with 69:9).[8] One wonders, however, why John would not have used the word "water" (ὕδωρ) if this is actually meant. The correct interpretation is probably somewhere in between; it is probably neither poison nor a refreshing drink. On the one hand, the drink does coincide with Jesus' death and so may appear to be life-taking. On the other hand, Jesus' death enables life for those who believe in him, so the vinegar is ultimately—and ironically—life-giving.

Irony is also present in the expression of Jesus' thirst. In John 4:10–14, he offers living water that will quench thirst forever.[9] In John 7:37–39, he again offers living water to all that thirst. Jesus says this: "Let anyone who is thirsty come to me, and let the one who believes in me drink. As the scripture has said, 'Out of his heart shall flow rivers of living water.'" The narrator explains that Jesus is talking about the spirit, which believers would receive after his death.

---

[5] See Brown, *Gospel*, 930; Witkamp, "Thirst," 489–510; S. Moore, *Literary Criticism and the Gospels: The Theoretical Challenge* (New Haven: Yale University Press, 1989), 159–70; R. Brawley, "An Absent Complement and Intertextuality in John 19:28–29," *JBL* 112 (1993): 427–43; Daly-Denton, *David*, 220–221.

[6] Hodges, "Food," 612–67. The Gospel implies a negative comparison between the delicious wine (οἶνος) provided in 2:1–11 and this vinegar (ὄχος).

[7] The Gospel of Peter describes the mixture of gall and vinegar as if it were a poison to hasten death (16).

[8] "Thirst," 494.

[9] The death of Jesus is connected to his encounter with the Samaritan woman at five points. First, Jesus says that he is thirsty (4:7; 19:28). Second, both events occur at noon (4:6; 19:14). Third, Jesus is described as a source for a flow of water (4:13; 19:34). Fourth, Jesus is engaged in finishing the work of God (4:34; 19:30). Fifth, the event has an eye-witness who testifies about Jesus, thus bringing others to belief (4:39; 19:35), as one who speaks the truth (4:18; 19:35).

In other words, the life-giving water is really the spirit that comes from Jesus after his death. The two ideas of water and spirit are brought together again in the crucifixion scene. At his death, Jesus bows his head and "gives up the spirit" (19:30); then, a soldier pierces his side and blood and water flow out (19:34). The flow of water (and blood) is again associated with the spirit. John 19:30–34 may, in fact, fulfill the prediction made in 7:37–39.[10] Though the Greek word, πνεῦμα, is the same in both John 7 and 19, the release of the spirit in John 19 seems to refer to the life-force that animates Jesus' flesh and not the Holy Spirit that is promised to believers in John 7.[11] Indeed, the Holy Spirit is explicitly given to the disciples in John 20:22: Jesus "breathed on them, and said, 'Receive the Holy Spirit.'" The release of the spirit and the water (and blood) in 19:30 thus seems to anticipate the gift of the Holy Spirit that would follow the resurrection.[12] Therefore, Jesus is understood to be a source of life-giving water (= spirit) at the very moment of his death; his request for a drink is thus ironic.[13]

Water is also associated with baptism and cleansing in the Gospel. John baptizes with water, but his baptism is surpassed by Jesus' baptism with the Holy Spirit (1:26, 31, 33; cf. 3:5). In the Wedding in Cana story, Jesus has the jars used for purification rites filled to the brim with water. He then turns this "cleansing" water into choice wine that is ingested (2:1–11). The blind man, whose blindness is attributed to sin by others (9:2, 34; cf. 9:40–41), receives his sight when Jesus sends him to wash the mud from his eyes with water (9:1–41). Water alone is not sufficient for healing, however, as the story of the lame man attests; Jesus, not the water, is the source of healing (John 5). At the Last Supper, Jesus washes the feet of the disciples to make them completely clean (13:1–30), but it is really his word and not the water that cleans them (15:3; cf. 1:1). Thus, in one sense, the water that flows from Jesus' dead body may be

---

[10] See Minear (*John*, 75–76); Bultmann, *Gospel*, 764, n.2.

[11] The blood and water are evidence of Jesus' corporeal death, refuting docetic Christianity. See, for example, G. Richter, *Studien zum Johannesevangelium* (Regensburg: Fredrich Pustet, 1977), 120–142. Cf. 1 John 5:6; Irenaeus, *adv. Haer.* 3.22.2).

[12] Hoskyns (*Fourth*, 532) proposes that Jesus gives the Holy Spirit to those present at the cross at the time of his death. More likely, it confirms that Jesus' spirit is available at death and anticipates the more precise giving of the Spirit in 20:22 (so Brown, *Gospel*, 931; Barrett, *Gospel*, 554; Beasley-Murray, *John*, 353).

[13] Many commentators argue (with more or less conviction) that the flow of water and blood from Jesus' side represents the institution of baptism and the Eucharist (e.g., Brown, *Gospel*, 913; Bultmann, *Gospel*, 678; E. Malatesta, "Blood and Water from the Pierced Side of Christ (John 19:34)," in *Segni e sacramenti nel Vangelio di Giovanni* (Roma: Editrice Anselmiana, 1977), 176; cf. Morris, *Gospel*, 820; Cullmann, *Worship*, 115. Barrett (*Gospel*, 557) argues that the sacramental reference is secondary to the fact that "the real death of Jesus was the real life of men." For a survey of arguments and Patristic citations, see Malatesta, "Blood," 171–81.

understood to have cleansing properties.[14]

Likewise, the outpouring of blood recalls earlier allusions to Jesus' death in the Gospel narrative. Given the strong Passover motif throughout the Gospel, the most likely point of reference is to the blood of the paschal lamb that is wiped on the doorposts to protect Israel from the angel of death. Like the paschal lamb, Jesus here sheds his blood to save from death those who believe (1:29, 36). Moreover, the bystanders offer vinegar to Jesus on a hyssop branch. Although the botanical identification of hyssop is uncertain today, 1 Kgs 4:33 describes it as a plant that grows on a wall. It was more likely a flexible vine than a rigid reed, and thus would be unsuitable to hold and extend a heavily laden sponge.[15] However, hyssop has theological importance that has a bearing on this passage, for it was used to smear the blood of the paschal lamb on the doorposts and lintels (Exod 12:22). Other paschal references, such as the absence of broken bones and the hour of Jesus' death, support this allusion.[16]

The letting of Jesus' blood also looks back to an earlier Passover in the Gospel narrative. In the Bread of Life discourse, Jesus makes this unconditional statement: "Unless you eat the flesh of the Son of Man and drink his blood, you have no life in you; whoever eats my flesh and drinks my blood has eternal life, and I will raise him up on the last day" (6:53–54). Jesus' blood is called "true drink" (6:55). As Jesus sheds his blood on the cross, then, he makes the way possible for believers to drink this "true drink" and to gain eternal life. In this way, both the water (chapter 7) and the blood (chapter 6) are understood to be life-giving drinks.[17]

THE ROLE OF THE DISCIPLES

The narrative focuses on the events of Jesus' trial and death. Nonetheless, several disciples serve as witnesses to his death. These include Jesus' mother

---

[14] Barrett (*Gospel*, 557) argues that Zech 13:1 lies behind the citation of John 7:37–39 and thus makes explicit the cleansing action of the "fountain opened for the house of David and the inhabitants of Jerusalem."

[15] Brown, *Gospel*, 909; Barrett, *Gospel*, 552. It is unlikely that ὑσσώπῳ has taken the place of ὑσσῷ (javelin or spear), a reading found in an 11th C. mss (476) and a 13th C. mss (1242). Based on the description of hyssop in *m. Parah* 12:1, F. G. Beetham and P. A. Beetham ("A Note on John 19:29," *JTS* 44 [1993]: 163–9) suggest that the hyssop was bound to a reed to give it substance. (The term "hyssop" is a metonymy used to describe the combination of the two.) The reed separates the handler from impurity, in the case of John 19, from corpse impurity. Brawley ("Intertextuality," 433–4) cites this as an example of "ungrammaticality" (or a conflict with normal reality) that drives interpretation to a metaphorical level.

[16] Brown, *Gospel*, 930.

[17] Minear, *John*, 76–77; Barrett, *Gospel*, 557.

and her sister, Mary the wife of Clopas, and Mary Magdalene. Apparently, the disciple whom Jesus loved is also present (19:25–26). From the cross, Jesus gives his mother over to the care of the beloved disciple (19:27). It is also likely the beloved disciple who witnesses the soldier piercing Jesus' side (19:35; cf. 21:24).[18] The pace of the narrative slows dramatically at this point. The narrator confirms the reliability of the witness: "his testimony is true, and he knows that he tells the truth" (19:35). Then two scripture passages are recalled, the first that no bones will be broken (cf. Ps 34:20; Exod 12:46; Num 9:12) and the second that "they will look on the one whom they have pierced" (19:36–37; cf. Zech 12:10). The witnesses, including the reader, gaze on Jesus for three full verses.

The narrator emphasizes the moment of Jesus' death by addressing the reader directly, saying that the witness testifies to these things so that "you also may believe" (19:35). The content of this belief is Jesus' death. Later, the narrator tells the reader that the Gospel is written so that "you may come to believe that Jesus is the Messiah, the Son of God, and that through believing you may have life in his name" (20:31). The content of belief in this latter citation is extended to include the identity of Jesus. Thus, the role of the disciples and by extension the readers is to come to believe in the death of Jesus and in his identity as the Messiah and Son of God. They respond to this belief by testifying to the things that they have seen. As we will see in John 21, this is understood as feeding others.

CONCLUSION

The Gospel of John constantly looks ahead to the death of Jesus as the event that will complete the work that the Father sent Jesus to do. Jesus does not go to his death unwillingly; instead, he moves steadily towards the cross in full knowledge of what will happen and in ultimate control. At the moment of his death, he fulfills the scriptures by expressing his thirst; he takes a drink and dies. Though it seems ironic that Jesus, who is able to provide living water, now expresses thirst, the Gospel speaks of a higher, spiritual thirst, namely, to do the work of the Father.

Despite John's frequent use of meal narratives and ingesting language, Jesus explicitly ingests something by mouth only once—at his death. Though his disciples offer him food to eat while in Samaria, Jesus says, "I have food to eat that you do not know about" (4:32). When the disciples question him further, he

---

[18] Barrett, *Gospel*, 557. Minear (*John*, 70–73) argues that the soldier who pierced Jesus is the one who testifies to what he has seen for he would be in a better position to observe the events.

tells them that his food is to do the will of God and to complete his work (4:34). As we see above, this work is to go to his death. It is fitting, therefore, that Jesus takes a drink when his work is complete, at the moment of his death.[19] This action, however, makes it possible for others to eat and drink that which Jesus offers, namely, eternal life.

Freedman points out that a motif has greater impact if it dominates climactic moments.[20] At the absolute pinnacle of the Gospel's plot, the ingesting motif again appears. The terse and final words of Jesus, "I thirst," emphasize the centrality of relationship between Jesus' death and the ingesting motif.

---

[19] Brown, *Gospel*, 929.
[20] "Freedman, "Motif," 127.

Chapter 8

Resurrection Breakfast (21:1–25)

The final chapter of this study addresses the final narrative in the Gospel of John, the Resurrection Breakfast. It is included in this study for obvious reasons. The narrative setting is explicitly a meal, and food is variously described, specified, and eaten. Again, the ingesting motif appears at a significant point in the narrative, in this case, at the Gospel's conclusion.

In John 21, seven of the disciples go to Galilee to fish. They fish all night but catch nothing. As the day begins, Jesus appears on the shore and directs them to cast their net on the other side of the boat. They do so and net such a large number of fish that they have trouble hauling their catch to shore. The beloved disciple then recognizes Jesus, and Peter swims to shore.[1] When the other disciples follow, they find fish and bread cooking over a charcoal fire. They add some of their own fish and eat breakfast with Jesus. After breakfast, Jesus asks Peter to feed and tend his sheep. Then he predicts the death of both Peter and the beloved disciple. In the closing words of the Gospel, the testimony of the beloved disciple is authenticated.

The narrative itself follows the usual pattern of a miracle story: the expression of a need, intervention, and the reaction of the participants.[2] We see this pattern in the Wedding in Cana: the wine runs out, Jesus turns water into wine, the steward is pleased, and the disciples believe. In the Feeding of the Multitude, the need for food arises, Jesus multiplies the bread and fish, and the people eat and believe. In the story of John 21, the disciples have no success fishing all night. Jesus intervenes, the disciples do as they are instructed and they catch a netful of fish. In response, the disciples know that it is the Lord who has appeared to them and has instructed them.

Some scholars believe that John 21 is an addendum to the rest of the Gospel.[3]

---

[1] S. Agourides ("The Purpose of John 21," in *Studies in the History and Text of the New Testament—in Honor of K. W. Clark* [ed. B. Daniels and M. Suggs; Salt Lake City: University of Utah, 1967], 128) argues that Peter's swim through the water alludes to his repentance and subsequent washing.

[2] Luke 5:1–11 tells a similar story of a miraculous catch of fish and the call of Peter but places it at the beginning of Jesus' ministry rather than after his crucifixion.

[3] For a survey of this question, see H. Drumwright Jr., "The Appendix to the Fourth Gospel," in *The Teacher's Yoke* (ed. L. Vardaman, et al: Waco: Baylor, 1964), 129–34; Morris,

This conclusion is based on two principal factors. First, the Gospel appears to conclude at 20:30–31: "Now Jesus did many other signs in the presence of his disciples, which are not written in this book. But these are written so that you may come to believe that Jesus is the Messiah, the Son of God, and that through believing you may have life in his name." The account in John 21 seems to be added as an after-thought. Second, chapter 21 is not closely connected to chapters 1–20 and can be read quite apart from them. For these two reasons, many scholars conclude that John 21 is an appendix, epilogue, or correction and that it should be treated separately from the rest of the Gospel.

Others scholars argue that John 21 is a part of the original Gospel. For example, Paul Minear[4] points out that there is no manuscript evidence to suggest that chapters 1–20 circulated without chapter 21.[5] Nor are there significant grammatical or lexical differences between chapters 1–20 and 21.[6] On the basis of this evidence, Minear proposes that the concluding statement in 20:30–31 applies only to the preceding chapter (i.e., chapter 20) and not to the entire Gospel. Thus, the "signs" mentioned in 20:30 refer, not necessarily to the miracles in John 1–12, but to the "signs" of Jesus' resurrection found in John 20: the empty tomb seen first by Mary (20:1–2), and then by Peter and the beloved disciple (20:3–10); the appearance of Jesus to Mary (20:11–18), then to the ten disciples behind locked doors (20:19–23), and then again to the disciples with Thomas (20:24–29). Therefore, he argues, John 20:30–31 does not conclude the Gospel, only chapter 20. Minear provides other reasons for including John 21 in the Gospel. Narrative strands connect chapter 21 in significant ways to the first 20 chapters of the Gospel. For example, chapter 21 finishes the stories of Nathanael (1:45–51; 21:2), Peter, and the beloved disciple.[7] It also continues themes that are developed throughout the Gospel, such as discipleship, the

---

Gospel, 858; Barrett, Gospel, 576–7; Brown, Gospel, 1077–85; D. M. Smith, The Composition and Order of the Fourth Gospel (New Haven: Yale University Press, 1965); M. Goguel, "Did Peter Deny His Lord? A Conjecture," HTR 25 (1932): 1–27. Because of the "clumsy" addition and some "differences in outlook," Barrett (Gospel, 576) argues that chapter 21 was added. Brown (Gospel, 1081) argues that it was earlier material incorporated into the Gospel later. See S. Smalley, "The Sign in John 21," NTS 20 (1974): 275–88. Bultmann (Gospel, 700–702) claims that there is no need for a third appearance story after 20:29.

[4] P. Minear, "The Original Functions of John 21," JBL 102 (1983): 85–98.
[5] Chapter 21 is found in the earliest manuscripts, including p66 and Tertullian.
[6] Barrett (Gospel, 576–7) lists words found in John 21 that are absent in John 1–20 and concludes that they do not serve as sufficient evidence that chapter 21 was written by a different author.
[7] Minear ("Functions," 85–98) suggests that they returned to Galilee (20:10) and were not present with the other disciples "behind locked doors" (20:19).

dualism of light and dark, and martyrdom.[8] The three denials of Peter in John 18 are balanced by the three questions of Jesus to Peter—"Do you love me?"—in John 21:15–17. Minear concludes that John 21 is an integrated part of the Gospel as a whole and an interpretation of the chapter should reflect this unity. Serge Besobrasoff rightly confirms that John 21 cannot be understood unless it is read in the context of the whole Gospel, drawing on themes introduced elsewhere (e.g., 10:1–18; 13:31; 17:1; 12:33; 18:32).[9] Needless to say, this study includes John 21 in its survey of the ingesting motif.

Scholars are equally divided over the unity of the narrative within John 21 itself, especially when they posit various redactive hands.[10] According to Raymond Brown, the strongest argument against the internal unity of John 21 is the shift in symbols from fish to sheep; these two symbols likely stem from separate traditions, he concludes.[11] Additionally, the narrative of John 21:1–14 has awkward plot anomalies. For instance, Jesus asks the disciples for some fish, but he already has some cooking on the fire (21:9–10); the beloved disciple and Peter recognize Jesus, but the other disciples later seem dubious (21:7, 12). These anomalies suggest to scholars that John 21:1–14 represents two or more narrative strands woven together into one, such as a Resurrection Breakfast story and a Miraculous Catch of Fish story. Rudolf Bultmann suggests that a redactor added the information about Peter and the beloved disciple in order to establish appropriate authority in the early church.[12] Wiarda, on the other hand, argues that the narrative of John 21 is held together by a concern for the development of Peter's role.[13] Peter's name heads the list of disciples, and it is his decision to go fishing (21:2–3), an activity that does not reflect either his previous employment (which the Gospel does not mention) or the mission Jesus has given the disciples

---

[8] J. Staley says that "we tend to want the text, the story to end at 20:30–31, with what seems to be a 'mouthy confession' of who Jesus is. But in fact, the story goes on, beyond 'mouthing the words' to 'what's that to you? You follow me!' That is, it is only when the 'confession' is linked to 'following' that the story can end (or, really begin). . . . From my reading of John, the rhetorical structure of Johannine 'signs' makes it highly unlikely that the 'author' could have ever thought John 20:30–31 was an adequate ending to the book." Email to Johannine List Serve, March 31, 2000. Smalley ("Sign," 275–88) agrees that John 21 is an epilogue but argues, nonetheless, that it both follows consistent Gospel patterns (statement, sign, witness) and develops messianic titles. It points both to Jesus' incarnation (the material details) and the resurrection (a post-resurrection meal). For this reason, it should not be excluded from a study of the Gospel.

[9] S. Besobrasoff, "John 21," *NTS* 3 (1956–1957): 132–6.

[10] For a discussion and survey of this question, see T. Wiarda, "John 21:1–23: Narrative Unity and Its Implications," *JSNT* 46 (1992): 53–71.

[11] *Gospel*, 1084. See also F. Neirynck, "John 21," *NTS* 36 (1990): 321–36.

[12] *Gospel*, 701–2. See Brown, *Gospel*, 1082; B. Bacon, "The Motivation of John 21:15–25," *JBL* 50 (1931): 71–80.

[13] "Narrative Unity," 55–71.

(12:25–26; 15:15–16, 27; 17:18, 20; 20:21). Peter actively responds to the miracle and Jesus' presence by jumping in the water (21:7). He reacts to a series of questions (21:15–17). He is confronted with a predicament and a command (21:18–19) and receives a rebuke (21:21–22). The chapter is also tied together by the continued presence of Peter, the beloved disciple, and Jesus. Accepting the view that John 21 is a unified narrative, this study will address the chapter as a whole.

The setting of John 21 is the Sea of Tiberias and, as such, evokes other feeding miracles in this Gospel. Cana, where the water was turned into wine, is in Galilee not far from the sea; the Feeding of the Multitude, followed by the Walking on the Water and the Bread of Life discourse, is centered explicitly on or by the Sea of Tiberias. By locating this narrative on the same lake, the Gospel invites comparison with the other narratives that occur in Galilee. For example, the role of the disciples develops from gatherers in John 4 and 6 to providers in John 21. (This will be explored fully below.) By locating the feeding miracles on the same lake, the Gospel also implies that Galilee is an important location for "ingesting Jesus," that is, for "coming to belief."[14] The Miraculous Catch of Fish thus takes its place comfortably on the Sea of Tiberias.

In John 21, the temporal setting is also mentioned, albeit briefly, as "after these things." This phrase is used in the Gospel five times to introduce a new narrative (3:22; 5:1; 6:1; 7:1; 21:1). The episode is described as "the third time that Jesus appeared to the disciples after he was raised from the dead" (21:14). There are, in fact, three previous appearances of the resurrected Jesus recounted in the Gospel: Jesus appears to Mary (20:11–18), to all disciples except Thomas (20:19–23), and to the disciples and Thomas a week later (20:24–29). If the encounter with Mary does not constitute "an appearance to the disciples [plural]," then this appearance in Galilee makes the third time Jesus appeared to the disciples after his death. Whereas the first two sightings take place on the first day of the week (Sunday), the day of the week is not specified in John 21. However, the time of the day is specified: the disciples go out to fish during the night and Jesus appears to them "just after daybreak."[15]

Jesus is often associated with the coming of light in the Gospel of John. Jesus is, indeed, the light that has come into the world (1:4, 9; 3:19; 12:35, 46). Those

---

[14] Brown (Gospel, 1094) explains this pattern by claiming that the Galilean meal narratives of bread and fish come from a separate tradition. See Meeks, "Galilee," 159–69.

[15] John 21:4. K. Cardwell ("The Fish on the Fire," ET 102 [1990]: 12–14) claims that the use of gematria to interpret the number 153 (i.e., the number of the fish caught) reveals the word, "day" (ἡμέρα). "Day" is used as a title for Jesus in the early church (e.g., Justin, Dialogues C, 4) and is associated with the appearance of the Logos in creation by Philo (Alleg. Interp. 1.21). Thus Jesus appears as the day dawns or Jesus is, in fact, the "day" appearing.

who believe in the light (i.e., Jesus) are children of light (12:36, 46), and they "do what is true" (3:21); they do not stumble in the darkness (8:12; 11:9–10; cf. 12:35; 13:30). In John 21, the disciples do not catch anything during the night, but when Jesus comes and "as the light began," they catch many fish (21:4–21; cf. 6:16). When they are in the presence of the light, i.e., Jesus, they receive abundantly.

The Miraculous Catch evokes two biblical passages. The first is the creation story in Genesis. There, too, the light comes into being (Gen 1:3; cf. John 1:4, 9; 3:19; 12:35, 46; 21:4), the waters teem with living things (Gen 1:20–21; cf. John 21:6), and dry land appears (Gen 1:9; cf. John 21:8–9).[16] The second passage, which possibly draws from Genesis 1, is Ezekiel 47:1–10. On a tour of the heavenly temple, Ezekiel sees water that gathers into a river flowing out from underneath the temple (cf. John 7:37–39). Wherever the river goes, living things swarm, especially many fish "of a great many kinds, like the fish (ἰχθύες, as in 21:6, 8, 11) of the Great Sea." On the banks of the river, people will stand (ἵστημι, as in 21:4) and fish (ἁλιεύω, as in 21:3). The point of the passage in Ezekiel is that, where God dwells, the waters teem with life. In John 21, where Jesus is, the waters also teem with life. The Miraculous Catch of Fish thus suggests the presence of the divine.

The multiplication of fish also recalls the feeding miracle in John 6. There, the multiplication of the fish evokes the lament of Moses that he would not find enough fish to feed all the people (Num 11:22). In John 21, however, the "enemy" is not the wilderness, nor the distance from home, nor the lack of money to buy food; the "enemy" is collectively the night, the sea and the disciples' ignorance. With the advent of Jesus come day, many fish, and knowledge.

Three separate words are used to refer to *fish* in this passage. First, those fish that are held in the net are referred to as ἰχθύς (21:6, 8, 11), the same word used in the LXX for the fish in Ezekiel 47. Second, the fish lying on the fire (21:9), ready for the fire (21:10), or distributed by Jesus (21:13) are called ὀψάριον. This is the same word used for the fish distributed by Jesus in the Feeding of the Multitude story (6:9, 11). Most likely, ἰχθύς refers to live fish and ὀψάριον refers to fish that are prepared for eating.[17] Third, Jesus' question from the shore to the disciples in the boat, "Children, you have no fish, have you?" (21:5), uses the word προσφάγιον, translated here as "fish" because of the context, but used

---

[16] These events occur on the first, fifth, and third days respectively. Is this a possible solution to the age-old question of the meaning of the number 153 in John 21:11?

[17] A. Pitta ("Ichthys ed opsarion in Gv 21:1–14: semplice variazione lessicale o differenza con valore simbolico?" *Biblica* 71 [1990]: 348–64) argues that ὀψάριον refers simply to the material fish; ἰχθύς refers to the redeemed who enter the unbroken net.

elsewhere in Greek texts to refer to a type of relish for bread.[18] The word itself may be broken down loosely into προς- ("in addition to") and -φάγιον ("eating"). Used only once in the New Testament, that is, in John 21:5, the word choice suggests that the food Jesus asks about, προσφάγιον, refers to food that is over and above the daily requirement.[19] It is food that makes ordinary fare more interesting and delicious; it enhances the flavor. Like the water that is turned into superior wine to the delight of the steward, the relish that Jesus seeks is a welcome addition to the feast.

The distribution of the food by Jesus also evokes the Feeding of the Multitude narrative in John 6. In John 6, Jesus "took the loaves, and when he had given thanks, he distributed them to those who were seated; so also the fish, as much as they wanted" (6:11). In John 21, "Jesus comes and takes the bread and gives it to them, and does the same with the fish" (21:13). These two passages have in common the following words: "Jesus," "take" (λαμβάνω), "bread" (ἄρτος), "distribute/give" (δια-δίδωμι), "fish" (ὀψάριον), and "likewise" (ὁμοίως). In both stories, Jesus distributes first the bread and then the fish to those present. Several differences should be noted, however. In the Feeding of the Multitude narrative in John 6, the verbs are in the aorist tense (completed action in the past). In the final narrative in John 21, the verbs are in the present tense. Most translators identify this as a historical present and thus give it the simple past tense in English, but this English translation loses the nuances of vivid and dramatic Greek storytelling that places the reader into the narrative action.[20] In that sense, the narrative lives on in the present. Secondly, in John 6 the bread is plural, but in John 21 it is singular (21:9, 13). As we have noted previously, the plural form of this noun appears only with reference to the Feeding of the Multitude account (6:5, 7, 9, 11, 13, 26). The singular noun is used consistently throughout the Bread of Life discourse, a discourse that refers to Jesus metaphorically as the "bread that comes down from heaven." It is used to refer to the bread which Jesus "hands over" to Judas (13:26), and again in this final narrative. It might be safe to assume, therefore, that the use of the singular noun has symbolic meaning that goes beyond the simple foodstuff and refers, in fact, to Jesus. Furthermore, in the Feeding of the Multitude story in John 6, the miracle occurs as Jesus distributes the bread and fish and is seen only after people are satisfied and the remnants are collected. In John 21, however, the miracle is evident with the catch of fish, and the meal is the outcome of the miracle already completed. In the same way, the miracle of Jesus' resurrection

---

[18] *Proverbia Aesopi* 98 P; POxy. 498, 33, 39; 736, 46; 89; 739, 7; 10; 12; 14; *BGU* 916, 22, etc. Bauer, *Lexicon*, 719.

[19] Cf. Brown, *Gospel*, 1071.

[20] J. Brooks and C. Winbery, *Syntax of New Testament Greek* (London: University Press of America, 1979), 87–88.

has already occurred, and the disciples now have an opportunity to eat the bread that has come down from heaven directly from the source. Jesus is again understood to be both the provider and the substance of the food that gives eternal life, confirmed by his presence after his resurrection.

THE ROLE OF THE DISCIPLES

In the narrative of the Miraculous Catch, the disciples have a larger role to play than in the other food and drink miracles. In the Wedding in Cana (2:1–12), the disciples are present but not as participants; their response is noted only as silent belief.[21] In the Feeding of the Multitude story (6:1–15), Andrew, one of the disciples, brings a small boy to Jesus with his five loaves and two fish. The disciples are instructed to have the people recline, Jesus distributes the food, and the disciples gather up what is leftover. Their role is relatively minor. In this final miracle concerning food and drink, the disciples are more active. They attempt to gather food themselves but are unsuccessful without the direction or presence of Jesus. They follow his instructions, but unlike the Feeding of the Multitude story, they are more actively involved in the miracle. They are "directed workers."[22] Their success, furthermore, depends on the participation of Simon Peter.

The word used to describe the action of the disciples is "draw" (ἕλκω), translated in the NRSV as "haul" (21:6, 11). This word is significant because it connects the various actions of Jesus to those of the disciples. In John 6:44, the word is used to describe what the Father does: he draws people to Jesus. "No one can come to me unless drawn by the Father who sent me." John 12:32 indicates that the occasion for drawing people is Jesus' own death: Jesus says, "I, when I am lifted up, I will draw all people to myself." Now, in John 21:6, the disciples are enlisted in the "drawing" of the fish, but they were "unable to draw in [the net]" because there are too many fish. They need Peter to help them: "Simon Peter went aboard and 'drew' the net ashore, full of large fish" (21:11). Given the use of ἕλκω elsewhere in the Gospel, it is possible that the fish

---

[21] The disciples are not mentioned in certain other miracle stories, such as the healing of the official's son (4:46–54) and the healing of the lame man (5:1–18). They are non-participant observers of the walking on the water (6:16–21) and the healing of the blind man (9:1–12).

[22] See also E. McDowell, "Lovest Thou Me? A Study of John 21:15–17," *RE* 32 (1935): 422–41. Only seven disciples are named here, rather than twelve (6:67), and included are Peter, Nathanael, Thomas, the sons of Zebedee, and two other disciples (21:2). Though they are mentioned elsewhere in the Gospel, this list does not include Philip or Andrew (1:40, 43; 6:7–8; 12:22), the other Judas (14:22), or the beloved disciple (but see vs. 7). The identity of the "two other disciples" is unknown.

symbolize people.[23] Therefore, the role of the disciples is to draw people to Jesus.

The action of "drawing" has its metaphorical parallel in the action of "gathering." In John 4:36, we have seen that the disciples are sent "to reap that for which they did not labor" and to "enter into the labor of others." Jesus does "preliminary work" (in this case, the sowing), and the disciples are commissioned to carry on with the next steps. Similarly, in John 6:12–13, Jesus does the preliminary work, multiplying the bread and fish, and the disciples become engaged in carrying the work forward; they gather up (συνάγω) the leftover bread fragments into twelve baskets. This action of drawing together or of gathering evokes images of the eschatological in-gathering of the dispersed children of God referred to in 11:52.[24] The image of hauling in a net full of fish therefore suggests that the disciples are to continue the work of Jesus by participating in the gathering or the drawing in of people to Jesus.[25]

The Role of Peter

According to Timothy Wiarda, the narrative of John 21 is held together by

---

[23] We see the same use of this "fishing for people" idea in Mark 1:17; Matt 4:19; Luke 5:1–11.

[24] See John 10:16. See discussion on John 6:12.

[25] The number of fish, 153, perhaps represents the number of people gathered in the Johannine community. The number is usually interpreted as having universal significance and interpretations fall into three main areas: historical, gematria, and allegorical. Historically, according to Jerome, the ancients believed that the total number of kinds of fish species was 153. The "153 fish," therefore, refers to the entire population of fish, or according to Jerome's commentary on Ezek 47:9–12 (*PL* 25, col. 474C), all manner of men. Unfortunately, the "ancients" themselves do not support the number of kinds of fish as 153. See R. M. Grant, *HTR* 42 (1949): 273. For example, Pliny identifies 74 kinds of fish (*Natural History*, 9.43). Using gematria, Cardwell ("Fish," 12–14) suggests "day" or "Simon" (= 76) and "fish" (= 77). O. T. Owen ("One Hundred and Fifty Three Fish," *ET* 100 [1988]: 52–54) suggests the site of Moses' commissioning, Pisgah. J. A. Emerton ("The Hundred and Fifty-Three Fishes in John 21:11," *JTS* 9 [1958]: 86–89 and 11 [1960]: 335–6) and P. Trudinger ("The 153 Fishes: A Response and a Further Suggestion," *ET* 102 [1990]: 12–14) suggest (En)Gedi and (En)Eglaim, the site of a miraculous catch of fish in Ezek 47:8–10. Others have suggested that 153 represents the sum of all numbers from 1 to 17 (10 = Ten Commandments, 7 = the gifts of the spirit) or that 153 dots can be arranged in an equilateral triangle with 17 dots on each side. As Morris (*Gospel*, 867) points out, "there seems no end to the 'meanings' that can be extracted from the number. But that John intended any of them is another matter." It is much simpler to accept the specific number as an indication that the testimony comes from an eye-witness and that it later was understood to have some kind of symbolic meaning, most likely of "universality." This is the position accepted by Schnackenburg, *Gospel*, 3:358, Brown, *Gospel*, 1076; Quast, *Reading*, 142. See the survey by Beasley-Murray, *John*, 401–4. Wiarda ("Narrative Unity," 67) sees only a narrative reference emphasizing the size of the catch of fish.

the development of Peter's role.[26] Peter, whose name heads the list of disciples, decides to go fishing and the other disciples follow his lead (21:2–3). He is the first to approach Jesus (21:7) and he responds obediently to Jesus' request for some of the catch (21:11). In spite of the fact that the disciples are already engaged in hauling in the fish, Peter is specifically identified as the one who hauls the net ashore without tearing the net (21:11). Peter appears to be the lead fisherman in this story, although there is no indication from the rest of the Gospel that this is his profession.

Peter's role is developed more explicitly in an after-breakfast conversation with Jesus. Three times Jesus asks Peter, "Simon son of John, do you love me?" (21:15, 16, 17); the first time he adds "more than these?" (21:15).[27] Peter responds each time with "Yes Lord, you know that I love you." The three-part sequence recalls Peter's denial in the courtyard of the high priest (18:17, 25, 27), which also takes place by a charcoal fire (18:18; cf. 21:9).[28] Where he once denies Jesus, Peter now affirms him. Peter is grieved (ἐλυπήθη) by the need for affirmation (21:17). After each affirmation of his love, Peter is given a command. In the first, he is told, "Feed my lambs" (βόσκε τὰ ἀρνία μου). In the second, "Tend my sheep" (ποίμαινε τὰ πρόβατά μου). In the third, he is told, "Feed my sheep" (βόσκε τὰ πρόβατά μου). In this dialogue, the focus shifts from fish to sheep, from sea creatures to land creatures. The role of Peter thus shifts from fishing to shepherding.

Biblical and post-biblical literature depicts the profession of sheep-herding positively. Many of the patriarchs, such as Jacob and Joseph (see Gen 47:3–4), were esteemed shepherds. Moses was a shepherd (Exod 3:1). Joshua (Num 27:16–17) and David (1 Sam 16:11; 2 Sam 5:2) are both called "shepherds" in their role as leader of Israel. Good shepherds will be provided to lead Israel (Jer 3:15; *1 Enoch* 85–90; 89:13, 20, 36–39; *Pss. Sol.* 17:23–46; *4 Ezra* 2:34), and those shepherds who "destroy and scatter the sheep" are cursed (Jer 23:1–4; Ezek 34:1–24; 37:22, 24). God is also seen to take on this role of gathering and leading the sheep (Ps 23:1; 80:1; Isa 40:11; Jer 23:3; Ezek 34:1–24; Sir 18:13, 14). Philo praises shepherds as leaders (*Agriculture* 27–59). In all these cases,

---

[26] See Wiarda, "Narrative Unity," 55–71.

[27] This last phrase (πλέον τούτων) may be read grammatically three ways: (1) Do you love me more than these others do? (2) Do you love me more than these things (i.e., boats, nets, fish)? Or (3) Do you love me more than you love these others? In the first and third, Peter's claim to superior love for Jesus may be challenged (see 13:8, 37; 18:10, 15). In the second, Peter is given an alternative occupation to fishing: feeding sheep. See Wiarda, "Narrative Unity," 60–65; McDowell, "Lovest," 433; cf. Brown, *Gospel*, 1069.

[28] Koester, *Symbolism*, 121; Smith, *John*, 395; P. Benoit, *Passion and Resurrection of Jesus Christ* (trans. B. Weatherhead; New York: Herder & Herder, 1969), 305; Besobrasoff, "John 21," 133.

the people are understood to be sheep that are gathered and protected by the shepherd; the shepherd is understood to be their leader.

Within the Gospel of John, the shepherd and sheep theme is developed in John 10. In John 10, the role of the "good shepherd" is described in contrast to thieves, bandits, and hired hands. A good shepherd enters the gate in the appropriate fashion (10:2); the gatekeeper admits him (10:3). He calls the sheep: they are his own (10:3); he knows their name (10:3, 27); he cares for them (cf. 10:13). He leads them (10:4), protects them (10:28), and provides pasture for them (10:13). He willingly lays down his life for his sheep (10:11, 15, 18) and gives them abundant life (10:10, 28). The sheep follow the shepherd because they know his voice (10:4, 27). They trust him (cf. 10:26). The thieves and bandits, in contrast, enter the sheepfold another way in order to steal, kill, and destroy (10:1, 10). The hired hand does not own the sheep nor care about them, so he runs away when he sees a wolf. The sheep are left unprotected; they are snatched by the wolf and scattered (10:12–13). The sheep belonging to the good shepherd do not follow a stranger (10:8); they run away because they do not know his voice (10:5). Jesus identifies himself as the good shepherd (10:11), ready to lay his life down for the sake of those who believe and follow him (10:11, 15, 17–18); they will have eternal life and never perish (10:28). In short, Jesus the shepherd provides life for those who follow him. In John 21:15–17, Jesus passes the role of shepherd on to Peter.

How does the Gospel understand Peter to feed the sheep of Jesus? We have seen in the study thus far that ingesting Jesus means to believe that Jesus is both the provider and the substance of food that gives eternal life. In other words, to eat Jesus means to believe that Jesus needed to die in order to give life. Peter's task is therefore "to feed Jesus" to the sheep, that is, to lead them to believe in the efficacy of Jesus' death. This he does by word and deed. As the spokesman for the disciples, he recognizes that Jesus has "the words of eternal life" (6:68).[29] He also does the works that Jesus has done (see 14:12; 13:14). The extreme act of love, according to the Gospel, is to give up one's life willingly for another (15:13), as Jesus does (10:17–18). With the pursuant description of his death, the Gospel implies that Peter does indeed demonstrate his love for others through death (21:18–19). In this way, Peter "follows" Jesus (21:19).

The way that John uses the word "follow" is different from the way that other New Testament texts use the word. Although the verb may be used simply in the literal sense as a person or thing coming after another, the Synoptic Gospels emphasize the act of following Jesus as forsaking all else (e.g., Matt 4:20–22; 10:38; 16:24; 19:21, 27; 27:55) and imitating Jesus' life (e.g., Matt 8:19–20;

---

[29] The testimony of others is highly esteemed in this Gospel. See 1:19–37, 41–51; 2:22; 3:11–12; 4:39–42; 5:31–47; 15:27; 19:35; 20:2, 18, 25, especially 20:31.

27:55). Many people "follow" Jesus because they want to be taught or because they seek healing (e.g., Matt 8:1; 12:15; 19:2). Sometimes they follow Jesus because they have been healed (e.g., Matt 20:34). Not all those who follow Jesus are his disciples (e.g., Mark 5:24; Matt 21:9). In other words, following and believing are not necessarily synonymous. But for the Twelve who leave everything and follow Jesus, the reward will be, "at the renewal of all things, when the Son of Man is seated on the throne of his glory," to "sit on twelve thrones, judging the twelve tribes of Israel" (Matt 19:28). The Synoptic tradition emphasizes the importance of forsaking one's former life for a reward in the future. Elsewhere in the New Testament, the verb "follow" (ἀκολουθέω) is rarely used.[30]

In the Gospel of John, the verb "follow" (ἀκολουθέω) is used differently. Of course, there are occasions when the word is used in its literal sense, such as in John 1:38 and 6:2. There is no comparable emphasis, however, that when one follows Jesus, one must forsake all else. The Gospel uses the image of sheep following a shepherd (10:4–5, 27): when a sheep follows a shepherd, it entrusts its life to him. Emphasis is placed, not on what is left behind, but on what lies in the present (security) and what will come in the future (eternal life). In John, personal possessions such as nets, boats, wealth, and family are not renounced;[31] instead, abundance and satisfaction are emphasized, not as a promise of reward but as a benefit of being in the presence of Jesus.[32] What is emphasized in the Johannine notion of following, however, is the willingness to love and to serve to the point of death. This is most clear in John 13:33–38.

> Jesus says to his disciples, "Little children, I am with you only a little longer. You will seek me; and as I said to the Jews, now I say to you, 'Where I go, you cannot come.' I give you a new commandment, that you love one another. Just as I have loved you, you also should love one another. By this everyone will know that you are my disciples, if you have love for one another." Simon Peter said to him, "Lord, where are you going?" Jesus answered him, "Where I am going you cannot follow me now; but you will follow me afterward." Peter said to him, "Lord, why can I not follow you now? I will lay down my life for you." Jesus answered, "Will you lay down your life for me? Very truly, I tell you, before the cock crows, you will have denied me three times."

This brief dialogue is set in the context of Jesus' approaching death (cf. 13:1) and refers to his imminent "departure" from the earth; Peter cannot follow him

---

[30] It is found in Acts 5 times in the usual sense and 6 times in Revelation, where the "Lamb" (14:4) and the "Word of God" (19:14) are followed.

[31] Cf. Wiarda, "Narrative Unity," 60–65.

[32] For example, Jesus turns 120–180 gallons of water into wine (2:6), feeds 5,000 until they were "satisfied" (6:10–12), and Nicodemus brings "about 100 pounds" of spices to bury with Jesus (19:39). Being in the presence of Jesus is also described in such terms as "walking in the light" (8:12) and "abiding" in him (6:56; 15:5–10).

"now" but will follow afterward. To follow Jesus means to follow to his death and his subsequent resurrection (14:3), as Peter indicates in 13:37 that he is willing to do. It is to follow the example of Jesus (see 13:14–15). As in John 21, the idea of following is also juxtaposed with the concept of love. Therefore, when Jesus says to Peter, "Follow me," it is not necessarily an imperative to give up his former profession, as some have argued,[33] but an imperative to love others to the point of his own death, a death that is described in the verse immediately preceding this one.[34]

Therefore, because he loves Jesus, Peter is to step into the role of shepherd. This requires that Peter "will do the works that Jesus does" (14:12; cf. 13:14); he will bring others to belief in Jesus both through his testimony and by following Jesus' example to the point of laying down his life for the sake of "his sheep."

The Role of the Beloved Disciple

In the context of this meal narrative, the role of the beloved disciple is also developed. He is one of the disciples who follows Peter's lead and goes fishing (21:3).[35] With the other disciples, he catches nothing until Jesus tells the disciples to cast the net on the other side of the boat (21:6). After the disciples catch a great many fish, the beloved disciple is the one who recognizes Jesus standing on the shore: "It is the Lord!" he says to Peter (21:7).[36] His testimony causes Peter to respond immediately: Peter jumps into the sea (21:7). With the other disciples, the beloved disciple follows Peter to shore, dragging the net full of fish (21:8). He shares the meal of bread and fish that Jesus prepares (21:12–13). With the rest of the disciples, he responds to Jesus' directions and participates in a miracle.

It is testimony to this miracle that sets the beloved disciple apart from his fellows. He is the one who puts his observations into words.[37] John 21:24 says that "this is the disciple who is testifying to these things and has written them, and we know that his testimony is true."[38] He is also the one who stands at the

---

[33] See, for example, Wiarda, "Narrative Unity," 61–63.

[34] See Besobrasoff, "John 21," 135.

[35] The Gospel identifies the characters in this narrative as "disciples" (21:1) and provides a list: Simon Peter, Thomas, Nathanael, the sons of Zebedee, and two other disciples. The beloved disciple must be counted among them for he is identified in verse 7. Is he one of the sons of Zebedee or one of the other two disciples? It is impossible to know.

[36] Barrett (*Gospel*, 580) notes that the beloved disciple's exclamation, "It is the Lord," corresponds to Jesus' self-identification as "I am" (6:35; 8:24, etc.).

[37] Bacon ("Motivation," 71–80) refers to the beloved disciple's testimony as "white martyrdom" (not requiring death) in opposition to Peter's "red martyrdom" (requiring death).

[38] J. Chapman ("We Know That His Testimony Is True," *JTS* 31 [1930]: 379–87) unconvincingly argues that the "we" is a "plural of majesty." In other words, the author (beloved disciple = John) needs no collaboration from others.

foot of the cross and sees Jesus die, testifying to the truth so that others might also believe (19:25–35; cf. 20:30). He has knowledge that the other disciples do not have: the identity of the betrayer (13:26), the nature of Jesus' death (19:34), the meaning of the empty tomb (20:8), and the identity of Jesus in this passage. His words instil confidence in those who hear (21:7, 12).[39] Unlike the impulsive Peter who moves right into the action, the beloved disciple sees, believes, and testifies (see also 20:3–10). His main role is thus to testify to the source of the food: "It is the Lord!"

The beloved disciple is identified, in part, as "the one who had reclined next to Jesus at the supper and had said, 'Lord, who is it that is going to betray you?'" This refers to the incident at the Last Supper in John 13:23 when Peter motioned to the beloved disciple to ask Jesus who would betray him. Jesus tells the beloved disciple that the betrayer is the one who will take his bread, referring to Judas. By recalling Judas, albeit indirectly, John 21 brings the contrast between the various disciples into the forefront of the narrative. Unlike Peter and the beloved disciple, the character Judas does not remain with Jesus, although his presence is preserved in the text by referring to him here. The backward glance to John 13:23 also underscores the love that exists between Jesus and this disciple: he is the one who "reclined next to Jesus."

Finally, the Gospel uses the beloved disciple as an example of another way to follow Jesus. In 1:38, Jesus turns (στραθείς) and sees two disciples following him. In John 21:20, Peter turns (ἐπιστραθείς) and sees the beloved disciple following them. The beloved disciple therefore is following Jesus without being told to do so.[40] The Gospel indicates, therefore, that the beloved disciple is one who already accomplishes the behavior expected of Peter, that is, to follow Jesus. He does this ultimately by testifying to the truth about Jesus. The Gospel thus presents the beloved disciple as a different, perhaps even better, kind of disciple than Peter.[41]

---

[39] Schnackenburg (*Gospel*, 3:355) incorrectly argues that the disciples recognize Jesus when he gives them bread to eat (21:13); in fact, the Gospel states that they know who he is before they eat.

[40] John 18:15–16 refers to "another disciple" who also followed Jesus. "Since that disciple was known to the high priest, he went with Jesus into the courtyard of the high priest, but Peter was standing outside by the gate. So the other disciple, who was known to the high priest, went out, spoke to the woman who guarded the gate, and brought Peter in." This would be another incidence in which Peter was unable to follow but followed afterward and in which "another disciple" was able to follow.

[41] O. Cullmann, *Peter: Disciple, Apostle, Martyr* (2d ed.; Philadelphia: Westminster, 1962), 28–31. Wiarda ("Narrative Unity," 68) argues that the presence of the beloved disciple in the narrative is to further the character development of Peter.

CONCLUSION

The conclusion of the Gospel is a report of both the final appearance of Jesus and the final meal. Setting this narrative in the context of a meal accomplishes various purposes. First, in recounting this miracle, it reaffirms that Jesus is able to provide abundant food even after death (cf. 2:1–12, 4:4–30, 6:1–15). Second, it passes on the role of feeding to the disciples, especially to Peter, and affirms the importance of Jesus' direction. It also affirms that there is more than one way to follow Jesus; the beloved disciple does this by testifying to the things that he has seen.[42] The emphasis has thus shifted from "receiving Jesus," that is, "believing in him" or "eating his flesh and blood," to extending the invitation to others and providing food for them to eat. In this final post-resurrection narrative, the ingesting motif again comes to the fore in the service of the Gospel's soteriology.

---

[42] Agourides ("Purpose," 127–32) argues that the demise of Peter and the beloved disciple was of great importance to the church of his day. Peter's martyrdom was held in high regard, so much so that the different kind of death experienced by the beloved disciple put his authority in question. Thus, the purpose of chapter 21 is to re-establish the authority of the beloved disciple. Cf. Wiarda, "Narrative Unity," 68.

Conclusion

This study began with a challenge by David Tracy to re-examine familiar metaphors without the constraints of traditional interpretations, a challenge that has been applied to the language of ingesting in the Gospel of John. To begin, the parameters of the study were set. The obvious references to water, bread, wine, grain, fish, supper, and breakfast were included, of course. But Freedman notes that words that are associated with these primary ideas should also be included in a study of a literary motif.[1] These associated words give shape to and extend the definition of the symbol or metaphor, even when the symbol or metaphor is not readily present; an "associational cluster" thus develops that, even when one word is mentioned, the whole motif is called into service. This study of the ingesting motif in the Gospel of John was thus extended beyond the explicit and obvious expression of eating and drinking, food and drink, feeding and serving, to include more subtle forms of ingesting language. It includes a study of those narratives that say little about eating and drinking but that take place in the context of a meal; the Supper at Bethany is such an example. It also includes reflection on passing references to words drawn from the domain of ingesting language. "Tasting death" and "being consumed" are examples. A related motif, the Passover, has also influenced choices in this study because it is so often connected to passages that feature ingesting language; it forms part of the "associational cluster." Freedman's definition of the literary motif has been used to extend the usual boundaries of studies on the ingesting motif in the Gospel of John, a feature that makes this study unique.

Freedman notes that a motif's effectiveness is determined by five factors. The first factor is rate of recurrence. The ingesting motif is indeed prevalent in the Gospel of John. There are six "meal scenes," defined as narratives in which eating and/or drinking ostensibly take place. These include the Wedding in Cana, the "lunch" in Samaria, the Feeding of the Multitude, the Supper in Bethany, the Last Supper, and the Resurrection Breakfast. Food and drink are explicitly mentioned: Jesus is said to provide wine, bread, fish, and water to characters in the narrative. Food and drink are also used as metaphors for Jesus: he is the "bread of life," the source of "living water," and (possibly as food) the "Lamb of God." Bread and water are particularly well-developed concepts. Thus, the ingesting motif does occur with frequency in the Gospel of John.

---

[1] See Freedman, "Motif," 124–9.

The second factor determining the effectiveness of a motif is its avoidability or unlikelihood. Could the use of this language be easily avoided, or is it demanded by the context? In some cases, the context in the Gospel does require reference to ingesting language. For example, Jesus' request for a drink in Samaria gives occasion for the conversation with the Samaritan woman. The lack of wine in Cana gives occasion for Jesus to perform a miracle. Jesus asks for a drink while he is dying. Although the narrative context supports ingesting language in these cases, it is significant that these stories are recounted at all. Narratives that refer to ingesting are selectively chosen out of many possibilities; they are given priority. The Gospel is explicit in stating that "*these* are written so that you may come to believe" (20:30, emphasis added). There are also instances when the context does not require ingesting language. In John 8:51–52, for example, the wording changes from one phrase in the mouth of Jesus to its parallel phrase in the mouth of the Jews; the first says "never see death," the second says "never taste death." The context of this passage does not require the change. In fact, the change draws attention to the ingesting motif. In the Cleansing of the Temple story, the context does not demand the use of ingesting language; it seems definitely out of place there, even if it is a citation of a Psalm that says, "Zeal for your house will consume me" (2:17). In the scene where the disciples and the resurrected Jesus enjoy roasted fish, the command to "feed sheep" seems oddly out of place. Sheep do not eat fish, after all, and the disciples are presented as fishermen, not shepherds. In the Last Supper, Jesus gives Judas a morsel "and with it Satan" (13:27). The association of these two actions is startling, for according to the narrative, Judas had already been influenced by the devil (6:70; 13:2) and Jesus' bread had already been declared to be life-giving (6:22–59). Therefore, the Gospel selects a significant number of stories that feature ingesting language, it adds ingesting language where it could otherwise be avoided, and it uses ingesting language in uncommon ways. This is another mark of an effective motif, according to Freedman.

The third mark of an effective motif is its use at climactic points in the narrative. In the Gospel of John, the ingesting motif is used in Jesus' introduction to the narrative "in the flesh" as the "Lamb of God" (1:29, 36), even if it is more of an allusion than a clear case of ingesting language. The ingesting motif marks significant moments in the life of Jesus: his first sign in Cana (2:1–11), his death (19:28–37), and his resurrection (21:1–25). It also occurs with increasing frequency as the narrative climax approaches Jesus' death (Anointing in Bethany, Last Supper, mention of the cup). At the ultimate climax of the plot, it appears again when Jesus takes a drink before he dies. In the final Gospel narrative, the ingesting motif is front and center. Therefore, according to Freedman's definition, the ingesting motif is effective because it occurs at significant and climactic moments in the plot.

The fourth criterion of motif effectiveness, according to Freedman, is the degree to which all of the occurrences cohere into a recognizable unit. In this study of the ingesting motif in the Gospel of John, several discernible patterns have been identified that demonstrate this cohesiveness. In particular, ingesting language provides a way to describe both the role of Jesus and the role of believers.

Two aspects of Jesus' role are expressed with ingesting language. First, Jesus provides food for others. He changes water into wine in Cana (2:1–12). He multiplies the loaves and fish in Galilee (6:1–15). He has fish already on the fire for the disciples at the Resurrection Breakfast (21:1–14). Furthermore, the food and drink that Jesus provides are superior in quantity and quality to "perishable food" (see 6:27). In Samaria, Jesus asks for water but then offers the woman his own "living water" (4:4–15). In the Feeding of the Multitude narrative, Jesus multiplies the small amount of food provided by a boy and satisfies over five thousand people (6:1–12). The Gospel underscores the superiority of the food and drink that Jesus has to offer. It is food and drink that "does not perish . . . but endures for eternal life" (6:27). The various banquet allusions suggest that this eating and drinking is understood to be an eschatological event (see John 2:1–11; 6:1–15; 12:1–8; 13:8; 21:1–14).

The second and more important aspect of Jesus' role that the ingesting motif develops is that Jesus offers himself as food, giving life to others through his death. He is the "bread that comes down from heaven" whose flesh must be "crunched" to be salvific (6:52–58). His flesh and blood are true food and drink (6:55). His death releases the living water and the spirit that give life (4:10; 7:37–39; 19:34). He falls to earth as a grain of wheat that produces much fruit (12:24). He is also possibly the paschal lamb whose sacrifice "takes away the sin of the world" (1:29, 36), a theme that is brought to the fore in the frequent references to the Passover festival and its activities (2:17; 6:4; 12:1–21:25). It may also be argued that Jesus is metaphorically "consumed" in place of the sacrificial animals in the temple (2:17). The inevitability and necessity of his death color every meal narrative, from the anticipation of his hour in Cana (2:4), to his anointing for death in Bethany (12:1–8), and to his final testimony and symbolic actions during the Last Supper (13:1–30). Thus, the Gospel presents Jesus as one who gives his life as food in order to feed those who believe in him. In this way the salvific role of Jesus is communicated through the ingesting motif.

The expected response of believers to Jesus is also communicated with the ingesting motif, and discernible patterns may be identified. Those who believe Jesus will "eat Jesus." This is made most explicit in the Bread of Life discourse.

Jesus says, "All who see the Son and believe in him may have eternal life; and I will raise them up on the last day" (6:40). Those who *believe* in Jesus will be raised. Later, Jesus says, "I am the bread that has come from heaven. Whoever eats of this bread will live forever; and the bread that I will give for the life of the world is my flesh (6:51). . . . Those who eat my flesh and drink my blood have eternal life; and I will raise them up on the last day" (6:54). Thus, those who *eat* Jesus will be raised on the last day. Eating Jesus is thus equated with seeing and believing in Jesus. The idea of drinking Jesus is less explicit but is suggested in John 4: Jesus offers "living water" that will become in others "a spring of water gushing up to eternal life" (4:14). Jesus himself is later identified as a source of water (7:37–39; 19:34). Though John 6 is the clearest expression of this motif pattern, it is reflected in John 4 as well.

This aspect of the ingesting motif as it relates to the role of the disciples is enhanced by the contrast that is established between those who are willing to "eat" Jesus and those who are not. This is most explicit in the Bread of Life discourse in which Jesus rebukes the people for only wanting perishable bread (6:25–34). Many reject him because they are unwilling to "eat his flesh" (6:52–58). Others want to "taste death" rather than life (8:52). Peter wants to prohibit Jesus from washing his feet (through the laying down of his life), though this washing is necessary if Peter wants "to share a portion with him" (13:8; cf. 18:10). To believe in Jesus thus requires the appreciation that Jesus must die. It is only then that Jesus is available to the believer as food and drink (6:40, 54).

Finally, the ingesting motif is used to describe the way in which believers are to respond: they are to feed others. This notion is introduced gradually throughout the Gospel. When John introduces Jesus as the "Lamb of God that takes away the sin of the world," the disciples hear and follow (1:35–51). In the Wedding in Cana, the disciples silently observe the miracle and then believe (2:10). In the Cleansing of the Temple story, they merely remember what Jesus had told them (2:13–25). In the Samaritan woman story, they ask questions about the food that Jesus has, for their food is useless (4:31–34). They are invited to gather an imminent harvest (4:35–38). In the Feeding of the Multitude, they prepare the people to eat and Jesus feeds five thousand. They gather up the pieces that are leftover "so that none will be lost" (6:1–15). They are taught that their dependence on Jesus will produce much fruit (15:1–17). This is demonstrated in the story of the Miraculous Catch of Fish: the disciples obey the words of Jesus and pull in a net full of fish aided specifically by Peter (21:1–8). Simon Peter is instructed to feed Jesus' sheep (21:15–17), even to the point of death (21:18–19). Throughout the Gospel, then, the ingesting motif is used as a vehicle to communicate the role of the disciples in feeding others.

The ingesting motif in the Gospel of John is thus a coherent vehicle through which the roles of Jesus and the disciples are communicated. The description of these roles is not limited to the ingesting motif, however; these same soteriological ideas are communicated in other ways throughout the Gospel using different motifs. Jesus is referred to as the "light" and those who walk in the light will have eternal life (1:4–5; 3:17–21; 9:5; 11:9–10; 12:35–36, 46). Jesus dwells among the people as the "word" (1:1–13); those who keep his word will not die but have eternal life (3:15–21; 5:24; 6:47; 8:51–52; 11:25–26). So, just as Jesus provides and is the food and drink that give salvation, he also provides the word(s)/light and is the word/light that gives salvation. Similarly, as those who eat Jesus feed others, those who believe because of what they have seen or heard are to testify so that others will believe (1:41, 45; 4:39–42; 12:22; 19:35; 20:2, 18, 24, 30; 21:24–25). Therefore, the soteriology that is conveyed by the ingesting language in the Gospel of John is consistent with the soteriology of the Gospel as a whole.

Finally, Freedman argues that the fifth criterion of an effective motif is "the appropriateness of the motif to what it symbolizes."[2] It is unclear what the ingesting motif refers to symbolically. Two main propositions have been made: to eat Jesus means to take the Eucharist and/or to eat Jesus means to internalize his words or his spirit.

This study has deliberately refrained from presuming at the outset that the ingesting language in the Gospel of John refers to the Eucharist. As this analysis of the ingesting motif has shown, the language of food and drink, the actions of eating and drinking, and the meal settings function in a complex way within the symbolic and theological world of the Gospel. Nevertheless, the question of the connection between the ingesting motif and the Eucharist, a ritual that entails eating and drinking, cannot be ignored.

The Eucharist, also known as the Lord's Supper or Communion, is described by the Synoptic Gospels and Paul. Matthew describes it this way:

> While they were eating, Jesus took a loaf of bread, and after blessing it, he broke it, gave it to the disciples, and said, "Take eat; this is my body." Then he took a cup, and after giving thanks he gave it to them saying, "Drink from it, all of you; for this is my blood of the covenant, which is poured out for many for the forgiveness of sins. I tell you, I will never again drink of this fruit of the vine until the day when I drink of it new with you in my Father's kingdom." Matt 26:26–30 (cf. Mark 14:22–25; Luke 22:14–23; 1 Cor 11:23–26)

These events occur during the same meal that Jesus predicted Judas' betrayal and Peter's denial. Identified as the Passover (Matt 26:17; Mark 14:12; Luke 22:8), this meal is followed by Jesus' arrest and crucifixion.

Like the Synoptic account, the Johannine account of the Last Supper includes the prediction of Judas' betrayal and Peter's denial, and Jesus is

---

[2] Ibid., 126–7.

arrested that same night. However, the meal is set on the night before Passover and does not include the institution of the Eucharist, only the foot washing and Farewell Discourse. The Eucharist is not associated with the Johannine Last Supper.

Many scholars agree that ingesting language in John 6 refers to the Eucharist of the early Christian tradition.[3] This conviction is based principally on John 6:11, which reads, "Then Jesus took the loaves and when he had given thanks, he distributed them to those who were seated, so also the fish, as much as they wanted" (ἔλαβεν οὖν τοὺς ἄρτους ὁ Ἰησοῦς καὶ εὐχαριστήσας διέδωκεν τοῖς ἀνακειμένοις ὁμοίως καὶ ἐκ τῶν ὀψαρίων ὅσον ἤθελον). The key words here are ἔλαβεν . . . τοὺς ἄρτους ("he took . . . the bread") and εὐχαριστήσας ("after giving thanks").[4] The same word and grammatical form, εὐχαριστήσας, is found in all the Last Supper accounts of the three Synoptic Gospels (Mark 14:23; Matt 26:27; Luke 22:17) and in 1 Cor 11:24. The Synoptic stories of the Feeding of the 4000 also use the word εὐχαριστήσας and a form of the verb λαμβάνω, suggesting that the Eucharist was associated with the feeding miracles (see Mark 8:6; Matt 15:36). Therefore, the Johannine Feeding of the Multitude story likely alludes to Eucharist traditions.[5]

This argument is strengthened by references to eating the flesh of Jesus and drinking his blood in the Bread of Life discourse that follows the Johannine story of the Feeding of the Multitude. In the Last Supper accounts of the

---

[3] Brown (*Gospel*, 248) supports a Eucharistic coloring of the Johannine account of the multiplication "beyond doubt." See Barrett, *Gospel*, 84–85; Schnackenburg, *Gospel*, 1:160–1; Koester, *Symbolism*, 99–100; Culpepper, *Gospel*, 163; Smith, *John*, 160–161; Cullmann, *Worship*, 93–102; Paschal, "Sacramental," 151–79. Cf. Matsunaga, "Anti-Sacramental," 516; Morris, *Gospel*, 344.

[4] Εὐχαριστία, a noun referring to thanksgiving, and its related verbal form εὐχαριστέω are technical terms for the Eucharist, or the Lord's Supper, in the early church. See Ign. *Phld.* 4; Ign. *Smyrn.* 7:1; 8:1; *Did.* 9:5; 10:1, 2; 14:1; Justin, *Apology*, 1.65–66. C. F. D. Moule ("A Note on Didache 9:4," *JTS* 6 [1955]: 240–243) points out parallel language between John 6 and the Didache's Eucharistic prayer.

[5] Some scholars have argued that the vine imagery in John 15 refers to the wine of Eucharist. This is unlikely as there is neither mention of wine nor of bread, only of a vine. Nor does the context lend itself well to Eucharistic thought: the focus is on the relationship between the Father, Jesus and the disciples, not on the ingesting of symbolic food. By association with John 6, John 21 has also been proposed to reflect Eucharist traditions. In both stories, Jesus multiplies bread and fish. He acts as the host and distributes the food. R. Pervo ("PANTA KOINA: The Feeding Stories in Light of Economic Data and Social Practice," *Religious Propoganda and Missionary Competition in the New Testament World* [edited by L. Bormann, D. Tredici, A. Strandhartigen; Leiden: Brill, 1994], 163–94) argues that the feeding stories are recounted in order to motivate the community to share resources with the poor. The food that is distributed "belongs to the Lord," so individuals have no further claim to private property. As a possible referent for the ingesting motif, this theory does not account for the recurring mandate to "eat Jesus."

Synoptics and 1 Corinthians, Jesus refers to the bread as his body and the wine as his blood. He tells his disciples that they must eat them. Similarly, in the Bread of Life discourse of John 6:26–71, Jesus states that the disciples must eat his flesh and drink his blood. Various phrases and ideas are thus common between the ingesting motif in the Gospel of John and the Synoptic and Pauline Eucharist traditions, though they are set in different narrative contexts.[6]

If the ingesting motif in the Gospel of John does indeed reflect Eucharist traditions, then the choice of ingesting language to describe the soteriological roles of Jesus and believers does seem quite appropriate. In fact, the Gospel of John is vague about what it actually means "to eat" Jesus and "to drink his blood." In John 6:60–70, the possibility arises that a believer "eats" Jesus by internalising his words, hearing and obeying, and passing on the words of Jesus.[7] This is quite compelling but does not explain the *choice* of ingesting language very well. In John 4:4–42, 6:63, 7:37–39, 19:30, the possibility arises that believers "eat" Jesus by accepting his spirit. This notion is confused by other references to the "Holy Spirit" that depict the spirit quite differently (see the description of the "Spirit of Truth" and the "Advocate" in John 14–16 and 20:22). In contrast, the symbolic actions of eating Jesus' body and drinking his blood are easily understood within the framework of the Eucharist tradition,[8] thus suggesting that the ingesting motif derives from and refers to the Eucharist.

Freedman has defined the literary motif and set forth the criteria of effectiveness. This study has identified those passages that, according to his definition, constitute the ingesting motif in the Gospel of John. The motif has been deemed effective on the basis of its rate of recurrence, its avoidability, its placement at critical junctures in the narrative, its cohesiveness, and its symbolic appropriateness in the Gospel. The study concludes that the ingesting motif is an effective vehicle for conveying the soteriology of the Gospel and ties this expression of soteriology to the Eucharist tradition.

David Tracy challenges literary critics to re-open the exploration of biblical

---

[6] The differences in terminology are rather insignificant. The verb κλάω ("break," Mark 14:22; Matt 26:26; Luke 22:19; 1 Cor 11:24) in the Eucharist accounts may be reflected in the noun, κλάσμα ("fragment") (John 6:12). See Brown, *Gospel*, 239. Instead of eating (ἐσθίω) the bread as Jesus' body (σῶμα), Johannine believers are to "crunch" (τρώγω) his flesh (σάρξ).

[7] J. Bowman ("Metaphorically Eating and Drinking the Body and Blood," *Abr-Nahrain* 22 [1983–4]: 1–6) argues that the Johannine references to the body and blood of Jesus point, not to his physical body nor to the sacraments, but to the words of Jesus' teaching. See Jeremias (*Eucharistic*) for a discussion of the Christian Passover.

[8] The fact that the Eucharist is not explicitly recounted in the Gospel of John should not preclude its influence here, for the Gospel assumes that his readers are familiar with other unexplained referents. Its liberal use of biblical citations and allusions is a good example of this assumption.

metaphors. This dissertation has taken up the challenge and has sought to understand the ingesting motif in the Gospel of John. The ingesting motif is found to be dynamic, creative, and provocative. It is dynamic because it builds coherence throughout the Gospel. It is creative because it provides a compelling way to imagine participation in the promises of Jesus. It is provocative because it requires a reader to accept or reject that which Jesus offers as the host. In fact, the ingesting motif has proven to be tensive and powerful figurative language. By chewing over the meaning of this literary motif and savoring its permutations, the reader may taste a bit of heaven.

Works Cited

Abbott, Edwin A. *Johannine Vocabulary*. London: Adam & Black, 1905.

Agourides, S. "The Purpose of John 21." Pages 127–32 in *Studies in the History and Text of the New Testament—in Honor of K. W. Clark*. Edited by B. L. Daniels and M. J. Suggs. Salt Lake City: University of Utah, 1967.

Ashton, John. *Understanding the Fourth Gospel*. Oxford: Clarendon, 1991.

Atwood, Margaret. *The Edible Woman*. Toronto: McClelland & Stewart, 1969.

Bacon, B. W. "The Motivation of John 21:15–25." *Journal of Biblical Literature* 50 (1931): 71–80.

Barrett, Charles Kingsley. "The Old Testament in the Fourth Gospel." *Journal of Theological Studies* 48 (1947): 155–7.

———. "The Lamb of God" *New Testament Studies* 1 (1954–5): 210–218.

———. *The Gospel according to St. John*. 2d ed. Philadelphia: Westminster, 1978.

———. "The Flesh of the Son of Man." *Essays on John*. Philadelphia: Westminster, 1982.

Bauckham, Richard. "The Beloved Disciple as Ideal Author." *Journal for the Study of the New Testament* 49 (1993): 21–44.

Bauer, Walter. *A Greek-English Lexicon of the New Testament and Other Early Christian Literature*. 2d ed. Translation and adaptation of the 4th ed. by William F. Arndt and F. Wilbur Gingrich. Revised and augmented by F. Wilbur Gingrich and Frederick W. Danker from Bauer's 5th ed., 1958. Chicago: University of Chicago Press, 1979.

Beasley-Murray, George. *John*. Word Bible Commentary 36. Waco: Word, 1987.

Beck, David. "The Narrative Function of Anonymity in Fourth Gospel Characterization." *Semeia* 53 (1991): 143–58.

Beetham, F. G., and P. A. Beetham. "A Note on John 19:29." *Journal of Theological Studies* 44 (1993): 163–9.

Benoit, Pierre. *The Passion and Resurrection of Jesus Christ*. Translated by B. Weatherhead. New York: Herder & Herder, 1969.

Bernard, John Henry. *A Critical and Exegetical Commentary on the Gospel according to St. John*. 2 vols. International Critical Commentary 28. Edinburgh: T&T Clark, 1928.

Besobrasoff, Serge. "John 21." *New Testament Studies* 3 (1956–7): 132–6.

Beutler, Johannes. "The Use of Scripture in the Gospel of John." Pages 147–62 in *Exploring the Gospel of John: In Honor of D. Moody Smith*. Edited by R. Alan Culpepper and C. Clifton Black. Louisville, Ky.: Westminster John Knox, 1996.

Blanchard, Yves-Marie. "Le repas de Béthanie (Jn 12, 1–11) au regard de l'ecclésiologie Johannique." Pages 227–37 in *Nourriture et repas dans les milieux Juifs et Chrétiens de l'Antiqité*. Edited by M. Quesnel, Y.-M. Blanchard, and C. Tassin. Paris: Cerf, 1999.

Blass, Friedrich, and Albert DeBrunner. *A Greek Grammar of the New Testament and Other Early Christian Literature*. Translated and Revised by Robert Funk. Chicago: University of Chicago Press, 1961.

Boismard, M.-É. "Le lavement des pieds." *Revue Biblique* 71 (1964): 5–24.

Bokser, Baruch M. "Was the Last Supper a Passover Seder?" *Bible Review* (1987): 24–33.

———. "Feasts of Unleavened Bread and Passover." Pages 755–65 in vol. 6 of *The Anchor Bible Dictionary*. Edited by David Freedman. 6 vols. New York: Doubleday, 1992.

Bolyki, János. "Die Tischgemeinschaften Jesu: Methoden und Ergebnisse. Perspektiven für die heutige Kirche." *European Journal of Theology* 3 (1994): 163–70.

Bonneau, Normand R. "The Woman at the Well: John 4 and Genesis 24." *The Bible Today* 67 (1973): 1252–9.

Bonsirven, Joseph. "Hora Talmudica." *Biblica* 33 (1952): 511–15.

Borgen, Peder. *Bread from Heaven: An Exegetical Study of the Concept of Manna in the Gospel of John and the Writings of Philo*. Novum Testamentum Supplement Series 10. Leiden: Brill, 1965.

Borig, Rainer. *Der wahre Weinstock*. Munich: Kösel, 1967.

Bowman, John. "Metaphorically Eating and Drinking the Body and Blood." Pages 1–6 in vol. 22 of *Abr-Nahrain*. Edited by T. Muraoka. Leiden: Brill, 1984.

Braun, Willi. *Feasting and Social Rhetoric in Luke 14*. New York: Cambridge University Press, 1995.

Brawley, Robert L. "An Absent Complement and Intertextuality in John 19:28–29." *Journal of Biblical Literature* 112 (1993): 427–43.

Brooks, James A., and Carlton L. Winbery. *Syntax of New Testament Greek*. London: University Press of America, 1979.

Brown, Edward K. *Rhythm in the Novel*. Toronto: University of Toronto Press, 1950.

Brown, Francis, with S. R. Driver and Charles A. Briggs. *A Hebrew and English Lexicon of the Old Testament*. Based on the Lexicon of William Gesenius as translated by Edward Robinson. Oxford: Clarendon, 1974.

Brown, Raymond E. "The Gospel of Thomas and St. John's Gospel." *New Testament Studies* 9 (1962): 155–77.

———. *The Gospel according to John*. 2 vols. Anchor Bible 29 and 29a. New York: Doubleday, 1966.

———. *Text and Interpretation*. Cambridge: Cambridge University Press, 1979.

———. *The Death of the Messiah*. 2 vols. New York: Doubleday, 1994.

———. *An Introduction to the New Testament*. New York: Doubleday, 1997.

Bultmann, Rudolf. *The Gospel of John*. Translated from the German by G. R. Beasley-Murray, R. W. N. Hoare, and J. K. Riches. Philadelphia: Westminster, 1964.

Burchard, Christoph. "The Importance of Joseph and Aseneth for the Study of the New Testament: A General Survey and a Fresh Look at the Lord's Supper." *New Testament Studies* 33 (1987): 102–34.

Byrne, Brendan. "The Faith of the Beloved Disciple and the Community in John 20." *Journal for the Study of the New Testament* 23 (1985): 83–97.

Cardwell, Kenneth. "The Fish on the Fire." *Expository Times* 102 (1990): 12–4.

Carey, George L. "The Lamb of God and Atonement Theories." *Tyndale Bulletin* 32 (1981): 97–122.

Carmichael, Calum M. "Marriage and the Samaritan Woman." *New Testament Studies* 26 (1980): 332–46.

Chapman, John. "We Know That His Testimony Is True." *Journal of Theological Studies* 31 (1930): 379–87.

Charlesworth, James H. "Testaments Often with Apocalyptic Sections: Introduction." Page 773 in vol. 1 of *Old Testament Pseudepigrapha*. Edited by James H. Charlesworth. New York: Doubleday, 1983.

Chatman, Seymour. *Story and Discourse: Narrative Structure in Fiction and Film*. Ithaca: Cornell University Press, 1978.

Chilton, B. D. "Isaac and the Second Night: A Consideration." *Biblica* 61 (1980): 78–88.

Clark, Douglas. "Signs in Wisdom and John." *Catholic Biblical Quarterly* 45 (1983): 201–9.

Coakley, James. "Anointing at Bethany and the Priority of John." *Journal of Biblical Literature* 107 (1988): 241–56.

Collins, J. J. "Testaments." Pages 325–55 in *Jewish Writings of the Second Temple Period*. Edited by Michael Stone. Philadelphia: Fortress, 1984.

Collins, Raymond F. "Cana (Jn 2:1–12)—the First of His Signs or the Key to His Signs?" *Irish Theological Quarterly* 47 (1980): 79–95.

Corley, Kathleen E. "Jesus' Table Practice: Dining with 'Tax Collectors and Sinners,' Including Women." Pages 444–59 in *Society of Biblical Literature 1993 Seminar Papers*. Edited by E. Lovering. Atlanta: Scholars Press, 1993.

———. *Private Women, Public Meals: Social Conflict in the Synoptic Tradition*. Peabody, Mass.: Hendrickson, 1993.

Cothenet, Édouard. "La nourriture du Christ et la mission." Pages 181–91 in *Nourriture et repas dans les milieux Juifs et Chrétiens de l'Antiqité*. Edited by M. Quesnel, Y.-M. Blanchard, and C. Tassin. Paris: Cerf, 1999.

Crossan, John D. "It Is Written: A Structuralist Analysis of John 6." *Semeia* 26 (1983): 3–21.

Culler, Jonathan. "Commentary." *New Literary History* 6 (1974): 219–29.

Cullmann, Oscar. *Early Christian Worship*. Translated by A. S. Todd and J. B. Torrance. Studies in Biblical Theology 10. London: SCM, 1953.

———. "The Significance of the Qumran Texts." *Journal of Biblical Literature* 74 (1955): 222–4.

———. *The Early Church*. London: SCM, 1956.

———. *Peter: Disciple, Apostle, Martyr*. 2d ed. Philadelphia: Westminster, 1962.

———. *The Johannine Circle: Its Place in Judaism, among the Disciples of Jesus and in Early Christianity*. London: SCM, 1976.

Culpepper, R. Alan. *Anatomy of the Fourth Gospel*. Philadelphia: Fortress, 1983.

———. *The Gospel and Letters of John*. Nashville: Abingdon, 1998.

Daly, R. J. "The Soteriological Significance of the Sacrifice of Isaac." *Catholic Biblical Quarterly* 39 (1977): 45–75.

Daly-Denton, Margaret. *David in the Fourth Gospel: The Johannine Reception of the Psalms*. Leiden: Brill, 2000.

Daube, David. "Jesus and the Samaritan Woman: The Meaning of συγχράομαι." *Journal of Biblical Literature* 69 (1950): 137–47.

Davidson, Donald. "What Metaphors Mean." *Critical Inquiry* 5, no. 1 (1978): 31–47.

Davies, Philip R., and Bruce D. Chilton. "The Aqedah: A Revised Tradition History." *Catholic Biblical Quarterly* 40 (1978): 514–46.

Dentzer, Jean-Marie. "Aux origines de l'iconographie du banquet couché." *Revue archéologique* (1971): 215–58.

———. "Le motif du banquet couché dans le Proche-Orient et le monde grec du 7e au 4e siecle avant J.-C." *Bibliothèque des écoles françaises d'Athènes et de Rome* 246e. Rome, 1982.

Derrett, J. Duncan M. "The Zeal of the House and the Cleansing of the Temple." *Downside Review* 95 (1977): 90.

Derrida, Jacques. "White Mythology: Metaphor in the Text of Philosophy." *New Literary History* 6 (1974): 5–74.

Diel, Paul. *Symbolism in the Bible: The Universality of Symbolic Language and Its Psychological Significance*. Translated by Nelly Marans. San Francisco: Harper & Row, 1986.

Diel, Paul, and Jeannine Solotareff. *Symbolism and the Gospel of John*. San Francisco: Harper & Row, 1966.

Dillistone, Frederick William. *The Power of Symbols in Religion and Culture*. New York: Crossroad, 1986.

Dodd, Charles H. *The Interpretation of the Fourth Gospel*. Cambridge: Cambridge University Press, 1953.

———. *Historical Tradition in the Fourth Gospel*. Cambridge: Cambridge University Press, 1965.

Dreyfus, F. "Le thème de héritage dans l'Ancien Testament." *Revue des sciences philosophiques et théologiques* 42 (1958): 3–49.

Drumwright, H. L., Jr. "The Appendix to the Fourth Gospel." Pages 129–34 in *The Teacher's Yoke*. Edited by E. L Vardaman et al. H. Trantham volume. Waco: Baylor, 1964.

Dunn, James D. G. "Jesus, Table-Fellowship, and Qumran." *Jesus and the Dead Sea Scrolls*. Edited by James H. Charlesworth. New York: Doubleday, 1992.

Eliade, Mircea. *The Sacred and the Profane: The Nature of Religion*. Translated by W. Trask. New York: Harper & Row, 1961.

Emerton, J. A. "The Hundred and Fifty-Three Fishes in John 21:11." *Journal of Theological Studies* 9 (1958): 86–89.

———. "The Hundred and Fifty-Three Fishes in John 21:11." *Journal of Theological Studies* 11 (1960): 335–6.

Eslinger, Lyle. "The Wooing of the Woman at the Well: Jesus, the Reader and Reader-Response Criticism." *Journal of Literature and Theology* 1 (1987): 167–83.

Fenton, John C. *The Gospel according to John*. Oxford: Clarendon, 1970.

Fortna, Robert Tomson. *The Gospel of Signs: A Reconstruction of the Narrative Source Underlying the Fourth Gospel*. Cambridge: Cambridge University Press, 1970.

———. *The Fourth Gospel and Its Predecessor: From Narrative Source to Present Gospel*. Philadelphia: Fortress, 1988.

Freedman, William. "Literary Motif: A Definition and Evaluation." *Novel* 4 (1971): 123–31.

Friedman, Norman. *Form and Meaning in Fiction*. Athens: University of Georgia Press, 1975.

Gaffney, James. "Believing and Knowing in the Fourth Gospel." *Theological Studies* 26 (1965): 215–41.

Giblin, Charles H. "Suggestion, Negative Response, and Positive Action in St. John's Portrayal of Jesus." *New Testament Studies* 26 (1979–80): 197–211.

Glasson, Thomas F. *Moses in the Fourth Gospel*. London: SCM, 1963.

Goguel, Maurice. "Did Peter Deny His Lord? A Conjecture." *Harvard Theological Review* 25 (1932): 1–27.

Gooch, Paul D. *Dangerous Food: 1 Corinthians 8–10 in Its Context*. Waterloo: Wilfred Laurier University Press, 1993.

Goodenough, Edwin. *Jewish Symbols in the Greco-Roman Period*. Princeton: Princeton University Press, 1988.

Gray, G. Buchanan. *Sacrifice in the OT*. Oxford: Clarendon, 1925.

Guilding, Aileen. *The Fourth Gospel and Jewish Worship*. Oxford: Clarendon, 1960.

Hanson, Anthony T. "John's Use of Scripture." Pages 358–79 in *The Gospels and the Scriptures of Israel*. Edited by Craig A. Evans and W. Richard Stegner. Journal for the Study of the New Testament Supplement Series 104. Sheffield: Sheffield Academic Press, 1994.

Hayward, C. T. Robert. "The Present State of Research into the Targumic Account of the Sacrifice of Isaac." *Journal of Jewish Studies* 32 (1981): 135–7.

———. "The Sacrifice of Isaac and Jewish Polemic against Christianity." *Catholic Biblical Quarterly* 52 (1990): 292–306.

Hengel, Martin. "The Interpretation of the Wine Miracle at Cana: Jn 2:1–11." Translated by G. Schmidt. *The Glory of Christ in the New Testament.* Edited by L. Hurst and N. T. Wright. Oxford: Clarendon, 1987.

Heschel, Abraham. J. *Who Is Man?* Stanford: Stanford University Press, 1965.

Hill, David. *New Testament Prophecy.* Atlanta: John Knox, 1979.

Hodges, Horace Jeffery. *Food as Synecdoche in John's Gospel and Gnostic Texts.* Ph.D. diss., University of California, Berkeley, 1995.

Hoskyns, Edwyn C. *The Fourth Gospel.* 2d ed. London: Faber & Faber, 1947.

Hultgren, Arland. "The Johannine Footwashing (Jn 13:1–11) as a Symbol of Eschatological Hospitality." *New Testament Studies* 28 (1982): 539–46.

Jameson, Fredric. *The Political Unconscious: Narrative as a Socially Symbolic Act.* Ithaca: Cornell University Press, 1981.

Jensen, Robin M. "The Binding or Sacrifice of Isaac: How Jews and Christians See Differently." *Bible Review* 9 (1993): 42–51.

Jeremias, Joachim. *The Eucharistic Words of Jesus.* Translated by N. Perrin. London: SCM, 1966.

Jones, Larry Paul. *The Symbol of Water in the Gospel of John.* Journal for the Study of the New Testament Supplement Series 145. Sheffield: Sheffield Academic Press, 1997.

Jonge, Marinus de. "The Use of the Word 'Anointed' in the Time of Jesus." *Novum Testamentum* 8 (1966): 132–48.

———. "Messiah." Pages 777–88 in vol. 4 of *The Anchor Bible Dictionary.* Edited by David N. Freedman. 6 vols. New York: Doubleday, 1992.

Juel, Donald. *Messianic Exegesis: Christological Interpretation of the Old Testament in Early Christianity.* Philadelphia: Fortress, 1988.

Jung, Carl G. *Psychology and Religion.* New Haven: Yale University Press, 1938.

Just, Arthur A. *The Ongoing Feast: Table Fellowship and Eschatology at Emmaus.* Collegeville, Minn.: Liturgical, 1993.

Kittel, G., and G. Fredrich, eds. *Theological Dictionary of the New Testament.* Translated by G. W. Bromiley. 10 vols. Grand Rapids: Eerdmans, 1964–76.

Koester, Craig R. *Symbolism in the Fourth Gospel: Meaning, Mystery, Community.* Minneapolis: Fortress, 1995.

Kysar, Robert. "Johannine Metaphor—Meaning and Function: A Literary Case Study of John 10:1–8." *Semeia* 53 (1991): 81–111.

Leal, Juan. "El simbolismo histórico del IV Evangelio." *Estudios Biblicos* 19 (1960): 329–48.

Lee, Dorothy A. *The Symbolic Narratives of the Fourth Gospel: The Interplay of Form and Meaning.* Sheffield: JSOT, 1994.

Léon-Dufour, Xavier. "Le signe du temple selon Saint Jean." *Recherches de science religieuse* 39 (1951): 155–75.

———. "Towards a Symbolic Reading of the Fourth Gospel." *New Testament Studies* 27 (1981): 439–56.

Liddell, Henry G., Robert Scott, and H. S. Jones. *A Greek-English Lexicon.* Oxford: Clarendon, 1968.

Lightfoot, Robert Henry. *St. John's Gospel: A Commentary.* Oxford: Oxford University Press, 1957.

Lindars, Barnabas. *New Testament Apologetic: The Doctrinal Significance of the Old Testament Quotations.* London: SCM, 1961.

———. *The Gospel of John.* London: Butler & Tanner, 1972.

Little, Edmund. *Echoes of the New Testament in the Wine of Cana in Galilee (John 2:1–11) and the Multiplication of the Loaves and Fish (John 6:1–15): Towards an Appreciation.*

Cahiers de la Revue Biblique 41. Paris: Gabalda, 1998.

Malatesta, Edward. "Blood and Water from the Pierced Side of Christ (19:34)." Pages 165–81 in *Segni e sacramenti nel Vangelio di Giovanni*. Edited by Puis-Ramen Tragan. Studia Anselmiana 66. Rome: Editrice Anslemiana, 1977.

Malina, Bruce, and Richard L. Rohrbaugh. *Social Science Commentary on the Gospel of John*. Philadelphia: Fortress, 1998.

Manns, Frédéric. "Le lavement des pieds." *Revue des sciences religieuses* 55 (1981): 149–69.

Marsh, John. *Saint John*. Harmondsworth: Penguin, 1968.

Martyn, J. Louis. *History and Theology in the Fourth Gospel*. 2d ed. Nashville: Abingdon, 1979.

Matsunaga, Kikuo. "Is John's Gospel Anti-Sacramental: A New Solution in Light of the Evangelistic Milieu." *New Testament Studies* 27 (1981): 516–24.

McDowell, Edward A., Jr. "'Lovest Thou Me? A Study of John 21:15–17." *Review and Expositor* 32 (1935): 422–41.

McMahan, Craig Thomas. "Meals as Type Scenes in the Gospel of Luke." Ph.D. diss., Southern Baptist Theological Seminary, 1987.

McKinlay, Judith. *Gendering Wisdom the Host: Biblical Invitations to Eat and Drink*. Journal for the Study of the Old Testament Supplement Series 216. Sheffield: Sheffield Academic Press, 1996.

Meeks, Wayne. *The Prophet-King: Moses Traditions and the Johannine Christology*. Leiden: Brill, 1967.

———. "Galilee and Judea in the Fourth Gospel." *Journal of Biblical Literature* 85 (1966): 159–69.

———. "The Man from Heaven in Johannine Sectarianism." *Journal of Biblical Literature* 91 (1972): 44–72.

Meeûs, X. de "Composition de Lc.14 et genre symposiaque." *Ephemerides theologicae lovanienses* 37 (1961): 847–70.

Menken, Martinus J. J. "The Translation of Psalm 41:10 in John 13:18." *Journal for the Study of the New Testament* 40 (1990): 61–79.

Meshorer, Ya'akov. *Jewish Coins of the Second Temple Period*. Tel Aviv: Am Hassefer, 1967.

Michaels, J. Ramsey. "John 12:1–11." *Interpretation* 43 (1989): 287–91.

———. "Betrayed and the Betrayer: The Uses of Scripture in John 13:18–19." Pages 459–74 in *The Gospels and the Scriptures of Israel*. Journal for the Study of the New Testament Supplement Series Series 104. Edited by C. Evans and W. R. Stegner. Sheffield: Sheffield Academic Press, 1994.

Mildenberg, Leo. *The Coinage of the Bar Kokhba War*. Typos, 6. Edited and translated by Patricia Erhart Mottahedeh. Aarau: Sauerländer, 1984.

Minear, Paul S. "The Original Functions of John 21." *Journal of Biblical Literature* 102 (1982): 81–98.

———. *John: The Martyr's Gospel*. New York: Pilgrim, 1984.

Moloney, Francis J. *Belief in the Word: Reading John 1–4*. Minneapolis: Fortress, 1993.

———. *Signs and Shadows: Reading John 5–12*. Minneapolis: Fortress, 1996.

Moore, Stephen D. *Literary Criticism and the Gospels: The Theoretical Challenge*. New Haven: Yale University Press, 1989.

Morgan, Robert. *Biblical Interpretation*. Oxford: Oxford University Press, 1988.

Morris, Leon. *The Gospel according to John: The English Text with Introduction, Exposition and Notes*. New International Commentary on the New Testament. Grand Rapids: Eerdmans, 1971.

Moule, C. F. D. "A Note on Didache 9:4." *Journal of Theological Studies* 6 (1955): 240–243.

Mounce, William D. *Basics of Biblical Greek: Grammar*. Grand Rapids: Zondervan, 1993.

Motyer, Steve. "Method in Fourth Gospel Studies: A Way Out of the Impasse?" *Journal for the Study of the New Testament* 66 (1997): 27–44.

Negoitsia, Athanase, and Constantin Daniel. "L'Agneau de Dieu est le Verbe de Dieu." *Novum Testamentum* 13 (1971): 24–37.

Neirynck, Frans. "John 21." *New Testament Studies* 36 (1990): 321–36.

Nickelsburg, George W. E. *Jewish Literature between the Bible and the Mishnah*. Philadelphia: Fortress, 1981.

O'Day, Gail R. "John." Pages 381–93 in *Women's Bible Commentary: Expanded Edition*. Edited by Carol A. Newsom and Sharon H. Ringe. Louisville, Ky.: Westminster John Knox, 1998.

Odeberg, Hugo. *The Fourth Gospel: Interpreted in Its Relation to Contemporaneous Religious Currents in Palestine and the Hellenistic-Oriental World*. Amsterdam: Grüner, 1968.

Olsson, Birger. *Structure and Meaning in the Fourth Gospel: A Text-Linguistic Analysis of John 2:1–11 and 4:1–42*. Translated by Jean Gray. Lund: C. W. K. Gleerup, 1974.

O'Rourke, John J. "Two Notes on John's Gospel: Jn 19:13 *eis ton topon*; *phagein* and *pinein* in John." *Catholic Biblical Quarterly* 25 (1963):124–8.

Owen, O. T. "One Hundred and Fifty Three Fishes." *Expository Times* 100 (1988): 52–54.

Painter, John. "Johannine Symbols: A Case Study in Epistemology." *Journal of Theology of South Africa* 27 (1979): 26–41.

Pamment, Margaret. "The Fourth Gospel's Beloved Disciple." *Expository Times* 94 (1983): 363–7.

Paschal, R. Wade. "Sacramental Symbolism and Physical Imagery in the Gospel of John." *Tyndale Bulletin* 32 (1981): 151–79.

Pattengale, Jerry A. "Aenon." Page 87 in vol. 1 of *The Anchor Bible Dictionary*. Edited by David N. Freedman. 6 vols. New York: Doubleday, 1992.

Perkins, Pheme. "The Gospel according to John." Pages 942–85 in *New Jerome Biblical Commentary*. Edited by R. E. Brown, J. A. Fitzmyer, and R. E. Murphy. London: Geoffrey Chapman, 1989.

Pervo, Richard. "PANTA KOINA: The Feeding Stories in Light of Economic Data and Social Practice." Pages 163–94 in *Religious Propoganda and Missionary Competition in the New Testament World*. Edited by L. Bormann, D. Tredici, and A. Strandhartigen. Leiden: Brill, 1994.

Phillips, Gary. "This Is a Hard Saying. Who Can Be a Listener to It? Creating a Reader in John 6." *Semeia* 26 (1983): 23–56.

Porter, Stanley E. *Idioms of the Greek New Testament*. 2d. ed. Sheffield: Sheffield Academic Press, 1999.

Pitta, Antonio. "Fish on the Fire." *Biblica* 71 (1990): 348–64.

Prat, Ferdinand. "Les places d'honneur chez les Juifs contemporains du Christ." *Recherches de science religieuse* 15 (1925): 512–22.

Quast, Kevin. *Reading the Gospel of John: An Introduction*. New York: Paulist, 1991.

Rasmussen, David M. *Symbol and Interpretation*. The Hague: Martinus Hijhoff, 1974.

Reinhartz, Adele. "Great Expectations: A Reader-Oriented Approach to Johannine Christology and Eschatology." *Journal of Literature and Theology* 3 (1989): 61–76.

———. "Jesus as Prophet: Predictive Prolepses in the Fourth Gospel." *Journal for the Study of the New Testament* 36 (1989): 3–16.

———. "The Gospel of John." Pages 561–600 in vol. 2 of *Searching the Scriptures: A Feminist Commentary*. Edited by Elisabeth Schüssler Fiorenza with Ann Brock and Shelley Matthews. New York: Crossroads, 1994.

Rhoads, David. "Narrative Criticism and the Gospel of Mark." *Journal of the American Academy of Religion* 50 (1982): 411–34.

Richards, Ivor A. *The Philosophy of Rhetoric.* Oxford: Oxford University Press, 1936.

Richter, Georg. *Studien zum Johannesevangelium.* Regensburg: Friedrich Pustet, 1977.

Ricoeur, Paul. "Metaphor and the Main Problem of Hermeneutics." *New Literary History* 6 (1974): 95–110.

———. *Interpretation Theory: Discourse and the Surplus of Meaning.* Fort Worth: Texas Christian University Press, 1976.

Ringe, Sharon. *Wisdom's Friends: Community and Christology in the Fourth Gospel.* Louisville, Ky.: Westminster John Knox, 1999.

Roberts, Edgar V. *Writing Themes about Literature.* 6th ed. Englewood Cliffs, N.J.: Prentice Hall, 1988.

Roberts, J. H. "The Lamb of God." Pages 41–56 in *The Christ of John: Essays on the Christology of the Fourth Gospel.* Potchefstroom: Pro Rege, 1971.

Robinson, Bernard P. "Anointing by Mary of Bethany." *Downside Review* 115 (1997): 99–111.

Robinson, J. A. T. "The Significance of the Footwashing." Pages 144–7 in *Neotestamentica et Patristica, eine Freundesgabe, Herrn Professor Dr. Oscar Cullmann zu seinem 60. Geburtstab überreicht,* Novum Testamentum Supplement Series 6. Leiden: Brill, 1962.

———. "The 'Others' of John 4:38." Pages 61–66 in *Twelve New Testament Studies.* Studies in Biblical Theology 34. London: SCM, 1962.

Rosenberg, Roy A. "Jesus, Isaac, and the Suffering Servant." *Journal of Biblical Literature* 84 (1965): 381–8.

Sabbe, M. "The Footwashing in John 13 and Its Relation to the Synoptic Gospels." *Ephemerides theologicae lovanienses* 58 (1982): 279–308.

Sandy, D. Brent. "John the Baptist's 'Lamb of God' Affirmation in its Canonical and Apocalyptic Milieu." *Journal of the Evangelical Theological Society* 34 (1991): 447–59.

Schnackenburg, Rudolf. *The Gospel according to St. John.* 3 vols. Translated by Kevin Smyth. New York: Seabury, 1980.

Schneiders, Sandra. "Symbolism and the Sacramental Principle in the Fourth Gospel." Pages 221–35 in *Segni e sacramenti nel Vangelio di Giovanni.* Edited by Puis-Ramen Tragan. Studia Anselmiana 66. Rome: Editrice Anselmania, 1977.

———. "History and Symbolism in the Fourth Gospel." Pages 371–6 in *L'Evangile de Jean: Sources, redaction, theology.* Edited by M. de Jonge. Gembloux: Leuven University Press, 1977.

———. "The Foot Washing (John 13:1–20): An Experiment in Hermeneutics." *Catholic Biblical Quarterly* 43 (1981): 76–92.

Schoeps, Hans Joachim. "The Sacrifice of Isaac in Paul's Theology." *Journal of Biblical Literature* 65 (1946): 385–92.

Scott, Martin. *Sophia and the Johannine Jesus.* Sheffield: JSOT Press, 1992.

Segovia, Fernando. "John 13:1–20, the Footwashing in the Johannine Tradition." *Zeitscrift für die neutestamentliche Wissenschaft und die Kunde der älteren Kirche* 73 (1982): 31–51.

Smalley, Stephen S. "The Sign in John 21." *New Testament Studies* 20 (1974): 275–88.

———. "Salvation Proclaimed 8: John 1:29–34." *Expository Times* 93 (1982): 324–9.

Smith, Barry D. "The Words of Institution: Jesus' Death as Eschatological Passover Sacrifice." Ph.D. diss. McMaster University, 1988.

Smith, Dennis E. "The Historical Jesus at Table." Pages 466–86 in *Society of Biblical Literature 1989 Seminar Papers.* Edited by David Lull. Atlanta: Scholars Press, 1979.

———. "Social Obligation in the Context of Communal Meals: A Study of the Christian

Meal in the First Century in Comparison with Greco-Roman Communal Meals." Th.D. diss., Harvard Divinity School, 1980.

―――. "Meals and Morality in Paul and His World." *Society of Biblical Literature Seminar Papers* 20 (1981): 319–39.

―――. "Table Fellowship as a Literary Motif in the Gospel of Luke." *Society of Biblical Literature* 106 (1987): 613–38.

―――. "The Messianic Banquet Reconsidered." Pages 64–73 in *The Future of Early Christianity*. Edited by B. Pearson. Minneapolis: Fortress, 1991.

―――. "Messianic Banquet." Pages 788–91 in vol. 4 of *The Anchor Bible Dictionary*. Edited by David N. Freedman. 6 vols. New York: Doubleday, 1992.

Smith, Dwight Moody. *The Composition and Order of the Fourth Gospel*. New Haven: Yale University Press, 1965.

―――. *John*. Nashville: Abingdon, 1999.

Soskice, Janet. *Metaphor and Religious Language*. Oxford: Clarendon, 1985.

Spicq, C. "La charité est amour manifeste." *Revue Biblique* 65 (1958): 358–70.

―――. "ΤΡΩΓΕΙΝ: est-il synonyme de ΦΑΓΕΙΝ et d'ΕΣΘΙΕΙΝ dans le Nouveau Testament?" *New Testament Studies* 26 (1979–80): 414–9.

Staley, Jeffrey Lloyd. *The Print's First Kiss: A Rhetorical Investigation of the Implied Reader in the Fourth Gospel*. Atlanta: Scholars Press, 1988.

Steele, E. Springs. "Jesus' Table Fellowship with Pharisees: An Editorial Analysis of Luke 7:36–50, 11:37–54 and 14:1–24." Ph.D. diss., Notre Dame University, 1981.

Stemberger, Günter. *La symbolique du bien et du mal selon Saint Jean*. Paris: Seuil, 1970.

Steinbeck, John. *Grapes of Wrath*. New York: Penguin, 1992.

Stone, Michael, editor. *Jewish Writings of the Second Temple Period*. Philadelphia: Fortress, 1984.

Swancutt, Diana M. "Hungers Assuaged by the Bread from Heaven: 'Eating Jesus' an Isaian Call to Belief: The Confluence of Isaiah 55 and Psalm 78 (77) in John 6:22–71." Pages 218–51 in *Early Christian Interpretation of the Scriptures of Israel: Investigations and Proposals*. Edited by Craig A. Evans and James A. Sanders. Journal for the Study of the New Testament Supplement Series 148. Sheffield: Sheffield Academic Press, 1997.

Teeple, Howard M. *The Mosaic Eschatological Prophet*. Philadelphia: Society of Biblical Literature, 1957.

Tillich, Paul. *Dynamics of Faith*. New York: Harper & Row, 1957.

Torrey, Charles. "In the Fourth Gospel the Last Supper Was the Paschal Meal." *Jewish Quarterly Review* 42 (1952): 237–50.

Tovey, Derek. *Art and Act in the Fourth Gospel*. Journal for the Study of the New Testament Supplement Series 151. Sheffield: Sheffield Academic Press, 1997.

Tracy, David. "Metaphor and Religion." *Critical Inquiry* 5, no. 1 (1978): 91–106.

Trudinger, Paul. "153 Fishes: A Response and Further Suggestion." *Expository Times* 102 (1991): 11–12.

Vermes, Geza. *Scripture and Tradition in Judaism*. Leiden: Brill, 1961.

―――. "New Light on the Sacrifice of Isaac from 4Q225." *Journal of Jewish Studies* 47 (1996): 140–146.

Villescas, J. "John 2:6: The Capacity of the Six Jars." *Bible Translator* 28 (1977): 447.

Wead, David. *Literary Devices in John's Gospel*. Theologischen Dissertationen 4. Basel: Friedrich Reinhart Kommissionsverlag, 1970.

Webster, Jane. "Transcending Alterity: Strange Woman to Samaritan Woman." *Feminist Companion to the Johannine Literature*. Edited by A.-J. Levine. Sheffield: Sheffield Academic Press, forthcoming.

Wellek, René, and Austin Warren. *Theory of Literature*. 3d ed. New York: Harcourt Brace & World, 1956.

Weiss, Herold. "Foot Washing in the Johannine Community." *Novum Testamentum* 21 (1979): 298–325.

Wheelwright, Philip. *The Burning Fountain: A Study in the Language of Symbolism*. Bloomington: Indiana University Press, 1954.

Wiarda, Timothy. "John 21:1–23: Narrative Unity and Its Implications." *Journal for the Study of the New Testament* 46 (1992): 53–71.

Wilckens, Ulrich. *Das Evangelium nach Johannes*. Das Neue Testament Deutsch 4. Göttingen: Vandenhoeck & Ruprecht, 1998.

Witkamp, L. T. "Jesus' Thirst in John 19:28–30: Literal or Figurative?" *Journal of Biblical Literature* 115 (1996): 489–510.

Wright, R. B. "Psalms of Solomon." Pages 639–50 in vol. 2 of *The Old Testament Pseudepigrapha*. Edited by James H. Charlesworth. New York: Doubleday, 1985.

Yee, Gail. *Jewish Feasts and the Gospel of John*. Wilmington, Del.: Michael Glazier, 1989.

Young, Frances M. *The Use of Sacrificial Ideas in Greek Christian Writers from the New Testament to John Chrysostom*. Cambridge: Patristic Foundation, 1979.

Zeitlin, Solomon. "The Last Supper Was an Ordinary Meal in the Fourth Gospel." *Jewish Quarterly Review* 42 (1952): 251–60.

Indices

OLD TESTAMENT

NEW TESTAMENT

John, continued		13:7	67, 108,	13:23	97, 103,
12:23–24	39		110, 114,		104, 117,
12:24	4, 20, **59–**		115, 117		145
	64, 78,	13:8	33, 105,	13:24	104, 117
	149		108, 111,	13:26	99, 120,
12:25	72, 79		113, 114,		125, 138,
12:25–26	20, 115,		119, 121,		145
	136		141, 149,	13:26–30	104
12:26	112, 116		150	13:27	88, 104,
12:27	39	13:8–10	108		118, 120,
12:31	78	13:9	115		148
12:38	73	13:10	108, 118,	13:28	103, 120
12:42	80		122	13:29	94, 99,
12:48	110	13:10–11	123		102, 117
12:49–50	59	13:11	106, 118,	13:30	88, 102,
13:1	39, 43,		125, 126		114, 120,
	67, 88,	13:12	71, 102,		131, 137
	102, 105,		103, 104,	13:31	125, 135
	106, 115,		106, 107,	13:31–17:26	102
	117, 122,		110	13:33	78
	125, 126,	13:12–17	116	13:33–38	143
	143	13:13–17	109	13:36	116
13:1–3	117	13:14	142, 144	13:36–38	105
13:1–4	123	13:14–15	144	13:37	34, 107,
13:1–11	5	13:15–18	118		114, 141,
13:1–14:31	2	13:16	62		144
13:1–19:16	125	13:17	110	13:38	107
13:1–30	24, 25,	13:18	83, 106,	14:1–3	105
	93, **101–**		113, 114,	14:2–3	115
	122, 102,		118, 119,	14:3	112, 144
	125, 126,		120, 125	14:4	106
	128, 149	13:18–19	126	14:6–16	61
13:2	94, 99,	13:19	120	14:8–9	34
	102, 106,	13:20	62, 118	14:8–10	81
	125, 148	13:21	86, 120,	14:10	16, 60,
13:3	106, 120		125		123
13:4	104, 107	13:21–30	105, 123,	14:10–12	125
13:4–5	106, 107		126	14:11	60
13:5	108	13:22	118	14:12	16, 62,
13:5–11	102				142, 144
				14:13	117

INDEX OF MODERN AUTHORS

Printed in the United States
1001500007B